Francis Grose, Thomas Astle

The Antiquarian repertory:

A miscellany intended to preserve and illustrate several valuable remains of old

times: adorned with elegant sculptures- Vol. 1

Francis Grose, Thomas Astle

The Antiquarian repertory:
A miscellany intended to preserve and illustrate several valuable remains of old times: adorned with elegant sculptures- Vol. 1

ISBN/EAN: 9783337713300

Printed in Europe, USA, Canada, Australia, Japan

Cover: Foto ©Thomas Meinert / pixelio.de

More available books at **www.hansebooks.com**

THE

ANTIQUARIAN REPERTORY:

A

MISCELLANY,

INTENDED TO PRESERVE AND ILLUSTRATE

SEVERAL VALUABLE

REMAINS

OF

𝔒𝔩𝔡 𝔗𝔦𝔪𝔢𝔰.

ADORNED WITH ELEGANT SCULPTURES.

VOL. I.

LONDON:

Printed for the Proprietors, and Sold by FRANCIS BLYTH, No. 87, *Cornhill*; and T. EVANS, No. 54, *Paternoster-Row*.

1775.

INTRODUCTION.

IT has long been the fashion to laugh at the study of Antiquities, and to consider it as the idle amusement of a few humdrum, plodding fellows, who wanting genius for nobler studies, busied themselves in heaping up illegible Manuscrips, mutilated Statues, obliterated Coins, and broken Pipkins; in this the laughers may perhaps have been somewhat justified, from the absurd pursuits of a few Collectors, but at the same time an argument deduced from the abuse or perversion of any study, is by no means conclusive against the study itself; and in this particular case I trust I shall be able to prove, that without a competent fund of Antiquarian Learning, no one will ever make a respectable figure, either as a Divine, a Lawyer, Statesman, Soldier, or even a private Gentleman, and that it is the *sine quâ non* of several of the more liberal professions, as well as many trades; and is besides a study to which all persons in particular instances have a kind of propensity, every man being, as Logicians express it, " *Quoad hoc,*" an Antiquarian.

Let us begin then with the Divine. His profession indispensibly obliges him to be an Antiquarian in the most extensive sense of the word, and to consider this Globe, and all things in it, from their very infancy. The formation of which being so minutely recorded in the Holy Scriptures, seems to give a sanction to the pursuit. How will he defend the truth of the
Prophecies

Prophecies from the cavils of Infidels, how shew the harmony between the sacred and prophane writers, without a thorough knowledge in History and Chronology; and how are these to be acquired but by the study of Ancient Monuments, Statues, Coins, Manuscripts and Customs?

In a more limited view, considering him as a Member of the national Church. He ought to be minutely acquainted with the Ecclesiastical Antiquities, which serve for the foundation of the ceremonials he daily performs, and the vessels, utensils and garments he constantly wears and makes use of. And in order to be enabled to manage his own property, or that of any Church over which he may preside, an insight into the Monastick History and Terms are absolutely necessary. He should also be enabled to read the ancient charters and deeds of endowment, be conversant in the weights, measures, customs and immunities of former times, all which are expressed in a language totally unintelligible to a mere classic Scholar, and are only to be attained by a course of Antiquarian researches.

That a thorough knowledge of the national Antiquities is indispensibly necessary for every man of the Law, seems so self-evident a proposition, that an attempt at proofs would rather obscure than demonstrate it. What is the *Lex non Scripta*, or Common Law, but a series of ancient customs? Does not the origin of almost every writ in use depend on some piece of Ancient History? And how can a Judge or Advocate expatiate on the spirit of any statute, without knowing the history of the manners, customs, and even vices of the times when it was framed? What, besides a liberal arrangement of these matters, which may be called Legal Antiquities, has made the Commentaries of Judge Blackstone so universally read, and so justly admired?

Let us next turn to the Statesman and Legislator; here we find his very being depends on the knowledge of History and Antiquities. It is not simply the retaining in the memory a succession of events, catalogues of tyrants, plagues, battles and revolutions; but clear ideas of the laws, customs, opinions, arts, arms and commerce of the different æras; from these he may draw the causes of the subversion of kingdoms, popular commotions, or the spirit that actuated the several Ministers in the treaties of alliances

alliances made by them. This knowledge is to be collected from the confideration of Ancient Ufages, Arms, Coins, Medals, Utenfils, Buildings and Infcriptions.

As a Member of either Houfe he ought to know the rules, precedents and orders of that community, or, in other words, the Parliamentary Hiftory and Antiquities. If he is a Peer, his perfonal attendance in the great ceremonials require him to be mafter of that part of Antiquarian Knowledge which fettles all forts of precedency.

A general knowledge of Antiquity is profeffionally neceffary to a Soldier; without it, it will be impoffible he fhould receive the leaft benefit from the relations of former fieges or battles, in which to make proper deductions he fhould take into his confideration the Ancient military buildings, engines, weapons, both offenfive and defenfive, together with the difcipline of the times. Adequate ideas of the former can only be gained by a critical examination of Ancient forts and caftles; and a proper judgment of the latter formed from public arfenals, Ancient coins, fepulchral monuments, acts of parliament, illuminated manufcripts and old chronicles. Owing to too great a neglect of thefe enquiries, few Officers are able to give a rational account of many of their parade motions and ceremonials, which though they to them may feem arbitrary, were neverthelefs founded on convenience and neceffity.

To the private Gentleman nothing can be more ornamental than a tincture of this knowledge in general, or more ufeful than an accurate acquaintance with the Antiquities of his country in particular; without it he cannot underftand its hiftory, neither is he qualified ably to ferve as a Member of Parliament or Juftice of the Peace, or even as a Juror; a proper execution of all thefe offices in different degrees requiring an acquaintance with the conftitution, laws and cuftoms of our anceftors, and thefe cannot be obtained but by the perufal of Ancient records, coins and monuments, which at the fame time that they inftruct, ferve to fix in the memory the æra of the different events, and Hiftory of the times in which they were conftructed.

Even as a man of pleasure some smattering of this knowledge is required. Would he appear at a masquerade in any particular old English character, if he has not some standard for the forming of his dress, he may personate King Alfred in the ruff, short jacket, shoulder belt, and quail pipe boots, worn in the reign of Charles the Second.

The professors of Architecture, Sculpture or Painting, cannot go on a moment in their respective professions without more than a moderate share of Antiquarian Learning. If the first is employed to construct a Gothic ruin in a garden, or is desired to repair an Ancient church or cathedral, without this, he would jumble together the different stiles of Saxon, Norman and modern Gothic. Or suppose the Painter was to represent the battle of Hastings, he might perhaps draw the Conqueror in the character of a French Mareschal, his large peruke and drapery waving in the wind, he, serenely smiling amidst the flight of bursting bombs, cannon balls and vollies of small arms, brandishing his truncheon in one hand, whilst the other, garnished with a laced ruffle, is placed a kimbo on his hips. In short, to make use of their own terms, this deficiency would betray them constantly into a violation of the *coutume*.

The want of Acquaintance with these matters often causes theatrical heroes and princesses to fall into manifest absurdities. To this we owe the tye wig of a Mark Anthony, and the ample hoop and chased watch of the beautiful Cleopatra. I will not, however, charge them with the frequent solecisms seen in the furniture of the mimic palaces and apartments, these being the works of the scene painter; but for want of attention to this kind of propriety, I have more than once seen the chamber of a Roman Lady decorated with a harpsichord, whilst the chimney has been loaded with china josses and mandarines, beneath a picture representing the taking of Porto Bello, the battle of Culloden, or some other similar Anachronisms.

I have said that every man is naturally an Antiquarian, and to every ones own breast I appeal for a proof. Is he possessed of an Ancient

seat

(vii)

feat, does he not earneftly defire to know its hiftory and the fucceffion of his predeceffors in that manfion, and if it has been the fcene of any remarkable tranfaction, does not he read every thing concerning it with particular avidity; and can he refrain enquiring and making himfelf mafter of every circumftance and place of action; and does not this propenfity even extend to the parifh or town wherein he lives. Let any one go to Runny Mead, or Bofworth Field, there is not a clown that refides thereabouts, however rude, but can tell him the fpot where the Barons affembled, and where Richard fell.

In cultivating the ftudy of Antiquities, care muft be taken not to fall into an error, to which many have been feduced, I mean that of making collections of things which have no other merit than that of being old, or having belonged to fome eminent perfon, and are not illuftrative of any point of hiftory. Such is the Scull of Oliver Cromwell, preferved in the Afhmolean Mufeum at Oxford, and pieces of the Royal Oak, hoarded by many loyal old ladies. That Oliver had a fcull and brains too would have been allowed without this proof; and thofe who have confidered the Royal Oak do not, I believe, find it effentially different from the wood of a common kitchen table. Thefe may be rather ftiled Reliques than Pieces of Antiquity, and it is fuch trumpery that is gibed at by the ridiculers of Antiquity.

Having thus, I hope, pointed out the importance of the ftudy of Antiquities, let me fay a word of the following Work.

This Collection is meant as a Repofitory for fugitive pieces, refpecting the Hiftory and Antiquities of this country. In the courfe of it care fhall be taken to admit only fuch Views as may be depended on, and have never before been publifhed, and which, at the fame time that they pleafe the eye, fhall reprefent fome remains of Antiquity, fome capital Manfion, or ftriking Profpect. The Portraits fhall introduce to the public acquaintance only fuch perfons as have figured in fome eminent ftation, or been remarkable for their abilities, ftations, or accidents in life. And the Letter-Prefs fhall convey either original effays, or extracts from books, whofe price and

fcarcity

(viii)

scarcity have rendered them accessible only to a few. Any Gentlemen possessed of Drawings, Coins, or Manuscrips, with which they would chuse to oblige the Public, may, by sending them to the Publisher, have them, if consistent with the plan, elegantly executed; and if incompatible or improper, immediately returned.

The cheapness and singularity of this undertaking will, it is hoped, recommend it to the public favour, to deserve which neither pains nor expence shall be spared; and the Editor begs leave to assure the Purchasers, that should he be so happy as to meet with success, he will, instead of flagging, redouble his efforts to please.

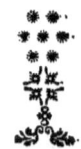

THE

ANTIQUARIAN REPERTORY.

The following curious Account of the Ordinances used at Tournaments, asalso that respecting Battles in Lists, or legal Duels, were copied by the late ingenious William Oldys, *Esq; Norroy King of Arms, from a* M S. *marked* I. 26. *in the Library of the College of Arms, or Herald's Office, London.*

The Ordinances Statutes and Rules made and enacted by John Erle of Worcestre constable of England by the Kinges commandement at Windesore the 14th Day of May in the vith Yere of his noble reigne, to be observed and kepte in all manner of Justes of peace Royall, within this Realme of England, before his highnefs or lieutenant by his commandement or licence, had from this Time forth, reserving alwais to the Quens highnes, and to the ladies there present, the attribution, and Gifte of the price, after the maner and forme accoftomed, the merrites and demerites attribute according to the articles followenge.

FIRSTE, whoso breaketh most Speares, as they ought to be broken, shall have the Price.

Item, who so hitteth thre tymes in the heaulme shall have the Price.

Ite, who fo meteth two tymes Coronoll to Coronoll, fhall have the Price.

Ite, who fo beareth a man downe with Stroke of Speare, fhall have the Price.

How the Price fhould be Lofte.

Firfte, who fo Striketh a Horfe fhall have no Price.

Ite, whofo Striketh a man his Back turned, or Difyarmyed of his Speare, fhall have no Price.

Ite, who fo hitteth the Toyle or Tilte thrife fhall have no Price.

Ite, whofo unheaulmes himfelf twice fhall have no Price withowt his horfe faile him.

How Speares broken fhalbe allowed.

Firfte, who fo breaketh a Speare between the Saddell and the Charnell of the heaulme fhalbe allowed for one.

Ite, who fo breaketh a Speare from the Charnell upward fhall be allowed for two.

Ite, who fo breaketh a Speare fo as he ftrike him down or put him out of his Saddell or difarme him in fuch wife as he maye not runne the nexte cowrft after fhalbe allowed for three Spears broken.

How Speares broken fhalbe Difallowed.

Firfte, who fo breakethe on the Saddell fhalbe difallowed for a Speare breakinge.

Ite, who fo hites the toyle or tilte once fhalbe difallowed for two.

Ite, who fo hitteth the toyle twice for the fecond tyme fhalbe abafed thre.

Ite, who fo breaketh a Speare within a foote of the Coronoll fhalbe judged as no Speare broken, but a good attempte.

For the Price.

Firfte, who fo bearethe a man downe owte of the Saddell or putteth him to the earthe, horfe and man, fhall have the Price, before him that ftrikethe Coronoll to Coronoll two tymes.

Ite, he that ftriketh Coronoll to Coronoll two tymes fhall have the Price before him that ftrikethe the Sight thre tymes.

Ite, he that ftrikethe the Sight thre tymes fhall have the Price before him that breakethe mofte Speares.

Ite,

THE ANTIQUARIAN REPERTORY. 11

Ite, yf there be any man that fortunetly in this wife fhalbe demed he bode longeſt in the feeld heaulmed and ranne the faireſt cowrſe and gave the greateſt ſtrokes, helpinge himſelf beſt with his Speare.

WHEREAS your moſt noble grace haſte moſte habondantly given unto fowre maydens of your moſte honorable Courte the caſtell caled Loyall to diſpoſe accordinge to their pleaſures, they have moſt lyberallye given the garde and cuſtodie of the ſame unto a captaine, and with him 15 gentlemen, of whom I ame the Officer of Armes, and have by them in commandement to certifie, unto your moſte noble Grace under their fourme, that wheras thei Stranngers evermore, ſervinge, to Ladies for the famous renown of this your noble court, hathe departed their forre contries for to ſe that ſame youre cowrte therin to ſerve unto ladies accordinge to their cuſtome under your protection and favour. That yt might pleaſe your Grace they have undertaken the Defence of the ſame to knowe and underſtand the fourme and manner under the whiche to the beſte of their power lyke after the facion of their contrie thei purpoſe by your favorable ſuffrance to Defend and Keype the ſame againſt all comers, gentlemen of name and of armes.

Firſte, in the place before the holde without ſhall ſtand an Unycorne white and with his fore legges ſuſtaynenge iiij ſheldes the one white ſignyfienge to the Juſtes that is to Saye who toureth that to be anſwer'd courſts at the tilte with haſtinge Harnoys and Double Pieces by one of the Caſtell, the ij zede Signyfienge to the tourney, that is to ſaye who tourhethe that to be anſwer'd xij Strokes with the Sworde edge and Point rebated, the iij Yellowe Signyfyieng to the Barriars that is to ſaye who Toureth that to be anſwered at the Barrere xij Strokes with one hand Sworde the Poynte and edge rebated the iiijth blow Signifienge to the Aſſaulte and who tourhith that to aſſaulte the ſaid caſtell with Suche weepons as the ſaid gentlemen ſholl occupie that is to Saye Sworde target and morriſpike with the Edge and Pointe Rebated.

Item yt ſhalbe Lawfull for the aſſaulters to Deviſe all manner of Engynes for the wynenge of the ſaid Caſtell engyn or tole to breake the Grownd or howſe with all only xcepted.

Ite that no man aſſaulte the Caſtell with pike Sword Shott no throw other than ſhalbe lefte by the Unycorne a Patrone and Example.

Item none do meddell with fier neyther within nor without but to fire there gunes.

Ite,

Ite. yf any of the approchars or defendors be taken to Paye for his Ranſom thre yardes of Right Sattin to the Taker and every Captayne xiii yardes

Ite in any dayes that this enterpriſe ſhalbe don to begin at one of the cloke at after none, and to Continew until ſeven of the Clock at afternone,

Moreover yt is to be underſtood that the firſte day of this enterpriſe ſhall begin on St John's Daye which is the xxvijth Daye of Novembre now next commynge and to End on new Year's Daye at vi of the Clock at After none.

Wheras divers noble Perſons have enterpriſed and taken upon them to hold Juſtes Roiall and tourney, the iiijth and   th Daye of November at weſtend as plainlie appeere by their Articles, and at ſo noble a Feaſte dyverſe & Sondrie exerciſes of armes are uſed, therefore and to thee Intent that if there be any gentlemen or other men of Armes that preſent not themſelves at the ſaid Daies of Juſtes or torneye there be vi gent, that will make them diſporte the xiith daye of novembre, according to theſe Articles followeng yf yt ſo pleaſe the Kinges highneſs for whoſe Pleaſure the Quenes and all the Ladies they undertake the ſaid enterprice and Eſpecially for the pleaſure of their redoubted Lady and faireſt princeſſe the eldeſt Daughter to our Sovereigne Lord the kinge.

Firſte in the Place appointed for the ſaid Juſtes and tourney there ſhalbe ordeyned againſt the ſaid xijth Daye a good nombre of Speares and Swordes ſuche as ſhall pleaſe the Kinges Grace, and the ſaid vi Gent ſent in the ſame Place in haſtinge harniſes to anſwer other vi gent in this nam'd wiſe,

The vi comers ſhall take a Speare and a Sword every of them in like wiſe the vi gent. puttinge themſelves in Range Directly againſt their fellowes every man his Speare on his thighe and his ſword where yt ſhall Pleaſe him and then at the Sownde of the trumpete to Charge and runne together oll at once every man to his fellowe that ſhall ſtande againſt him and ſo Pas throughe.

Ite, the cowrſe with the Spears paſſed every man to take to his Sworde and do his beſt, only the foyne except, choſinge his fellow by fortune as it ſhall happen, and ſo to continew untill the Tyme that the kinge ſhall comand to reaſt.

Ite yf any man of armes breake his Sword or loſe yt by any fortune he maye retorne to the Skaffold where the Herehaults be and there Receave an other and ſo Enter into the tourney againe, Alſo yt ſhall not neede that every man confyne to ſtill in fightinge with him whome he ſhall firſte encounter but if he will maye alſo ſerche to and fro taking his adxantage, and Helpinge his fellow

fellow if neede be, alwaies defended that no man Laye hand on other but only with his Sworde to do his befte nor twaine to fett uppon one alone unleft yt be in aydinge of his fellow as above.

Ite, If yt hap that there com to anfwer this enterprife more than the nombre of vi. yt fhalbe at the Kinges pleafure if the Said gent fhall anfwer them at Suche daies as fhall Pleafe his grace or ells to be devided halfe with them and thother half againft them alwaie obfervinge the faid Articles

Ite If any man be difarmed he maye withdrawe him felfe if he will but once Paft the Barres he maye not com agayne into the torney, for that Daye, Alfo there fhall no man have his Servant within the Barres with any peece of har-hois for no man fhalbe within the faid barres but fuche as fhalbe affigned by the Kinges Grace.

Ite who fhall befte demeane him felfe at thee fame arte of armes fhall have a Sword garnifhed to the valew of iij hundred crownes or under.

Ite every man that will be at the faid tourney fhall Delyver his name to one of the thre Kinges of Armes by the Lafte daye of October which fhall declare to them if any Doubte be made to the faid Articles

Ite, if any man ftrike a horfe with his Speare he fhalbe put owt of the torteye withowt any favour incontinent and if any Slaye an horfe he fhall paye to the owner of the faid horfe an hundred crownes in recompence alfo yt is not to be shought that any man will ftrike an Horfe willingly for if it do it fhall be to his Great Difhonor.

Therefore the faid vi Gentlemen befeche the Kinges noble Grace that this bill of the faide articles figned with his mofte noble hande may be a fufficent warrant and comandement unto his Officers of Armes to make proclamation thereof as well in his mofte noble cowrte as in all fuch other places as fhalbe mofte Requyfite.

EVER in cowrte of Great Kynges are wonte to com Knights of Dyvers nations and more to this cowrte of England where is mayntayned knyghthood and feats of armes valliantly for the fervice of Ladies in more higher Degrees and Eftates then in any realme of the worlde It befeemeth well to Don Francifco de Mendoza and Carflaft De la Vega that here bettar than in any place thei may fhew their great Defire that they have to ferve their Ladies They Saye that they will mayntayne to fight on foote at the barriars with footmens harnois iij pufhes with a Pike and xii Strokes with a Sworde in the Place appoynted before the cowrte gate the twesday being the iiijth Daye of December from xii of the Clocke untill fix at night to all noble men or knighte that will com to the faid combates with the condicions that here followe requyring thefe Lordes, The Erle of Arrondell the Lord Clynton and Garde Lopos de Padilla and Don Pedro de Cordoua that they wilbe Judges of their triumphes.

Firft he that cometh mofte gallauntly foorthe not bringinge any golde or filver tyne for counterfait woven or embroidered nor no gold Smythes worke on him fhalbe given a brooche of gold.

Ite he that fighteth beft with the pike fhall have a ringe of Golde with a ruby in yt.

Ite he that fighteth beft with a fword fhall have a ringe of Gold with a Dyamonde.

When they fhall iointly fight together accordinge to the appoyntment he that then dothe mofte valiantly fhall have a Ringe with a Dyamonde.

Ite he that giveth a ftroke with a Pike from the girdle downward or under the barriar fhall win no price.

Ite he that fhall have a clofe gauntlett or any thinge to faften his Sworde to his Hande fhall win no price

Ite he that his fword falleth owt of his hand fhall winne no price

Ite he that Stayeth his hand in fight on the barriars fhall win no price.

Ite. whofoev. fhall fight and fheweth not his Sword to the Judges fhall win no price.

Yet it is to be underftood that the challengers maye wyn all thefe prifes agaynfte the firfte comers Defendants and more the mofte gollaunte as yt is afore expreffed

The mayntenars maye take ayde or Affiftance of the noble men and of fuche as they fhall thinke befte.

Moreover that all fuche triumphes as are agreed uppon by the challenger and allowed by the prince fhalbe puplifhed by the Kinge of Armes of the province in fuche places as fhalbe appoynted by the Prince, And alfo that the nexte night after any triumphes is ended the Gifte of the prifes is to be pclaymed by the faid King of Armes in the pfence chamber after the Second cowrfe be ferved the manner wherof hearafter followethe.

O yes,

THE ANTIQUARIAN REPERTORY.

O yes, O yes O yes, we lett to underſtand to all princes and princeſſes Lordes Ladies and Gentlewomen of this noble cowrte and to all others to whom yt appertaynethe that the nobles that this Daye have exerfiſed the feates of Armes at the Tilte Tornoy and barriars, have every one behaved them ſelves moſte vallyanntly in Showeng their prowes and valour worthie of Greate Proiſe

And to begine, as towchinge the brave entre of the Lorde —— made by him very gallantly the Kinges Majeſtie more brave then he and above all the Erle ———, unto whom the Price of a very Riche ring is given by the Quenes Majeſtie by the adviſe of other princeſſes Ladies and gentlewomen of this noble cowrte

And as towchinge the valyantnes of the piques the Duke M hathe very valyantly bhaved him ſelfe, the Erle of P. bettar than he and above all others the erle of D, unto whome the Price of a Ringe of Golde with a Ruby is Given by the moſte hige & Mightie princes the Quene of England by the Advice aforeſaid

And as towchinge the valyantnes of the Sworde ——— Knight hathe very well behaved him ſelfe The Erle N Bettar than he and Sir J P Knight above all the reſte unto whome is given the Price of a Ringe of Golde with a Dyamond by the Quenes moſte Excellent Majeſtie by the adviſe of other princeſſes Ladies and Gentlewomen.

And as towching the valyantnes of the Sworde at the foyle Sir W R Knight hathe very valyanntly behaved himſelfe, The Marquis C bettar then he and above all others the Kinges Majeſtie, unto whome was Given the Price of a ringe of Golde with a Dyamond by the Quenes Majeſtie, by the adviſe of other princes Ladies and Gentlewomen

Finally towchinge the valiancie of the Pique the poynte abated Thomas P hathe well and valyantly behaved him ſelf, Charles C better than he and above all others Z S, unto whom was Given by the Quenes Majeſtie a ringe of Gold by the Adviſe of other Princes Ladies and Gentlewomen.

Fees

Fees apperteyneng to the Officers of Armes at all thofe triumphes aforefaide.

FIRSTE yf any of the Sayd Challengers or defendante fall to the grounde horfe and all, the Said horfe ought to be the Officers of Armes

Item at all Juftes with Speares or axes that is made in thofe fields the Covertures of the Horfes behinde the Saddells, the Cotes of Armes of the Challengers or defendante, with all the Speares axez and Swordes broked and broken, the States whereon the faid Officers of Armes fit belonge unto them And furthermore the Kinge of Armes or herehault that PClameth the faid Juftes fhall have vi Elles of Skarlett and Duringe the faid Juftes their wages, and alfo all the banners Standards and cotes of Armes that be worne in that feeld that Daye belonge to the faid Officers.

Alfo what noble man fo ever he be that entreth into the faide feeld or Juftes, the firfte tyme, he ought to Give the Officers of Armes 6 crownes of Golde for the marfhallinge of his armes, that tyme and no more.

(To be continued.)

THE ANTIQUARIAN REPERTORY. 17

EXPLANATION of the MISCELLANEOUS PLATE.

THE numbers 1, 2, 3, 4 and 5 of this Plate exhibit diverſe rude figures, ſcratched on the chalk wall of the ſecond ſtory of Guildford Caſtle in Surry; tradition makes them the work of a great perſonage confined there, who uſed to beguile the tedious hours of his impriſonment by amuſing himſelf with theſe delineations. Who this great perſonage was, or at what time he was there confined, is not known, but the ſtile of theſe figures themſelves beſpeak them of no very modern date; ſeveral ſimilar to them were not long ago diſcovered in a ſubterraneous chapel at Royſton in Cambridgeſhire.

No. 1. repreſents St. Chriſtopher, with his ſtaff, carrying in his arms an infant Chriſt; the other figure, ſcratched on the ſide of his garment, having its head ſurrounded with a nimbus, or glory, ſeems to have been ſince added.

No. 2. ſhews the figure of a Biſhop, (as appears by his mitre) repoſing beneath an arch, over him is an antique crown, and beneath him an imperfect ſketch of Chriſt upon the croſs.

No. 3. is a ſquare Pillaſter, whoſe capital is decorated with ornaments in the Saxon ſtile, ſimilar to ſeveral in the Undercroft of the Cathedral of Canterbury.

No. 4. is a complete Hiſtorical Piece, repreſenting the crucifixion, where, though rudely executed, the fainting Virgin, and the Soldier piercing the ſide of our Saviour, are both delineated, as alſo the figure of St. John, who, by his joined and uplifted hands, ſeems in the attitude of praying.

No. 5. is a King, wearing a crown of a very ancient form, and holding an orb in his hand, near him is the defaced traces of another.

No. 6 and 7. ſhew two ſmall Loaves, or Cakes, annually diſtributed on Eaſter Sunday, at Biddenden church, in the Weald of Kent, when they bake fourteen buſhel of wheat, half in ſmall loaves, in memory of two ſiſters, who lived, as tradition ſays, 250 years ago, and who, according to the account given in that pariſh, were joined together at the ſhoulders and lower parts of their bodies; in this ſtate they lived many years, not without frequent quarrels, which ſometimes terminated in blows. At length one of them died, and her ſiſter, refuſing to be ſeparated, did not long ſurvive.

E.   At

At their deceafe they by will left certain lands, then let at fix, and now at twenty pounds per annum, out of the produce of which they directed thefe loaves to be provided; they are of different finenefs and forms, as may be feen by the two fpecimens here prefented.—The country people affemble in great numbers at the church where thefe loaves are diftributed.

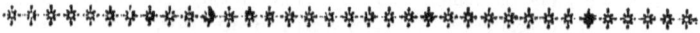

BLACK FRIARS BRIDGE.

THE Citizens of London, refiding about Fleet-ftreet and St. Paul's, long having experienced the inconveniency arifing from a want of communication with the Borough of Southwark, and an immediate outlet to the County of Surry, other than by the Bridges of London and Weftminfter, at length formed a defign to erect a Bridge in that neighbourhood, to which they were, it is faid, greatly induced by a fenfible Pamphlet attributed to Samuel Dicker, Efq; the proprietor of Walton Bridge, wherein the utility, and even neceffity of fuch an erection was demonftrated.

After fome affemblies of the Common Council, it was agreed, at one held February 22, 1754, that a Bridge fhould be built between thofe of London and Weftminfter, and a Committee was inftituted, confifting of the Aldermen, all the Deputies, and one Commoner of each Ward, who were empowered to confider on a proper plan and fituation.

In purfuance of thefe deliberations Black Friars was the fpot pitched upon, and January 13, 1756, a Petition was prefented to Parliament, in confequence of which an Act paffed, whereby the Mayor, &c. were empowered to raife 30,000l. per ann. on loans, until 160,000l. fhould be raifed, the intereft of which was to be paid by the tolls granted by the faid Act. The City was alfo authorifed to fill up the channel of Bridewell Dock, between Fleet-bridge and the Thames, making fufficient drains and fewers.

The Committee, after examining many plans, pitched upon one given by Mr. Robert Mylne, who was appointed Architect. The firft pile was driven January 7, 1760; and on the laft day of October the firft ftone was laid, with great folemnity, by the Lord Mayor and Committee, when feveral gold, filver, and copper coins of his late Majefty, were depofited under it, together with a filver medal given by the Roman Academy to Mr. Mylne, as a

prize

prize for his superior skill in Architecture. By order of the Court of Common Council a plate with the following inscription was likewise placed there; the propriety of its stile was severely criticised by the Literati, and with some humour ridiculed in a tract entitled City Latin.

Ultimo die Octobris, Anno ab Incarnatione
MDCCLX.
Auspicatissimo principe GEORGIO Tertio
Regnum jam ineunte,
Pontus hujus, in Reipublicæ commodum
Urbisque Majestatem
(Late tum flagrante Bello)
à S. P. Q. L. suscepti,
Primum Lapidem posuit
THOMAS CHITTY, Miles,
Prætor:
ROBERTO MYLNE, Architecto.
Utque apud posteros extet Monumentum
Voluntatis suæ erga Virum
Qui Vigori Ingenij, Animi Constantiâ,
Probitatis et Virtutis suæ felici quadam Contagione
(favente Deo
faustisque GEORGII Secundi Auspiciis)
IMPERIUM BRITANNICUM
In
ASIA, AFRICA et AMERICA,
Restituit, auxit & stabilivit,
Necnon Patriæ antiquum Honorem et Auctoritatem
Inter EUROPÆ Gentes instauravit;
Cives LONDINENSES, uno Consensu
Huic Ponti inscribi voluerunt Nomen
GULIELMI PITT.

TRANSLATED.

On the laſt day of October, in the year 1760,
and in the beginning of the moſt auſpicious reign of
GEORGE the Third,
Sir THOMAS CHITTY, Knight, Lord-Mayor,
laid the firſt Stone of this Bridge,
Undertaken by the Common-council of London
(in the height of an extenſive War)
for the public accommodation
and ornament of the City,
ROBERT MYLNE being the Architect.
And that there may remain to poſterity
a monument of this City's affection to the Man,
who, by the ſtrength of his Genius,
the ſteadineſs of his Mind,
and a kind of happy contagion of his probity and
Spirit,
(under the divine favour
and fortunate auſpices of GEORGE the Second)
recovered, augmented, and ſecured
The BRITISH Empire
in ASIA, AFRICA and AMERICA,
And reſtored the antient reputation
and influence of his country
amongſt the nations of EUROPE,
The Citizens of London have unanimouſly voted
this Bridge to be inſcribed with the Name of
WILLIAM PITT.

All the arches of the ſouthernmoſt half of the Bridge being completed, a temporary Bridge for foot-paſſengers was begun, and on the 19th of November, 1767, opened. The form and conſtruction of which will be better comprehended from the View here given, than can be conveyed by a verbal deſcription. The Drawing was taken Anno 1767, from a window in Black-
Friars

Friars Coffee-houſe, near the north-eaſternmoſt foot of the Bridge. The ſmall wooden hut there ſhewn was one of the toll houſes.

Although the building of the temporary Bridge coſt 2,167l. yet the tolls thereby collected not only replaced that ſum, but accumulated conſiderably towards the diſcharge of the annual intereſt for the great debt.

At length, within ten years and three quarters from the time of his being firſt employed, Mr. Mylne completed this Bridge, for which his ſalary and thoſe of his clerks amounted to 3762l. 10s. From the accounts laid before the Committee, it appears that the nett expence of building amounted to 152,840l. 3s. 10d. excluſive of 5,830l. for arching and filling up Fleet Ditch, and 2,167l. the coſt of making and altering the temporary Bridge.

The following deſcription of its form and dimenſions are given in Northouc's Hiſtory of London.

This Bridge conſiſts of nine arches, which being elliptical, the apertures for navigation are large, while the Bridge itſelf is low; when a perſon is under one of theſe arches, the extent of the vaults overhead cannot be viewed without awe! the dimenſions of this fabrick are as under:

	Feet	
Length of the Bridge from wharf to wharf —	995	Engliſh
Width of the central arch — — —	100	
Width of the arches on each ſide, reckoning from the central one toward the ſhore	98 93 83 76	
Width of the carriage way ———	28	total width
Width of the raiſed foot ways on each ſide —	7	42 feet
Heighth of the balluſtrade on the inſide —	4	10 inches

The upper ſurface of this Bridge is a portion of a very large circle; ſo that the whole forms one arch, and appears a gently ſwelling ground under foot all the way. Over each pier is a receſs or balcony, containing a bench, and ſupported below by two Ionic pillars, and two pilaſters; which ſtand on a ſemicircular projection of the pier, above high water mark; theſe pillars give an agreeable lightneſs to the appearance of the Bridge on either ſide. At each extremity of the Bridge ſpreads open the foot ways, rounding off to the right and left a quadrant of a circle, by which an open acceſs is formed, no lefs agreeable than ufeful on the approach. There are two flights of ftone fteps at each end, defended by iron rails, for the conveniency of taking water, each of which has a neat brick building befide the landing place at the top, as fhelters and privies for the watermen. Thefe ftairs, however, by conforming to the curvatures at the end of the Bridge, are more elegant than convenient; a flight of fifty narrow ftone fteps, without a landing place, muft be very tirefome to porters going up and down with loads, and no lefs dangerous in frofty weather, when, if a perfon flips down near the top, there is nothing to check their fall till they reach the water at the flood, or the bottom at the ebb of the tide. Befide the intrinfic merit of this Bridge, it has been obferved, that from its fituation it enjoys the concurrent advantage of affording the beft, if not the only true point of view for the magnificent cathedral of St. Paul, with the various churches in the amphitheatre extending from Weftminfter to the Tower.

The wooden frames on which the arches of this Bridge were turned, were very ingenioufly contrived for ftrength and lightnefs, allowing a free paffage for boats under them, while they were ftanding.

A curious model of one with the wood work under it, the foundation of the piers below, with the road and foot paffages over it, and two patterns for the rails on each fide, is preferved in the Britifh Mufeum.

Within thefe few years the toll gates next the City have been taken off, fo that the Citizens enjoy the privilege of walking the whole length of the Bridge, and enjoying the frefh air, gratis.

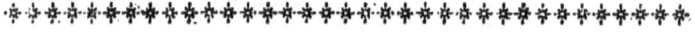

BOLTON HALL,

ONE of the feats of his Grace the Duke of Bolton, is fituated in a moft beautiful valley called Wenfley-Dale, in the North Riding of Yorkfhire, ten miles from Richmond, and four from Middleham. The environs of this feat, however worthy to be celebrated, feem not, till of late, perhaps from its diftant retirement, to have lived in defcription; but now its rural fcenes, antiquities, and other objects of curiofity, are called forth, and befides the

pencil

pencil of the Artist, have succefsfully exercised, both the pen of the Mufe, the Antiquary, and the Traveller.*

This houfe was finifhed about the year 1678, by Charles, Marquis of Winchefter, afterwards created Duke of Bolton, fon of John, the fifth Marquis, who fo gallantly defended his houfe at Bafing, in Hampfhire, during the civil wars in the reign of Charles the Firft.

The manfion is built with ftone, and although it cannot boaft the elegance of fome of our modern erections, yet does not want that fober dignity which befpeaks refpect, added to which, the apartments and offices are both fpacious and convenient.

The great dining, and an adjoining fmaller room, were finifhed by Artifts from Italy—and though near a century has elapfed fince their conftruction, do not differ much from the modern ftile of decoration.

The pleafure gardens, which have been formed at a great expence, are laid out in the old tafte, including yews, holly, fifhponds, and a fpouting fountain, and agree with the ftile of the building. The gardens rife in terraces behind the houfe, and with firs and other trees fhelter the manfion from the keen northern winds; they, in their turn, are fenced on that quarter, by gradual afcents; and laftly, at about the diftance of two miles, by a ridge of high perpendicular rocks, regularly continued like a fortification, and bordered below with fhrubbery and wood, which bound the northernmoft fide of Wenfley-Dale.

The furrounding grounds are well wooded, and at the diftance of 200 yards to the fouth, the river Eure runs parallel to the houfe; a range of lofty hills, or rather mountains, part romantically black and barren, and part beautifully verdant, and diverfified with trees, clofe the profpect, and terminate the valley to the fouth. Near the top of thefe hills is a temple, or hunting tower, which commands a moft enchanting and extenfive view.

The Duke, befides this feat and its demefnes, with an antient caftle, elegantly engraved and hiftorically defcribed in the Antiquities of England, poffeffes a very valuable property, being owner of ten contiguous manors.

The annexed View fhews the fouthern afpect of the houfe, which overlooks the parks, feverally appropriated in times paft for red and fallow deer; but the laft kind only now remain. In former ages fo fond were the noble

owners

---

* See Maude's Wenfley-Dale, Grofe's Antiquities, Young's Northern Tour; and we are informed that Mr. Pennant is now clofing the Eulogium of this Vale with his Obfervations.

owners of this fort of inclofure, probably from the diverfion which the Chace afforded, that the fences were faid to have meafured fixty miles, which grounds, although many are now divided, feverally retain the appellation of Park. That now denominated Capplebank, properly ufed as a park, is diftinguifhed by a gradually climbing avenue from the houfe, until the afcent becomes abrupt, and terminates the horizon at the diftance of about a mile and a half; this circumftance, combined with fome ftriking objects on the fide view, give the profpects a kind of romantic air, unufually pleafing and picturefque.

In this retirement lived, during the agitated reign of James the Second, that Marquis of Winchefter, who, by feigning a temporary indifpofition for political purpofes, contributed fo much towards effecting the Revolution. Even now near the manfion, in the deep folitude of a woody dell, is to be feen the ruin of a houfe, which the Marquis built, and to which he ufed occafionally to retreat, in the awful hours of night, to enjoy that taciturnity and to cultivate that character he then found fo convenient and neceffary to affume.

THE

ANTIQUARIAN REPERTORY.

ELY HOUSE.

THE ancient building here represented stands in Holborn, and was once the town Manſion or Palace of the Biſhops of Ely. Its demeſnes were formerly very extenſive, and its gardens, according to Stowe, and after him * Shakeſpear, famous for ſtrawberries.

In the reign of Queen Elizabeth, the ground whereon ſtands Hatton, Croſs and Kirby-ſtreet, Great and Little Charles-ſtreet, Hatton-garden, and Hatton-wall, was arbitrarily taken from this houſe by that Queen, and granted to her favourite, Sir Chriſtopher, afterwards Lord Hatton, Chancellor of England, who ingratiated himſelf with his Royal Miſtreſs by his excellence in a qualification, not very eſſential to his profeſſion—namely, dancing.

To aſſign any particular date to the erection of this houſe would perhaps be impoſſible, the different parts of which it conſiſts having been the work of

* Vide Richard the Third, where he makes the Duke of Glouceſter ſay,
    ' My Lord of Ely, when I was laſt in Holbourn
    ' I ſaw good ſtrawberries in your garden there,——
    ' I do beſeech you ſend for ſome of them.'——

The reprefentation of the ftory here related is engraved on both fides of the fame Plate; in one Selwyn appears with a hat on his head, and in the other he is bareheaded, but with fpurs on, a circumftance wanting in the former. From this double reprefentation fome have thought he performed this feat more than once, others with more probability attribute it to the firft Engraving not having been approved of by the family, as deficient either in likenefs or fome other circumftance, wherefore a fecond might be done, and to fave the expence of a frefh Plate, was executed on the back of the former, which opinion receives fome confirmation from the four holes, feen at the corners of the Plate, by which it was immoveably faftened down, fo that only one fide could be viewed. In this Drawing both fides of the Plate are fhewn.

Beneath his feet, and thofe of his wife and children, is the following infcription in the ancient black letter.

Here lyeth ye bodye of John Selwyn gent. keeper of her Maties Parke of Otelands under y^e Right honorable Charles Howward Lord Admyral of England his good Lord & Mr. who had iffue by Sufan his Wyfe v Sunes & vi Daughters all lyving at his Death & departed out of this World the 27th Day of Marche Anno Domini 1587.

The

The ACCOUNT of the ORDINANCES used at TOURNAMENTS, &c. &c. continued.

TO his right highe and mightie Lorde and Liege Rychard by the Grace of God Kinge of Englande and France, Lorde of Ireland and Acquytaine Thomas Duke of Glofter your Coneftable of England Shewethe that wheras many batteyles within Liftes have been in this your Realme of England as well as late in the tyme, and prefence of my right worthie Lorde and father your Grandfather whom God Pardon, as in this your Tyme and Prefence more then hathe ben longe tyme before, and it is very apparannte that many oughte to have ben And for that yt is the greatefte arte that may be in Armes and that to your righte excellent royall Majeftie appertayneth the Soveregnetie Jurifdicion and Knowledge fo that yt be grounded by Juftice and Equitie to Yo honorable renowne in whom all Juftice oughte to remayne and be, Wherefore for that there are dyvers maners, coftomes and orders eftablyfhed in dyvers Partes and Contries as well within your Subjection as otherwhers wherfoever, howbeit this your faid Realme had never any eftablifhmente coftomes or Ordynance of armed Batteyles within liftes in your tyme nor yet in the Tyme of your noble Progenytors olbeyt they were wife valyant and jufte. Nevertheles becawfe that yo your heirs and Succeffors may the bettar do Juftice and equytie to all fuche as in Lyke feates of Armes fhall have to do before you as well your Leges and Subjects as others whatfoever I your faid humble Liege and conftable do offer unto your royall Majeftie this litle booke of the order and maner of combatinge in Liftes not Denyenge but that it is not fo wifely nor with fo good advifement and difcretion made but that yt maye eafely be amended Requyreng your nobleffe as humbly as I maye or can that of your bengnytie yt might Pleafe your Grace to furvey, examyne correcte and amend the faid booke, Shewenge your opinyon as yt fhall feeme good with the Delyberation and Advifement of the wifefte, moft valyant and fufficient Lordes and Knightes of your Realme who in feates of Armes have the Greatefte knowledge, Albeit I have enterprifed this worke, I have not Don the fame to take upon me fuche knowledge or Skill, that I ame hable to accomplyfhe fuche a matter but for that yt be-

longeth

longeth to my office Although that thofe which were in the fame office before me did never write the fame howbeit they were wife and difcreete ye farre more than I am, Wherefore I requyre your royall Matie and all my companyons and freindes wch the faid book fhall fee or heare that you and they will hold me xcufed if there be any thinge more or leffe added to the fame then ought to be, for accordinge to the litle Power and Knowledge that I have, I have made the fame befechinge your highnes my right excellent and right worthie Lorde that the Saide Booke maye be xamyned correfted and amended of you your Grace valyant and Sufficient Lordes and Knightes of yo' Realme who in feates of armes have the greateft knowledge, as aforefaid further maye yt pleafe you to eftablyfhe, approve ordeyne and confirme the faid booke to be kept in your faid realme of England for you your heirs and Succeffors being Kinges of England as to whome of Right it appertayneth.

 FIRSTE, the quarrells and billes of the Challenger and Defendante fhalbe Pleaded in the cowrte before the Coneftable and Marfhall, an if they can not prove their cawfe neyther by witnes nor otherwife, but difcide their quarrell by force the one to prove his entent uppon the other, and th'other in like cafe to Defende, the Coneftable hathe power to appointe the battaile as Chief vycaire or Captaine Under God and the Kinge, The battaile being appoynted the Conftable fhall affigne them the Daye and Place in Sorte that yt be not within xl. Daies after the battaile appointed unleft yt be by the confent of the Challenger and Def. awardinge them how many weapons thei fhall have that is to Saye Glayve Longefword Short Sworde and Dagar Alfo the faid Challenger and Defendante fhall finde Sufficient Sureties and Pledges that every of them fhall come at their faide Daye, the Challenger to Trie his proofe uppon the Defendante and the Def. in his Defence uppon the Challenger, And that the howre be appointed to the Challenger and that he be in the Liftes at leafte by the howre of Pryme to make his Proofe and Difcharge his Sureties and the Def. to do in lyke cafe and that neyther of them do hurte, damage laye in waight nor do the other any Grevance or anoyance by them or any of their frendes well willers or others whatfoever before the howre appoynted to the battaile.

 The Kynge fhall find the feelde to fight in and the Liftes fhalbe made and Devifed by the Coneftable, and yt is to be Confidered that the Liftes muft be 60 pace long and 40 pace brode in good order and that the Grownde be harde,

harde, ſtable and firme, and equally made without great Stones the grownde flatt and that the Liſtes be ſtrongly barred abowte with one Dore in the eſte an other in the Weaſte with good and ſtronge barres vij foot hyghe or more that a Horſe can not leape over them.

The Daye of the battaile the Kinge ſhalbe in a ſtate upon a Highe Skaffolde and a Place ſhalbe made for the Conſtable and Marſhall at the foote of the Stears of the ſaid Skaffolde where they ſhall ſit and then the Surities of the Challenger and Defendante ſhalbe called into the Liſtes and preſent in the Cowrte before the Kinge as Priſonars untill the Challenger and Defendante be come into the Liſtes and have made their Aſſurance.

When the Challenger comethe in his Torneye he ſhall come to the Eaſte gate of the Liſtes in ſuche manner as he will fight wth his Armour and Weapons as is appoynted by the Cowrte and there he ſhall remayne untill that he be led awaye by the Coneſtable in ſorte that when he is com to the Gate the Coneſtable and Marſhall ſhall go thether and the Coneſtable ſhall aſke him what man he is that is come, armed to the Doore of the Liſtes, what is his name, and Wherefore he is come, and the Challenger ſhall anſwer, I am Suche a one, A de F the Challenger that is com hether Er for to accompliſhe Er, Then the Conſtable openynge the umbrell of his heaulmet and Perceavinge him to be the Same man wch is the Challenger ſhall cawſe the Doore of the Liſtes to be opened and Suffer him to Enter with his ſaid Armour weapons victualls and other Lowable Neceſſaries abowte him and Alſo his Cownſaill with him and then he ſhall bringe him before the Kinge and to his State wheere he ſhall attend untill the Defendant be come.

In the like ſorte ſhalbe donne to the Defendante but that he ſhall enter in at the weſte dore of the liſtes

The Coneſtables Clarke ſhall write and put in regeſter the Comynge of and the howre of the entrance of the Challenger, and how he entered into the liſtes a foote or on horſe backe withe the Coolor of the Horſe and how the horſe is armed leſte anye thinge ſholde happen by weaknes of the horſe or harnes and Alſo the harnes of the Challenger and howe he is armed and with how many weapons he entrithe the Liſtes and what victualls or other lowable neceſſaries he bringethe into the Liſtes withe him.

In the like ſorte ſhalbe donne to the Defendante.

Further that the Conſtable cawſe goode heede to be taken that no man neyther before nor behinde the Challenger or Defendante ſhall bringe any more weapons or victualls than are appointed by the Cowrte.

If fo be that the Defendant come not in tyme at the Daye howre and tyme lymeted by the Cowrte the Coneftable fhall comande the marfhall to cawfe him to be called at the fower Cornars of the Liftes, the which Crie fhalbe made there in manner and forme followenge, Oies, Oies, Oies, E de B Defendant come to the tourneye the which yow have enterprifed this Daye to difcharge the Sureties before the kinge, the Coneftable and Marfhall do encounter in your Defence A de F the Challenger in that he hathe furmyfed the

And if that he com not then in tyme he fhalbe caled the feconde tyme in the lyke manner and in the ende he fhall faye come the Daye Paffethe to Moche and if he come not at that tyme he fhalbe caled agayne the Thirde tyme but yt fhalbe betwen the highe third and Middaye in the Same manner as before and in the Ende he fhall faye the Daye paffethe to Moche and the howre of Middaye is at hand fee that you come at that howre of Middaye at the fartheft uppon perrill that maye Enfue.

Albeit that the Coneftable have appointed the howre and tyme unto the Defendant to Com to his torney, nevertheles though he tarry untill myddaye the Judgment ought not to Pas againft him whether yt be in Cafe of Treafon or otherwife but yt is not fo with the Challenger for yt behoveth him to kepe his howre and tyme lymeted by the Cowrte withoutt any p'longinge or excufe whatfoever whether yt be in cafe of Treafon or otherwife.

The Challenger and the Def* beinge entred into the Liftes with their armour weapons victualls other lowable neceffaries and cownfailes as they are affigned by the Cowrte the Coneftable fhall knowe the Kinges Pleafure whether he will appointe any of the Lordes or Knightes of honor to the Saide parties to heare their othe or whether he will that the faid othe be made before him or before the Conftable and Marfhall within the Liftes, the Which thinge beinge donne the Coneftable and Marfhall fhall veve the Speares of the faid Challenger and Defendant and fhall cawfe them to be cut and Sharpned of equall meafure as fhalbe after reherfed.

Then the Challenger and Def* beinge by the conftable ferched for their weapons that thei be allowable withowt any manner of engyne in them Difallowable and if they be otherwife then reafon requyreth then thei fhalbe taken awaye cleerely for reafon good faithe nor Lawe of Armes ought not to Suffer any falfe engyne or treachery in fo greate a Deede, further yt is to be noted that the Challenger or Def* maye arme themfelves as Surely upon their bodies as fhall feeme good to them and to have a targe or pravis in the Liftes

becawft

becawſt yt as but Armure ſo that it be withowt any engyne in hit diſallowable if the one have yt and thother not and if yt fortune that the one of them wolde make his Glayve ſhorte within the meſure of the Standard yt neverthelefs the other maye have yt of the meaſure of the Standard if he will demand yt of the Cowrte, but as towchinge the Speares which has the Meaſure of the Standard the one ſhalbe made of equall meaſure after the other.

And then the Coneſtable ſhall ſende by the Marſhall furſte for the Challenger and his Cownſaile to make his Othe, and before the ſaid othe, the Coneſtable ſhall aſke him whether he will proteſte any more and if he will that then he put yt in Writinge for from thence foorthe he ſhall not make any other Proteſtation.

The Conſtable ſhall have his Clarke redie in his preſence and ſhall Laye before him a booke open and then the Conſtable ſhall cawſe his ſaide Clarke to Reade the ſaide bill of the Challenger a lowde and the bill beinge redde the Coneſtable ſhall ſaye to the Challenger A de F thow knoweſt this bill well and this the warrante and gage that thou gaveſt into owr Cowrte ſo ſhall thow laye thi right hande upon theſe Saincts and ſhall ſware in manner and forme followenge.

Thou A de F ſhalt Sware that this thei bill is trewe in all poynts and Articles conteyned in the ſame from the begynnyng to the Ende and that thow entendeſt to prove the ſame this daye uppon the ſaid E de B Def^t ſo God the healpe and all the Saincts.

This beinge ended the Marſhall ſhall cawſe him to be led backe into his Place and the Conſtable ſhall cawſe the Def. to be caled by the Marſhall and the lyke ſhalbe don to the Def. as before to the Challenger.

Afterwardes the Conſtable ſhall cawſe the Challenger to be caled agayne by the Marſhall and ſhall cawſe him to laye his hande as before uppon the booke and ſhall ſaye A de F, thow Shalt Sweare that thow ne haſte nor ſhalt have more weapons abowte the, ne on thie bodie nor within theſe Liſtes, other then are aſſigned the by the Cowrte that is to Saye Glayve Longſword Short Sworde and Dagger, nor any other Knyfe Smale or greate, ne ſtone of vertue ne herbe ne charme, experience carrecte, or enchantment by the ne for the by the whiche thow truſteſte the bettar to vanquyſhe the ſaide E de B, thine adverſarie whiche ſhall com agaynſt the within the Liſtes this daye in his Defence, and that thow truſteſte in no other thinge but only in God in the bodie

and

and thi Rightfull quarrell fo God the healpe and all Sainctes, after the faide othe beinge ended he fhalbe led agayne to his Place.

In the like Sorte fhalbe don to the Defendant.

The whiche othes beinge ended, and their Chamberlains and Pages being taken awaye, the Coneftable fhall cawfe by the marfhall bothe the Challenger and Def' to be Called who fhalbe brought and garded by the Conftable and Marfhalls men before them, and the Coneftable fhall Saye to bothe parties thowe A de F the fhalt take E de B Defendant by the right hand and he the in lyke cafe charginge you and every of you in the Kinges name upon perill that maye enfue and upon perill to lofe your quarell, that whofoever yt is that is fownde in Defawte, that neyther of you be fo hardie to do to the Other any hurte troble or Grevance nor to thretten any other myfchef at this tyme by the hand uppon perill beforefaid This charge beinge ended the Coneftable Shall cawfe them to Clafpe their handes together and to laye their lefte handes upon the booke Sayenge to the Challenger A de F challenger thow fwearefte by the faithe that thow geveft in the Hande of thine Adverfarie E de B Defendant and by all the Sainctes that you touche withe youre lefte hand that this prefent Daye you fhall do all your Power by all meanes that you can Devife to prove your entente againfte E de B Defendant your Adverfarie to make him yelde into your handes and fo he to Crie or Speake or ells to Make him Die by your hande before you Depart owte of thefe Liftes by the Tyme and fonne appoynted you by this cowrte by your faith, and fo God you healpe and all Sainctes.

Then he fhall Saye to the Defendant E de B Defendant you fweare by the faithe that you give into the hand of your Adverfarie A de F the Challenger and by all the Sainctes that you touche with your lefte hande that this prefent daye you fhall ufe all your Strenght pollycie and Connynge in the befte forte that you maye or can to defend your felfe againfte A de F the Challenger your adverfarie in that he hathe furmyfed, the fo God the healpe and all Sainctes.

The Othes beinge ended and every of them led to his place their cownfelors and frendes beinge taken awaye from them, there fhalbe certaine appoynted by the Coneftable and Marfhall to Garde them, and yt is to be noted that then the Sureties of bothe parties ought to be difcharged of their Suretiefhip if they will requyre yt of the Cowrte.

Then

Then Afterwardes the coneftable fhall comand the Marfhall to Make a Proclamation at the 4 cornars of the liftes in manner and forme followenge Oies, Oies, Oies, we charge and commande you in the behalf of the Kinge the Coneftable, and Marfhall that no man weyther of great or fmall Eftat of what condition or nation foever he be, be fo hardie from hencefoorthe to approche the liftes by 4 foote nor to fpeake one worde, to make any cowntenarce Signe likelehood or noyfe wherby any of the parties A de F challenger and E de B defendant maye take advantage of eche other upon perill to lofe their Life and goods at the Kinges Pleafure.

That done the coneftable and Marfhall fhall cawfe the liftes to be voyded of all manner of perfons except their lieutenante and two knights for the Coneftable and one for the Marfhall, who fhalbe armed uppon their bodies but they fhall have no knyves or Swordes abowt them nor any other weapons wherby the Challenger or Defendante maye have any Advantage whether yt be by negligence or otherwife by not kepinge them but the two Lieutenants of the Coneftable and Marfhall ought to have in their handes eyther of them a Speare withowt Iron, for to Parte them if the Kinge wolde cawfe them to ftaye in their Fightinge whether it be to reft or otherwife howfoer it be.

The Challenger beinge in this Place garded and accompanied by Suche as be apoynted by the Coneftable and Marfhall and the Defendante in lyke manner bothe parties beinge made redie appareiled and accompaned by their Kepers aforefaid the Marfhall with the one partie and the Coneftables Lieutenant with th'other the Coneftable Sittinge in his place before the Kinge as his generall vicayre and the parties beinge redie to fight as ys faid the Coneftable fhall by comandement of the kinge faye with a lowde voyce let them go and refte a While let them go agayne and refte a While, Let them go and Do their indevoir in Godes name, That beinge faide every man fhall Departe frome bothe parties fo theye maye encownter, and Do what fhall Seeme to them befte.

The Chalenger nor Defendant maye not eate nor Drinke from thenceforthe without Leave or Lycence of the Kinge for any thinge that myght happen albeit they wolde agree to hit by Affent within themfelves.

Thencefoorth yt is to be confidered Diligently of the Coneftable that if the kinge will cawfe the Parties fightinge, to be parted, to refte or tarrye for what cawfe foever it be, that he take good regard how theye are parted that they be bothe in one Eftate and Degree in all thinges if the Kinges would

Suffer

Suffer or cawſe them to go together agayne and alſo that he harken well and have good regard to them whether they Speake to Eache other to render or otherwiſe for the witneſſinge and Reporte of the wordes from thenſeforthe apperteynethe unto him and unto none other.

And if the Battayle be in caſe of treaſon he whiche is Convicte ſhalbe unarmed in the liſtes by the comandement of the Coneſtable and a pece of the Liſtes broken in reproche of him uppon the whiche he Shalbe Drawen owt with horſes from the Same place where he is unarmed throughe the liſtes unto the Place of execution where he ſhalbe hedded or hanged accordinge to the Manner of the country the Whiche thinge aperteynethe to the Marſhall to Surveue and perform by his Ofice and to put the Same in execution and to be by untill yt be Donne and fully ended as well for the Challenger as Defendant for good faithe righte and Lawe of Armes will that the Challenger encurre the Lyke Danger that the Defendant ſhould if he be vanquiſht and overcome.

If ſo be that the caſe be for any other cryme he whiche is convicte or overcome ſhalbe unarmed without the Liſtes at the place of Execution whether yt be to be hanged or hedded as well the Challenger as the Defendant as yt is ſaid accordinge unto the uſage of the Contry but he ſhall not be Drawen unleſſe yt be in caſe of Treaſon.

Alſo yf yt be for any facte or action of armes he that is convicte and overcome ſhalbe unarmed as ys aforeſaid and put foorthe of the Liſtes withowt any execution.

And yf it fortune that the kinge will take the Quarrell in hande and cawſe them to agree withowt Suffringe them any more to fighte, then the coneſtable taking the one Partie, and the Marſhall th'other oughte to bringe them before the Kinge and he Shewing them his mynde the Coneſtable and Marſhall ſhall leade them to one of the Doores of the Liſtes in Suche Sorte with their weapons horſe and Armour as they were fownd when the kinge toke the Quarrell in hande, And ſo they ſhall be ledde owte of the Doore equally ſo that the one go not owte before the other in no wiſe for after that the Kinge hathe taken up the quarrell yt were Diſhoneſte that the one partie ſholde receave more Dyſhonor than thother for yt hathe ben ſayd by Divers auncient wryters that he whiche goethe firſt owte of the Liſtes hathe the Dyſhonor, the Same as ys as well in caſe of Treaſon as otherwiſe.

Alſo

THE ANTIQUARIAN REPERTORY.   37

Alſo their oughte to be falſe liſtes withowte the principall Liſtes between the which the Conſt. & Marſhall ſarvantes and the Kings Sargeants of Armes oughte to be to kepe and Defende if any man ſholde make any offence or troble contrary to the Proclamation made in the Cowrte or any thinge that Might be contrary to the Kinges Roiall Majeſtie or Lawe of Armes, and thoſe people ought to be armed in all Points.

The Coneſtable ſhall have there ſo many men of armes as are needfull and the Marſhall ſhall have alſo by the Aſſignment of the Coneſtable ſo many as are requyſite, whiche people ſhall have the garde as is aforſaid, and the Kinges Sargeante of Armes ſhall have the keping of the Dore of the Liſtes and the areſts yf any be made by the Comandement of the ſaid Conſt. and Marſhall.

Farther if there be any meate or Drinke myneſtred to the Challenger or Deft. or any other Lawfull neceſſaryes, after the cownſelors frendes and Pages of the Challenger and Def^t. are taken awaye as afore ys ſaide, the Saide admyniſtration dothe belonge to the herehaults and alſo the Proclamation made within the Cowrte and Liſtes.

The wch Kinges herehaults and Purſuyvants ſhall have a Place appointed for them by the Coneſtable and Marſhall as nere to the Liſtes as thei maye well be made, ſo that theye maye ſe all the Deede and be redy if thei be caled to do any thinge.

The fees of the Kinge of Armes of the province and the other Officers of Armes is all the weapons horſes & Armour the wch they had medled wthall and let fall to the Grownde after thei are entred into the Liſtes as well of the Challenger as Def^t. and Alſo all horſes weapons and armour of him that is convict whether yt be the Challenger or Def^t wth the Liſtes Scaffold and Tymber uſed at the ſaid Battaile.

The OTIIE of the HERAULDE at ye tyme of his Creation before his Sovereigne.

From PHILPOT.

FIRSTE, ye fhall fwear, that ye fhalbe true to the moft high and Mighty Prince, the Kinge our Souvereigne Lord, and yf you have any knowledge, or hear any Imagination of Treafon or Language or Words that might found to the Derogation or hurt of his Eftate and highnefs (which God Defend) you fhall in that cafe as haftily and as foon as it is to you Poffible Difcover and Shew it unto his highnefs or to his Noble and Difcreet Councel and to conceal it in no Wife, Alfo you fhall Promife and Swear that you fhall be converfant and ferviceable to all Gentlemen to Do their commands to their Worfhip and Knighthood by your good Counfel that God has Sent you and ever Ready to Offer your Service unto them.

Alfo you fhall Promife and Swear to be Secret and Keep the Secrets of Knights Efq^{rs}, Ladies and Gentlewomen as a Confeffor of Arms, and not to Difcover them in any Wife except it be for Treafon as it is before faid.

Alfo you fhall Promife and Swear if fortune fall you in Diverfe Lands and Countries wherein you go or Ride that you find any Gentleman of Name and of Arms that hath Loft his Goods in Worfhip & Knighthood in the Kings Service, or in any other Place of Worfhip and is fallen into Poverty you fhall aid Support and Sucour him in that you may, & if he afk you of your Good to his Suftenance you fhall give him Part of fuch Good as God hath fent you to Your Power, and as you may bear.

Alfo you fhall Promife and Swear if you be in any Place that you hear any Langugge between Party & Party that is not Worfhipfull Profitable nor Virtuous that you keep your Mouth clofe, and Report it not forth but to their Worfhip and the Beft.

Alfo you fhall Promife & Swear if fo be you be in any Place that you hear any Debate or Languge Difhoneft between Gentleman & Gentlewoman the Which you be Privy to If fo be you be Required by Prince Judge or any other to bear Witnefs unlefs that the Law will needs compel you fo to Do you fhall not without Licence of Both Parties and When you have Leave

you

you fhall not for any favour Love or awe but fay the Sooth to Your Knowledge.

Alfo you fhall Promife and Swear to be True & Secret to all Gentlewomen Widdows & Maidens, and in Cafe that any Man would Do them Wrong or force them or Difinherit them of their Livelyhood & they have no Goods to Purfue them for their Right to Princes or Judges if the Require you of Supportation you fhall Support them, with your Good Wifdom & Counfel to Princes and Judges.

Alfo you fhall Promife and Swear that you fhall forfake all Places of Difhonefty the Play of Hazardy & the common Haunt of Going into Taverns & other Places of Debates, Efchewing Vices and Takeing you to Virtues to Your Power this Article & all other Articles above faid you fhall Truly Keep fo God you help and Holy Doom and by this Book and Crofs of this Sword that belongeth to Knighthood.

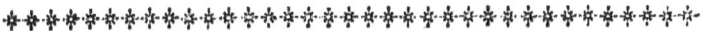

The OTHE of a HERAULDE abridged.

Taken from Vincent's Collection in the College of Arms.

FIRSTE ye fhall fwear to be true to y^e Kinge our Souveregn Lord whofe Arms you bear, and to his heyres and Succeffors, And all fuche Articles as apperteyneth to a Heraulde to be Kept you fhall well and truly obferve & keep in every Poynt therof, as well as yf they were read to you Article by Article, fo God you help and holydome and by this booke, and by the Croffe of the Sworde, y^t belongeth unto Knighthood.*

    * This is the Oath as now read.

To the EDITOR of the ANTIQUARIAN REPERTORY.

SIR,

THE annexed Differtation on the Etymology of the Names of Places in Ireland, was drawn up by a Gentleman, well verfed in the Language and Antiquities of that country. If you think it falls within the plan of your Work, you are extremely welcome to print it.

I am, Sir, your's, &c.

Hertford, March 27, 1775.   C. L.

THAT the Names of Places in Ireland, in common with other countries, had originally fome meaning, is not to be doubted, but the Etymology of moft of them, is, or feems to be, totally forgot: however, there are many places whofe fituation or qualities ftill point out the original meaning of their names, viz.

Such as begin with, Agha, are denominated from a plain field adjacent, as Aghanacloighe, i. e. Aghnacloy. Stonefield, Aghalean, Broadfield, &c. &c. Names in Anagh denote a hill furrounded with a morafs or fen; of which there are great numbers, as Anaghfamhri, Anaghfavry; Summer Ifland, Anaghruagh, Anaghroe, Red Ifland, &c. &c.

Such as begin with Ath are denominated from O Ford, as Ath Cliath, the Irifh name for Dublin. Athlone, Athboy, Atherdee, &c. &c.

Such as begin with Baile, i. e. a town, village, or habitation, are denominated from fome quality of the place, or from fome original proprietor, as Ballydonelly, now Caftle Caulfield, formerly O Donelly's Town, Ballymagavran, i. e. Magavran's-town, &c. &c.

Such as begin with Inis, denote their being iflands or peninfulas, as Inifkillin, Inifawen, &c. &c.

Such as begin with Coille, Killy, indicate the place to have been a wood, of which there are numbers almoft in every country, as Killebreftel, Killereafk, &c. &c.

Such

Such as begin with Dovie, Derry, appear to have been detached woods, which are so numerous in most countries, that it would be endless to mention them.

All places beginning with Knock are hills, as Knockbān, Whitehill; Knockruagh, Knockroe, Redhill, &c. &c.

There are in every country numbers of places that begin with Mullagh, which is another word for hill, as Mullaghbān, Whitehill, &c. &c.

There are also numbers that begin with Tully, which signifies the steep side of an hill. Wherever a place begins with Dun, it is evident, that place must have, at least, the remains of some old strength, natural or artificial, as Dungannon, Dunleer, Dundrum, Duncannon, &c. &c.

Lis, or Rath, are the Irish names for the Danish earthen forts, so numerous all over the kingdom, and give names to numbers of places, as Lismere, Lisgleen, Rathfriland, Rathdowny, &c. &c.

There are some places that begin with Magh, which signifies an extended plain, as Maghnealta, by those who do not understand Irish wrote Moynalty, in the county of Meath, and some others, which manifestly discover the origin of their names.

Some names of places begin with Glen, which signifies a valley, whether wide or narrow, between a ridge of mountains, as Glenarm, Glendalle, &c. In Scotland whole countries are called Glens, as Glengarry, Glencoe, Glenlivet, Glenlyon, &c. &c.

Carrick is the Irish for a rock, and consequently all towns or places beginning with Carrick have some rock or craggy place adjacent, as Carrickfergus, Carrickmacross, Carricknasure, &c. &c.

Tuam, is general, is where a river runs out of a lake; and there are some towns from thence called Tuam, one particularly, the see of an Archbishop, with some others.

Drum, a long ridge of a hill, from whence many places are denominated, as Drumquin, Drumahare, &c.

Stra, Hibernicé Strath, a plain on the side of a river, from which some places are denominated, as Strabane, Stranorlan, Stranocum, &c.

WESTMINSTER ABBEY.

THIS picturesque groupe of building is composed of elegant specimens of both ancient and modern magnificence. Westminster-Abbey and Hall, being among the most beautiful ancient buildings in this kingdom, and the Bridge, is justly esteemed not inferior to any structure of that kind in Europe.

Thorneie, or the West-Minster, so called, the first from the small island wherein it stood, and the second from its situation with respect to London, was built, as it is said, on the ruins of an old heathen temple, dedicated to Apollo, (which had also been a church in the time of King Lucius) by Sebert, King of the East-Saxons, about the year 610, being instigated thereunto by the encouragement and solicitations of his mother, brother, and sovereign, King Ethelbert, and of Mellitus, Bishop of London; it was dedicated to St. Peter, who, as the Legend says, consecrated it himself, the night before that ceremony was to have been performed, according to the king's order, by Mellitus.

This church being destroyed in the Danish wars, was restored Anno 958, by King Edgar, and Dunstan, Bishop of London, and twelve monks placed therein, who were but meanly provided for till King Edward the Confessor began Anno Dom. 1049, to rebuild this Church and Abbey, which he finished and amply endowed before the year 1066, from whence it continued in the hands of the Monks of the order of St. Benedict, till the general dissolution.

This edifice was greatly improved by King Henry the Third, who in the year 1200, began to erect a new chapel to the Blessed Virgin; and about twenty years after, finding the walls and steeple of the old structure much decayed, he pulled them all down, with a design to enlarge and rebuild them in a more regular manner, but he did not live to accomplish it, nor was it compleated till about the year 1285, about fourteen years after his decease, and this is the age of the oldest part of the building now standing.

About the year 1502, King Henry the Seventh began that magnificent Chapel, called after his name, for a burial place for himself and posterity, for which purpose he pulled down the Chapel built by Henry the Third, and

THE ANTIQUARIAN REPERTORY. 43

an adjoining houſe, called the White Roſe Tavern. This chapel, like the former, he dedicated to the Bleſſed Virgin.

At the general diſſolution, the annual revenues of this Monaſtery were eſtimated according to Dugdale, 3471l. os. 2d. q. A M S. vol. makes it 3033l. 17s. od. q. And Speed reckons it at 3977l. 6s. 4d. ob. q. King Henry the Eighth in the 32d year of his reign, erected a Biſhop's ſee here (to whoſe dioceſe was aſſigned the county of Middleſex) and a Cathedral, conſiſting of a dean, and twelve prebendaries. The biſhoprick was ſunk in the year 1550, but the chapter continued ſix years after, when they were forced to give place to the Abbot, and Black Monks, who were re-eſtabliſhed here by King Philip, and Queen Mary. In 1560 it was again changed into a collegiate church, in which form it ſtill continues, conſiſting of a dean, and twelve ſecular prebendaries, to which alſo belong petty canons, and other members of the choir, to the number of thirty; two ſchool-maſters, forty king's ſcholars, twelve almſmen, and many officers and ſervants. The offices of the monaſtery were converted to diverſe uſes.

This Abbey, beſides great riches, had diverſe privileges, and immunities, ſuch as ſanctuary to all perſons, let their offence be ever ſo enormous. Exemption from the juriſdiction of the Biſhops of London, and by a bull of Pope Nicholas the Firſt, it was conſtituted the place for the inauguration of the kings of England.

The Abbey church meaſures in length 360 feet within the walls, 72 feet in breadth at the nave, and at the croſs one hundred and ninety five. The whole is a moſt ſtriking inſtance of the beauty of Gothic architecture, and the ſolemnity of the ſcene receives a very conſiderable addition from the multitude of fine monuments both ancient and modern contained therein.

The two fine towers which make ſo conſpicuous a part of this view, are modern, but add greatly to the beauty of this venerable ſtructure.

The next in point of antiquity, is Weſtminſter-Hall, originally built by William Rufus, as an addition to the palace of Weſtminſter, but becoming ruinous, was Anno 1397, rebuilt by King Richard the Second, and is eſteemed one of the largeſt rooms in England, ſupported by pillars, it being 270 feet in length, and 74 broad. The roof is reckoned a maſter piece of art.

The Bridge, offers itſelf next to our conſideration; the firſt ſtone of which was laid on the 29th of January 1738-9, and it was compleated in November, 1747.

1747. The expence of its erection, which was raifed by feveral lotteries, amounted to 389,500l. The architect was Charles Labelye, a Switzer, by birth.

"This Bridge," fays the author of London and its environs defcribed, "is univerfally allowed to be one of the fineft in the world. It is adorned and fecured on each fide by a very lofty and noble baluftrade; there are receffes over every pier, which is a femi-octagon; twelve of them are covered with half domes, viz. four at each end, and four in the middle. Between thefe in the middle are pedeftals, on which was intended a group of figures; this would greatly add to the magnificence, by making the centre more principal (which it ought to be) and giving it an air of grandeur fuitable to the city to which it belongs; a great number of lamps are fo agreeably difpofed on the top of the receffes, as at once to contribute to the purpofes of ufe and beauty. This magnificent ftructure is 1223 feet in length, and above 300 feet longer than London-Bridge; the afcent at the top is extremely well managed, and the room allowed for paffengers confifts of a commodious foot way feven feet broad on each fide, paved with broad moor ftone, and raifed above the road allowed for carriages; this laft is thirty feet wide, and is fufficient to admit the paffage of three carriages, and two horfes, on a breaft, without the leaft danger.

"The conftruction and diftance of the piers from each other are fo managed, that the vacancies under the arches allowed for the water way, are four times as much as at London-Bridge, and in confequence of this, there is no fall, nor can the leaft danger arrive to boats in paffing through the arches; the piers, which are fourteen, have thirteen large and two fmall arches, all femicircular. Thefe with two abutments conftitute the bridge, whofe ftrength is not inferior to its elegance.

"The length of every pier is feventy feet, and each end is terminated with a faliant angle againft either ftream. The breadth of the two middle piers is feventeen feet at the fpringing of the arches, and contains three thoufand cubic feet, or near two hundred tons of folid ftone; and the others on each fide regularly decreafe one foot in breadth, fo that the two next to the largeft are each fixteen feet, and fo on to the two leaft next the fides, which are no more than twelve feet wide at the fpringing of the arches.

"The centre arch is feventy-fix feet wide, and the others decreafe in width four feet on each fide, fo that the two next to the centre arch are feventy-

"two

"two feet wide, and so on to the least of the large arches, which are each
"fifty two feet wide, and the two small ones in the abutments close to the
"shore, are about twenty feet in width.

"The foundation of the Bridge is laid on a solid and firm mass of gravel,
"which lies at the bottom of the bed of the river, but at a much greater depth
"on the Surry, than the Westminster side; and this inequality of the ground
"required the heights of the several piers to be very different, as some have
"their foundations laid at five feet, and others at fourteen feet under the bed
"of the river. The piers are all four feet wider at their foundation than at
"the top, and are founded on the bottoms of wooden cases, formed of the
"most substantial work, eighty feet in length, twenty-eight in breadth; and
"these timbers are two feet in thickness. The caisoon, or wooden case, in
"which the first pier was built, contained one hundred and fifty loads of
"timber, and forty thousand pound weight is computed to be always under
"water in stone and timber.

"The materials are much superior to those commonly used on such occa-
"sions, the inside is usually filled up with chalk, small stones or rubbish, but
"here all the piers are the same on the inside as without, of solid blocks of
"Portland stone, many of which are four or five tons weight, and none less
"than a ton, except the closers, or smaller ones intended for fastening the
"others, one of which has its place between every four of the large ones.
"These vast blocks are perfectly well wrought for uniting; they are laid in
"Dutch terrace, and also fastened together with iron cramps, run in with
"lead. All this iron work is however entirely concealed, and so placed that
"none of them can be affected by the water.

"It is also worthy of remark, that the soffit of every arch is turned and built
"quite through with blocks of Portland stone, over which is built and bond-
"ed in with it, another arch of Purbeck stone, four or five times thicker on
"the reins, than over the key; and by this secondary arch, together with
"the incumbent load of materials, all the parts of every arch are in equili-
"brio, and the whole weight so happily adjusted, that each arch can stand
"single, without affecting or being affected by the other arches. In short,
"between every two arches, a drain is contrived to carry off the water and
"filth, that might in time penetrate and accumulate in those places, to the
"great detriment of the arches.

"Though the greatest care was taken in laying the foundation deep in the gravel, and using every probable method to prevent the sinking of the piers, yet all this was in some degree ineffectual, for one of them sunk so considerably when the work was near compleated, as to retard the finishing it a considerable time. This gave the highest satisfaction to those who had opposed this noble work; but the Commissioners for building the Bridge, immediately ordered the arch supported by that pier, to be loaded with incredible weights, till all the settlement that could be forced was made; after this the arch was rebuilt, and has ever since been as secure as the rest."

In this view too appears the tower of the church of St. Margaret, built about the year 1064, by King Edward the Confessor, for parochial service, rebuilt in the reign of Edward the First, thoroughly repaired and beautified Anno 1735, 350ol. being granted by parliament for that purpose; and lastly again repaired in the year 1758, when the inhabitants purchased a beautiful glass window, made by order of the magistrates of Dort, in Holland, and intended for a present to Henry the Seventh, for his chapel, but he dying before it was finished, it was set up in the church of Waltham-Abbey, in Essex. At the dissolution it was removed to New-Hall, in that county, and remained there till sold by John Olmius, Esq; for the sum of 400 guineas. The subject is a crucifixion, and near the bottom are the portraits of King Henry the Seventh, and his Queen, from original pictures sent purposely to Dort. A print of this window has been published by the Antiquarian Society.

༺ ༻

Copy of the Letters Patents of King Richard y" 3ᵈ. whereby he did Incorporate In one Body Pollitique all the Kings Heraults and Pourſoiv" of Armes and Gave them a Howſe in London to Reſort unto and Dwell in called Cold Harbore in the firſt Yere of his Reign.

RICHARD by the Grace of God King of England and of France Lord of Ireland &c. to all that theſe prent Writeing ſhall come ſend^{eth} Greeting know you that we of our Eſpecial Grace and Certain Knowledge and our mere Motion and alſo upon Certain Conciderations ſpecially moveing have Geven and Granted for us and our Heirs as much as in us ys, to our well beloved John Writh otherwiſe called Garter King of Armes of Engliſhmen

Thomas

Thomas Holme Otherways call'd Clarenceux King of Arms of the South Parts, John Moore otherwife Norroy King of Armes of y[e] North, Richard Champney otherwife call'd Glofter King of Armes of Wales, and to all other Heraults and Purfuivants at Armes that they and their fucceffors that is to fay Garter King of Arms of Englifhmen, King of Armes of the South King of Armes of the North, King of Armes of Wales, and all other heraults and Pourfuivants of Armes which fhall for the Time being be one body Corporate in Deed and name and that they may have a Perpetual Succeffion and alfo that they may have and Exercife a Certain common Seal for their Bufinefs and the Expedition thereof and that they and their Succeffors be named for and by the Name of Garter King of Armes of Englifhmen, K of A. of the South, K of A. of the North and K of A. of Wales and other Her[ts]. and Pours[ts]. of Armes and that they and their Succeffors by the fame names be Able Perfons haveing Knowledge in the Lawe that they have and bear that name for Ever, and that the f[d]. Garter K of A. of Engl[n]. K of A. of the South. K of A. y[e] North. and K of A. of Wales and other Her[ts]. and Pours[ts]. at Armes and their Succeffors by the fame Names whatfoeer Lands Tenements Hereditaments and Poffeffions Goods and Chattels that they have and for the Lands Tenements Rents and Poffeffions, Rightes Goods and Chattels, whatfoeer they be, in all manner of Actions Caufes Demands Complaints and Pleas as well Real and Perfonal as other of what foeer Kind Conditions or Nature they be of in all manner of Courts Afore all manner of Juftices or Judges Spiritual or Temporal may for eer Plead be Impleaded anfwer and be anfwer'd even fo and in like manner as other our liege People Perfons able and Haveing Knowledge in the Lawe may and be Accouftom'd to Plead and be Impleaded and to Anfwer and to be Anfwered

And that the forefaid G. K of A. of Englifhmen K of A of S. K of A of N. K of A of W. and other Herl[ds] and other our Purfui[ts]. at Armes and their Succeffors at their Pleafure may Dwell together and at Days Places and Times convenient and meet as Often and when hit fhall Pleafe them to Affemble and Meet together to Intreat or Communicate and agree amongft themfelves and alfo with other for Counfel and Advifement concerning the Good State Learning and Order of the Aforefaid Faculties.

And that they may have a certain Place and Manfion convenient for that Purpofe of our Special Grace and Mere Motion we have Given and Granted unto the fame Garter King of A. of Engl[n]. K. of A. of the S. K of A of the N. K. of A. of W. and to our Her[ts]. and Pours[ts]. of Armes one Meffuage with the Appurtynances in London in y[e] Parifh of All Saints, call'd Cold
Harbore

Harbore to have and to Hold the said Messuage with the Appertenances to the s^d G K of A. of Englishmen K. of A. of ye S. K. A. N. K. A. W. and Heralds and Purs^{ts}. of Arms and their Successors to ye use of twelve of the most Principal and most aproved of them for ye Time being for ever without Compte or any other thing there of to us or our heirs to be given or paid.

And moreover of our most Abundant Grace we have Granted and given Licence for us and our Heirs aforesaid as much as is in us to the Afors^d. G K of Armes of Englishmen, K of A of ye S. K of A of ye N. K of A of W. and to the Her^{lts}. and Pursuits of Arms and to their Successors that they those Lands Tenement Rents and Possessions which be now Holden of us in Capite to the Value of Twenty Pounds Sterling by the Yeare besides the Messuage aforesaid with the Appertinances of Whatsoever Person or Persons Seculer or Regular that they can get them to have and to hold to them and their Successors for ever, to the Intent to find a Chaplain convenient to celebrate daily within the Aforesaid Messuage or without at the Pleasure of ye K^s. of A^s. aforesaid for the Good Estate of us and Ann our Bedfellow and of Edward Prince of Wales our first begotten Son as long as we live and for our Souls when we shall depart this World and for the Good Estate of all Benefactors Kings of Armes aforenam'd as long as they live and for their Souls when they be departed and for all Christian Souls after the Discretion and Ordonance of ye s^d, G. K. of A. of English^n. K of A. of ye S. K of A. of ye N. K of A. of W. and other H. and Purs^{lts}. of Arms and their Succ^{rs}.

And all these Aforesaid without Impeachment lett Trouble or Greffe of us or our Heirs Justices Sheriffs Exheators Crownes Bayliffs or of any other of our Ministers and without any other the King's Letters Patents or any Manner of Inquisition upon any Breve or W^{rit} De ad Quod.—or any other Kings Commandement in that Part by any means to be Prosecuted Had made taken or Return'd, and without any fine or fee thereof to us or our Heirs to be made or Paid the Statute ordain'd of Lands and Tenements ad manum. mortuum. non . Or that Because Express mention of the True yearly Value of the Messuage Aforesaid, or other the Premises or any of them or of other Gifts or Grants by us or any of our Progenitors or our Predecessors Kings of England to the Aforesaid John Wryth Thomas Holme John Moore and Richard Champney or to any of them after this Time and in these Presents is not Contain'd any Statue Act ordance or Restraint to the Contrary Made Constituted or Whatsoever it be notwithstanding in Witness whereof we have Caused these our Letters Patents to be Made witness our self at Westminster the 2d Day of March the first Year of our Reign.

THE

ANTIQUARIAN REPERTORY.

To the EDITOR of the ANTIQUARIAN REPERTORY.

SIR,

NOTHING can be more foreign to the original meaning of many words, and proper names, than their prefent appellations, frequently owing to the hiftory of thofe things being forgotten, or an ignorance of the language in which they were expreffed. Who, for example, when the Crier of a Court bawls out, O yes, O yes, would dream that it was a proclamation commanding the talkers to become hearers, being the French word *Oyez, liften*, retained in our Courts ever fince the Pleadings were held in Law French. Or would any perfon fuppofe that the Head Land on the French Coaft near Calais, called by our feamen *Black Nefs*, could be fo titled from its French name of *Blanc-Nez*, or, *The White Headland*.

I have collected a few inftances of thefe perverfions, and as they contain a kind of Antiquarian Reading, I here fend them for your Repertory; if you approve of thefe, you may perhaps hear further from

Your's, &c. C. D—y.

HENRY VIII. having taken the town of Bullogne, in France, the Gates of which he brought to Hardes, in Kent, where they are ftill remaining.

ing. The flatterers of that reign highly magnified this action, which, Porto-Bello-like, became a popular subject for Signs, and the Port or Harbour of Bullogne, called Bullogne Mouth, was accordingly set up at a noted Inn in Holbourn; the name of the Inn long out-living the Sign and Fame of the Conquest, an ignorant Painter, employed by a no less ignorant Landlord, to paint a new one, represented it by a Bull and a large gaping human Mouth, answering to the vulgar pronunciation of Bull and Mouth. Perhaps the conceit of its allusion to the roarings and vociferations of a Quaker's meeting held there might not a little tend to make it maintain its usurped post. The same piece of history gave being to the Bull and Gate, originally meant for Bullogne Gate, and represented by an embattled gate, or entrance into a fortified town.

The Barber's Pole has been the subject of many conjectures, some conceiving it to have originated from the word Poll, or Head, with several other conceits, as far fetched and as unmeaning; but the true intention of that party-coloured Staff was to shew the master of the shop practised Surgery, and could breathe a vein as well as mow a beard, such a Staff being to this day, by every village practitioner, put into the hand of a patient undergoing the operation of Phlebotomy. The white Band which encompasses the Staff was meant to represent the Phillet, thus elegantly twined about it.

Nor were the Chequers (at this time a common sign of a public-house) less expressive, being the representation of a kind of Draught-board, called Tables, and shewed that there that game might be played. From their colour, which was red, and the similarity to a Lattice, it was corruptly called the Red Lettuce, which word is frequently used by ancient writers to signify an Alehouse.

The Spectator has explained the sign of the Bell Savage Inn plausibly enough, in supposing it to have been originally the figure of a beautiful Female found in the woods, called in French *La belle Sauvage*. But another reason has since been assigned for that appellation, namely, that the Inn was once the property of a Lady Arabella Savage, and familiarly called Bell Savage's Inn, probably represented, as at present, by a Bell and a Savage, or wild Man, which was a Rebus for her name, Rebus's being much in fashion in the 16th century, of which the Bolt and Tun is an instance.

The Three Blue Balls prefixed to the doors and windows of Pawnbrokers shops, by the vulgar humourously enough said to indicate that it is two to one that the things pledged are never redeemed, was in reality the Arms

of

of a fet of Merchants from Lombardy, who were the firft that publicly lent money on pledges. They dwelt together in a ftreet, from them named Lombard-ftreet, in London, and alfo gave their name to another at Paris. The appellation of Lombard was formerly all over Europe confidered as fynonimous to that of Ufurer.

At the inftitution of the Yeomen of the Guard, they ufed to wait at table on all great folemnities, and were ranged near the buffets; this procured them the name of *Buffetiers*, not very unlike in found to the jocular appellation of Beef-eaters, now given them; though probably it was rather the voluntary mifnomer of fome wicked wit, than an accidental corruption arifing from ignorance of the French language.

The opprobrious title of Bum-bayliffe, fo conftantly beftowed on the Sheriff's Officers, is, according to Judge Blackftone, only the corruption of Bound Bayliffe, every Sheriff's Officer being obliged to enter into bonds, and to find fecurity for his good behaviour, previous to his appointment.

A Cordwainer feems to have no relation to the occupation it is meant to exprefs, which is that of a Shoe-maker. But Cordonier, originally fpelt Corduanier, is the French word for that trade, the beft leather ufed for fhoes coming originally from Cordua, in Spain. Spanifh leather fhoes were once famous in England.

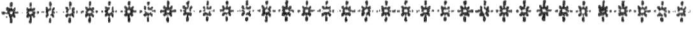

The LODGE in BUSHY PARK, MIDDLESEX.

THE Lodge here reprefented, was called the Upper Lodge; it was built, according to tradition, in the reign of King James the Firft, at which time there were three Parks, the Upper, Middle and Lower Parks; thefe have been fince joined.

It was firft inhabited by a Keeper of the name of Prodgies, who lies buried at Hampton. To that family fucceeded an Earl of Macclesfield, and to him Charles, Lord Hallifax, uncle to the father of the late Lord Hallifax. Lady North is the prefent Ranger.

In this building it is said King Charles the Second was once entertained by the then Keeper. It was, as report goes, repaired in the reign of King William the Third, who took great delight in the Palace of Hampton Court.

This Lodge was lately pulled down, and on its site a small building has lately been erected.

✤✤✤✤✤✤✤✤✤✤✤✤✤✤✤✤✤✤✤✤✤✤✤✤✤✤✤✤✤✤✤✤

At the West end of the Cathedral of Peterborough, in Northamptonshire, hangs a Portrait of old Scarlet, formerly Sexton of that church, copied from a more ancient Painting destroyed by time and damps, the fragments of which are still remaining. He is drawn at full length, having about him the insignia of his office, such as the mattock, spade, &c. Under the Picture are the following verses likewise hanging up against the wall.

  YOU see Old Scarlets picture stand on Hie,
   But at your feet there doth his bodie lie,
  His Grave Stone doth his Age and Death time Shewe
  His Office by his Tokens you may know
  Second to none for Strength and Sturdye Limm,
  A Scarebabe mighty Voice with Visage Grim
  Hee had enterr'd * two Queens within this Place
  And this Townes house-holders in his Lives Space
  Twice over: but at length his one turne came
  What he for others did, for him the same
  Was done: no Doubt his Soul doth live for aye
  In Heaven: though here his body's clad in clay.
    On a square stone below.
     July 2. 1594
      R S.
     Ætatis 98.

 * Catherine, divorced by Henry VIII. and Mary Queen of Scots, afterwards removed to Windsor.

                    Some

Some Account of the PEOPLE called GYPSIES.

THESE swarthy itinerants have spread themselves all over Europe, as is testified by various travellers of all nations, and every where, like the Jews, pretend to keep themselves as a distinct people, not intermixing with any but those of their own fraternity, and talking a gibberish or jargon peculiar to themselves, which is by some falsely dignified with the appellation of a language.

That they have so long subsisted seems a kind of reproach to all police, as they are universally considered in the same light, namely, that of cheats and pilferers,—witness the definition of them in Dufresne, and the curious etchings of them done by that ingenious artist Callot.

" Ægyptiaci," says the above cited author in his Glossary, " Vagi ho-
" mines, harioli ac fatidici, qui hac & illac errantes ex manus inspectione
" futura præsagire se fingunt, ut de marsupiis incautorum nummos corro-
" gent." The engraver does not represent them in a more favourable light than the lexographer, for besides his inimitable delineations of their dissolute manner of living, he has accompanied his plates with verses, which are very far from celebrating their honesty. Diverse severe laws have been enacted against them in different countries. They were driven out of France by an ordinance of the States of Orleans in 1560; and in a Provincial Council held at Terragona in the year 1591, there was the following decree against them, " Curandum etiam est ut publici Magistratus eos coerceant qui se
" Ægyptiacos vel Bohemianos vocant, quos vix constat esse Christianos,
" nisi ex eorum relatione, cum tamen sint mendaces, fures & deceptores &
" aliis Sceleribus multi eoram assueti." In England a very severe statute was framed against them, the 22d of Henry VIII. where they are described as " outlandish people, calling themselves Egyptians, using no craft nor feat
" of merchandize, who have come into the realm and gone from shire to
" shire and place to place in great company, and use great subtle, and crafty
" means, to deceive the people; bearing them in hand that they by palmestry
" could tell mens and womens fortunes, and so many times by craft and
" subtlety have deceived the people of their money, and also have com-
" mitted many heinous felonies and robberies." Wherefore they are directed to quit the kingdom, and not to return under pain of imprisonment,

and

and forfeiture of their goods and chattels; and upon their trials for any felony which they may have committed, they shall not be entitled to a jury *de medietate linguæ*; besides which it is enacted by statutes 1 and 2 Ph. and Mary, c. 4. and Eliz. c. 20. That if any such persons shall be imported into this kingdom, the importer shall forfeit 40l. And if the Egyptians themselves remain one month in this kingdom, or if any person, being fourteen years old, (whether natural-born subject or stranger) which hath been seen or found in the fellowship of such Egyptians, or who hath disguised him or herself like them, and shall remain in the same one month, at one or several times, it is felony without benefit of clergy. Sir Mathew Hale relates, that at one assize for the county of Suffolk, no less than thirteen Gypsies were executed upon these statutes, a few years before the Restoration.

Mr. Twiss, in his Travels through Portugal and Spain, says that in the last named kingdom, the Gypsies are tollerated, and frequently keep inns, at some of which he has occasionally lodged, without any injury or loss. His account of them is given in the following words:

" It may not be improper to mention the Gypsies, who are very numerous
" throughout Spain, especially about, and in Marcia, Cordova, Cadiz and
" Ronda. The race of these vagabonds is found in every part of Europe.
" The French call them *Bohemiens*, the Italians *Zingari*, the Germans *Zie-*
" *genners*, the Dutch *Heydenen*, (Pagans) the Portuguese *Siganos*, and the
" Spaniards *Gitanos*, in Latin *Cingari*. Their language, which is peculiar
" to themselves, is every where so similar that they undoubtedly are all de-
" rived from the same source; they began to appear in Europe in the fif-
" teenth century, and are probably a mixture of Egyptians and Ethiopians.
" The men are all thieves, and the women libertines, they follow no certain
" trade, and have no fixed religion: they do not enter into the order of
" society wherein they are only tollerated. It is supposed that there are up-
" wards of forty thousand of them in Spain, great numbers of whom are
" inn-keepers in the villages and small towns, and are every where fortune-
" tellers. In Spain they are not allowed to possess any lands, nor even to
" serve as soldiers. They marry among themselves; they stroll in troops
" about the country, and bury their dead under a tree. Their ignorance
" prevents their employing themselves in any thing but in providing for
" the immediate wants of nature, beyond which even their roguishness does
" not extend, and only endeavouring to save themselves the trouble of la-
" bour:

THE ANTIQUARIAN REPERTORY. 55

" bour: they are contented if they can procure food by shewing feats of
" dexterity, and only pilfer to supply themselves with the trifles they want;
" so that they never render themselves liable to any severer chastisement than
" whipping, for having stolen chickens, linen, &c. Most of the men have
" a smattering of physic and surgery, and are skilled in tricks performed by
" flight of hand. The foregoing account is partly extracted from le Voya-
" geur François, vol. XVI. but the assertion that they are all so abandoned
" as that author says, is too general; I have lodged many times in their
" houses, and never missed the most trifling thing, though I have left my
" knives, forks, candlesticks, spoons, and linen, at their mercy; and I have
" more than once known unsuccessful attempts made for a private interview
" with some of their young females, who virtuously rejected both the court-
" ship and the money."

Various are the accounts of the time and manner of introduction of this people into Europe, for it seems pretty clear that the first of them were Asiatics; some pretend they were brought hither by the Crusaders on their return from the Holy Wars, but to these it is objected that there is no traces of them to be found in history at that time, and that according to Munster they did not appear in this quarter of the globe till the year 1417; this date, which is adopted by Spelman, is by Sir William Blackstone supposed an error of the press, and that it ought to have been 1517, as Munster owns that the first of them he ever saw was in the year 1524. That author describes them as exceedingly tawny and sun-burnt, and in pitiful array: though they affected quality, and travelled with a train of hunting dogs after them, like nobles; he adds, that they had passports from King Sigismund of Bohemia and other Princes; ten years afterwards they came into France, thence passed into England. Probably from the passports here mentioned they might by the vulgar be stiled Bohemians.

Pasquier, in his *Referches*, l. 4. c. 19. relates the origin of the Gypsies thus: " On the 17th of April, 1427, there came to Paris twelve penitents,
" or persons, as they said, adjudged to penance, viz. one Duke, one Count,
" and ten Cavaliers or persons on horseback; they took on themselves the
" character of *Christians of the Lower Egypt*, expelled by the Saracens, who
" having made applications to the Pope, and confessed their sins, received
" for penance, that they should travel through the world for seven years,
" without ever lying in a bed. Their train consisted of 120 persons, men,
" women and children, which were all that were left of 1200, who came
" together

" together out of Egypt. Notwithstanding the abfurdity of the ftory, they
" had lodgings affigned them in the chapel, and people went in crowds to
" fee them. Their hair was exceedingly black and frizzled; their women
" were ugly, thievifh, and pretenders to telling of fortunes. The Bifhop
" foon afterwards obliged them to retire, and excommunicated fuch as had
' fhewn them their hands in order to have their fortunes told them."

Ralph Volaterranus making mention of them affirms, that they firft proceeded or ftrolled from among the Uxi, a people of Perfia.

Another, and the moft probable opinion is, that they were fome of thofe miferable Egyptians who, when their country was conquered by Sultan Selim, in the year 1517, rather than fubmit to the Turkifh yoke, chofe to difperfe themfelves in fmall parties over the world, fubfifting by begging, and their fuppofed fkill in chiromancy and magic, to which that nation had always pretence, and to the belief of which the grofs ignorance and fuperftition of the times were extremely favourable. This agrees very well with the time of their arrival in England, viz. about the year 1563, after having been expelled from France and Spain.

The firft comers, or their children, were probably foon reinforced by many idle perfons of both fexes; fwarthy fkins, dark eyes, and black hair, being the only qualifications required for admiffion; and fome of thefe might be heightened by the fun and walnut juice. Their language, or rather gibberifh, might foon be learned, and thus their numbers, in all likelyhood, quickly increafed till they became alarming, when thofe fevere ftatutes were promulged againft them, whofe great feverity prevented their intended effect, for when the purifhment inflicted by a law greatly exceeds the meafure of the offence, fuch law is rarely put in force, and the delinquents efcape with impunity. Had the punifhment been only hard labour, whipping, or imprifonment, it would have been much more efficacious.

Thefe ftrollers at prefent feem likely either to degenerate into common beggars, or, like fome of their brethren in Spain, to be obliged to take to a trade or bufinefs for a livelihood. The great encreafe of knowledge in all ranks of people, having rendered their pretended art of divination of little benefit to them, at leaft by no means fufficient to procure them fubfiftence, and fhould they attempt entirely to live by pilfering, the great quantities of provifion neceffary for their fupport when in large bodies could not be taken without alarming the country, and their numbers and affumed peculiarities would prevent their efcape.

MIS-

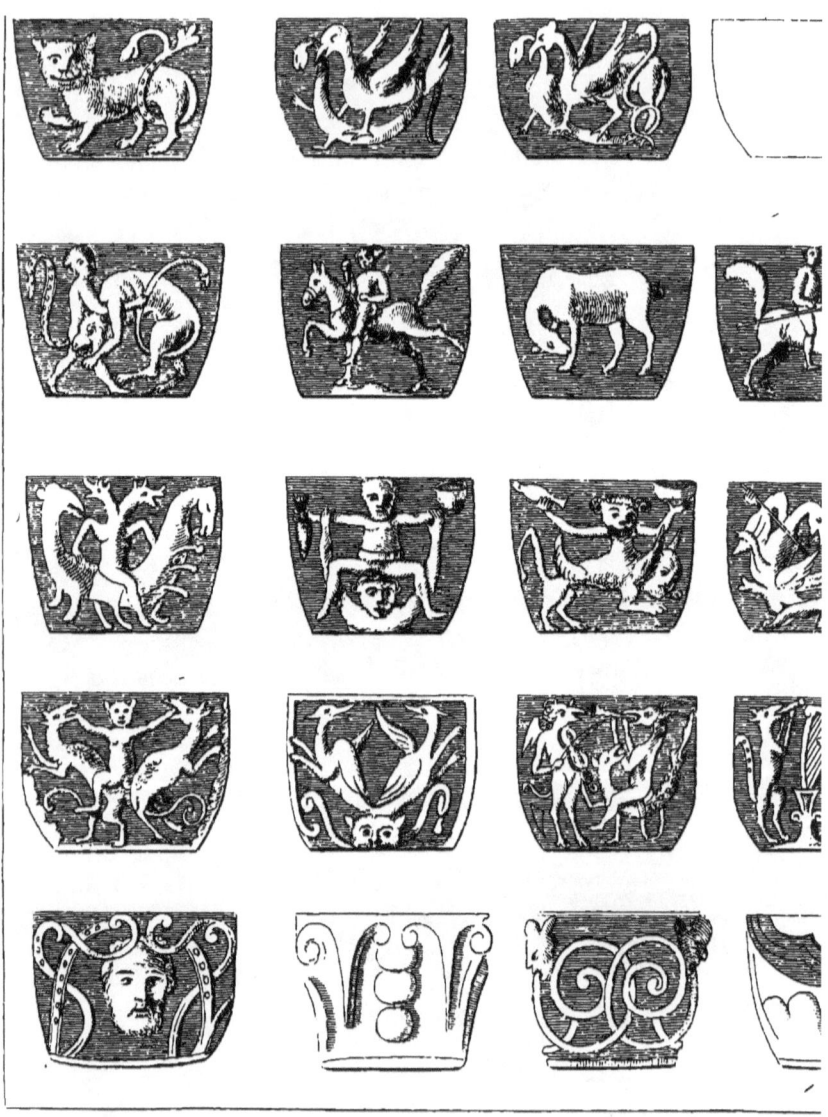

Saxon Capitals Engraved from an Original Drawing May 1 1775

THE ANTIQUARIAN REPERTORY. 57

MISCELLANEOUS PLATE.

THIS Plate contains Drawings of the different Capitals of the Ancient Columns in the French Church at Canterbury. Thefe Capitals are fquare, and one or two excepted have each of their faces ornamented with a different defign. Whether the grotefque figures have any hieroglyphical meaning, or are the grotefque whims of an irregular fancy, is not clear; from the ftrange affemblage of fome of the figures one would be almoft led to conjecture in the affirmative, though on the whole the negative is the moft defenfible opinion.

Thefe Columns are undoubtedly very ancient, and prior to the Norman ftile of building. The Rev. Mr. Goftling, in his ingenious book entitled, A Walk in and about Canterbury, feems to think them much older than is generally imagined, and that this building was not pulled down when the Church was repaired by Lanfranc, nor deftroyed by the fire in 1174.

From the great refemblance thefe bear to the Capitals of Grymbald's Crypt under the Ancient Church of St. Peter at Oxford, a print of which is in Leland's Collectanea, he feems to think them almoft coeval. Grymbald lived about the year 900, and was invited over to England by King Alfred to affift in reftoring Chriftianity, learning, and the liberal arts. " They " who compare the vault under our choir, with the defcription and print " given of Grymbald's Crypt (fays Mr. Goftling) will eafily fee, that the " fame defigners and the fame workmen could hardly have erected two build- " ings more ftrongly refembling each other than thefe, except that ours at " Canterbury is longer, and more profufely decorated, with variety of fancied " ornaments, the capitals of all the pillars being juft in fuch grotefque " tafte as that of the four given us in the Print of Grymbald."

Among the ornaments feveral Mufical Inftruments are apparent, not much differing in form from thofe now in ufe, except that blown by one of the animals in the fecond row from the bottom, fomewhat in the manner of a trumpet, which feems to be like the inftrument called a Shaum, a Drawing of which is given by Dr. Percy, in his Notes to the Northumberland-houfe Book.

P COPY

Copy from a Manuscript in the College of Arms, marked L. 14, page 226.
Printed in DUGDALE's Monasticon.

Of the BACON of DUNMOW PRIORY.

ROBERT FITZWALTER lived long beloved of King Henry the sonne of King John as also of all the Realme he betooke himself in his later dayes to prayer and deeds of Charity gave great and bountefull almes to the poore, kept greate hospetalite, and reedified the Decayed priorie of Dunmow, wth one Juga a most devoute and Religious woman, being in her kind his Auncetour had builded in which Priorie arose a Custome begune and instituted either by him or some other of his successors which is verified by a Common Proverb, or saying (viz) y^t he who repents him not of his marriage either sleeping or waking in a year and a Day may lawfully goe to Dunmowe and fetch a gamon of Bacon: it is most assured that such a Custome there was, and that this Bacon was Divided with such solemnitie and triumph as they of the Priory and the Townsmen could make. I have enquired of the manner of y^t. and can learne no more but that yt continued untill the Dissolution of that house as also the Abbey. That the ptie or Pilgrim for Bacon was to take his Oathe before the Prior, the covent and the whole towne, humbly kneeling in the Churchyard upon two hard poynted Stones, which Stones some Saye are there yet to be sene, in the prior's Church-yard, his oath was ministred with such long professe such solemn singing on him, wch Doubtlesse must make his Pilgrimage (as I tearme y^t) Painfull. After he was taken up upon Mens Shoulders and carried first aboute the Priory Churchyard and after Throughe the Towne, with all the Friers and Bretheren and all the Townesfolk Younge and Ould following him wth Shoutes and Aclamations, with his Bacon borne before him, and in Such Manner (as I have said) he was sent home with his Bacon, of Which I find that some had a gammon and others a fleeke, or a flitch, for proofe whereof I have from the records of the House found the Names of 3 severall persons that at severall tymes had yt.

A^o. 7 Edw. 4. M^d. quod Quidem Stephanus Samuell, de Ayston pva in Com Essex &c. whyche beinge in Lattaine entred in the Booke wch belonged to the house I have thus Englished. M^d. that one Steven Samuel of
Little

Little Ayſton in the Countye of Eſſex huſbandman came to the Priory of Dunmow on our Lady Day in Lent in the 7 yeare of King Edward the 4th and required a Gammon of Bacon and was ſworne before Roger Bulcott then prior and the Covent of this Place as alſo before a Multitude of other neighbours and there was Delivered unto him a gamon of Bacon.

A° 23. H. 6. M^d that one Richard Wright of Badbourghe neare the City of Norwich in the Countie of Norfolke yeoman came and Required of the Bacon of Dunmow namely the twenty Seaventh day of Aprill in the 23 Yeare of the Raigne of Henry the Sixth and according to the forme of the Charter was Sworn before John Cannon Prior of this Place and the Covent and many other neighbours and there was devided to him the Said Richard one fiitch of Bacon.

A°. 2 H. 8. M^d that in the yeare of our Lord 1510 Thomas Lefuller of Cogſhall in the Countie of Eſſex came to the Priory of Dunmow and required to have ſome of the Bacon of Dunmow on the 8 Day of September being Sunday in the Second yeare of King Henry the 8th he was according to the forme of the Charter ſworne before John Tils then Prior of the houſe and the Covent as alſo before a Multitude of Neighbours and there was devided unto the Said Thomas A Gamon of Bacon.

Heareby it appeareth that it was according to a Charter or Donation given according to by ſome conceited benefactor to the houſe, And It is not to be Doubted but that at ſuch tyme the bordering townes and Villages reſorted and were partakers of there paſtimes and laugh to Scorne the Poore man's paines.

The OATH.

You ſhall ſwear by the Cuſtom of our Confeſſion
That you never made any Nuptial Tranſgreſſion
Since you were married to your wife
By houſehold brawles, or contentious ſtrife
Or otherwiſe in bed or board
Offended each other in deed or word
Or ſince the Pariſh Clerk ſaid Amen
Wiſhed yourſelves unmarried agen
Or in a twelvemonth and a day
Repented not in thought any way

But

But continued true and in defire
As when you joined hands in the Holy Quire
If to thefe conditions without all fear
Of your own Accord you will freely fwear
A Gammon of Bacon you fhall receive
And bear it Hence with Love and Good Leave
For this is our Cuftom in Dunmow well known
Though the Sport be ours, the Bacon's your own.

This whimfical cuftom is not peculiar to Dunmow, a fimilar one prevails in the Manor of Wichnor in the county of Stafford, excepting that befides Bacon, Corn is alfo given to the happy pair, as may be feen in Blount's Jocular Tenures.

To the EDITOR of the ANTIQUARIAN REPERTORY.

SIR,

THE following gallant and almoft incredible action and fignal victory gained by an Englifh Captain, commanding one fmall privateer, over a large Turkifh fleet, is related by Roger, Earl of Caftlemayne, in his Account of the War between the Venetians and Turks, drawn up in form of a letter, dated 23^d May, 1666, and addreffed to King Charles the Second. As the book is rather fcarce, and the fact not much known, I have tranfcribed it for your work, and if you have a fpare corner fhould be glad you would infert it.

Yours, &c. B. L.

" Among the Englifh that fought bravely, Captain Thomas Middleton
" (who had his fhip hired in his fervice) did a moft prodigious action. It
" happened that the Admiral, intending a defign againft the Dardanels, put
" Middleton in fo defperate a place that he was in danger from land to be
" funk

" funk at every fhot. He advifed the Commander of it, and withal told
" him, that the peril of himfelf and fhip did not fo much trouble him as to
" be fet where it was impoffible for him to offend the enemy. Having no
" anfwer, or at beft a bad one, and feeing it could not prejudice the fleet,
" he drew off a little the veffel (his only livelihood) from the needlefs danger
" it was in. When the bufinefs was over, they difmiffed him (in a council
" of war) with the title of coward, and all the foldiers being taken away he
" was left only with fome 50 Englifh, to return home, or whither elfe he
" pleafed. He had not parted long from the Armata, but in a ftark calm
" met with 25 fail, of which 18 were the beft gallies the great Turk could
" make in all his fleet: Thefe crying out in derifion, that they would eat
" Englifh beef for dinner, fell upon him, wanting no affurance, being affift-
" ed with the ftillnefs of the air, and their own ftrength and number. But
" for all this confidence they miffed their aim, for after a long and fharp en-
" counter, the two Baffa's that commanded were killed, with 1500 to accom-
" pany them; and befides the many that were wounded, the whole fquadron
" was fo fhattered, that they had hardly oars to get off, and were all unfit to
" ferve, at leaft for that year. The Captain had neither wind, fails, nor
" tackle left to follow them; but with much-a-do he yet afterwards came fafe
" to Candie, and there prefented to the General a whole ton of falted heads
" of thofe he had killed, in their often boarding. His Excellency was afto-
" nifhed at the thing, and after all the careffes imaginable, he acquainted
" the Senate with it, who with univerfal confent ordered him a chain and
" medal of gold, as a teftimony of their high efteem and his own com-
" mendable valour. Middleton afterwards died on his journey home, leav-
" ing a fon, who commands here a fhip, and is very well efteemed by all
" the Nobility for his refolution and conduct."

The following Extract is taken from George Silver's Paradoxes of Defence, printed about the middle of the 16th Century, which exhibits a ſtriking Picture of the Manners of that Time, and elucidates ſeveral obſolete Words mentioned by Shakeſpeare, and other Ancient Writers. The Book is now become extremely ſcarce.

A Briefe Note of Three Italian Teachers of Offence.

I write not this to diſ-grace the dead but to ſhew their Impudent boldneſſe and inſufficiency in per-formance of their pro-feſſion when they were living; that from hence-forth this briefe note may be a remembrance and warning to beware of had I writ—

THERE were three Italian Teachers of Offence in my time. the firſt was Signior Rocko: the ſecond was Jeronimo, that was Signior Rocko his boy, that taught Gentlemen in the Blacke-Fryers, as Vſher for his Maiſter inſteed of a Man. The third was Vincentio. This Signior Rocko came into England about ſome thirtie yeares paſt: he taught the Noblemen and Gentlemen of the Court; he cauſed ſome of them to weare leaden ſoales in their Shoes, the better to bring them to Nimbleneſſe of feet in their fight. he diſburſed a great ſumme of mony for the leaſe of a faire houſe in Warwicke lane, which he called his Colledge, for he thought it great diſgrace for him to keepe a Fence-Schoole, he being then thought to be the only famous Maiſter of the Arte of Armes in the whole world. He cauſed to be fairely drawne and ſet round about his Schoole all the Noblemens and Gentlemens armes that were his Schollers, and hanging right under their armes their Rapiers, daggers, gloves of male and gantlets. Alſo, he had benches and ſtooles, the roome being verie large, for Gentlemen to ſit round about his Schoole to behold his teaching. He taught none commonly under twentie, fortie, fifty, or an hundred pounds. And becauſe all things ſhould be verie neceſſary for the Noblemen and Gen-tlemen, he had in his Schoole a large Square table, with a greene carpet, done round with a verie brode rich fringe of Gold, alwaies ſtanding upon it a verie faire Standiſh covered with Crimſon Velvet, with Inke, pens, pin-duſt, and ſealing waxe, and quiers of verie excellent fine paper gilded, rea-die for the Noblemen and Gentlemen (upon occaſion) to write their letters, being then deſirous to follow their fight, to ſend their men to diſpatch their buſineſſe. And to know how the time paſſed, he had in one corner of his Schoole a Clocke, with a verie faire large Diall, he had within that Schoole, a roome the which was called his privie Schoole, with manie weapons therein, where he did teach his Schollers his Secret fight, after he had perfectly taught them their rules. He was verie much beloved in the Court.

There was one Auften Bagger, a verie tall gentleman of his handes, not ftanding much upon his fkill, but carrying the valiant hart of an Englifhman, upon a time being merrie amongft his friendes, faid he would go fight with Signior Rocco, prefently went to Signior Rocco his houfe in the Blackfriers, and called to him in this manner: Signior Rocco, thou that art thought to be the only cunning man in the world with thy weapon, thou that takeft upon thee to hit anie Englifhman with a thurft upon any button, thou that takeft upon thee to come over the feas, to teach the valiant Noblemen and Gentlemen of England to fight, thou cowardly fellow come out of thy houfe if thou dare for thy life, I am come to fight with thee. Signior Rocco looking out at a window, perceiving him in the Street to ftand readie with his Sword and Buckler, with his two hand Sworde drawne, with all fpeed ran into the Street, and manfully let flie at Auften Bagger, who moft bravely defended himfelfe, and prefently clofed with him, and ftroke up his heeles, and cut him over the breech, and trode upon him, and moft grievoufly hurt him under his feet: yet in the end Auften of his good nature gave him his life, and there left him. This was the firft and laft fight that ever Signior Rocco made, faving once at Queene Hith he drew his Rapier upon a waterman, where he was throughly beaten with Oares and Stretchers, but the oddes of their Weapons were as great againft his Rapier, as was his two hand Sword againft Auften Baggers Sword and Buckler, therefore for that fray he was to be excufed.

Then came in Vincentio and Jeronimo, they taught Rapier-fight at the Court, at London, and in the countrey, by the Space of feaven or eight yeares or thereabouts. Thefe two Italian Fencers, efpecially Vincentio, faid that Englifhmen were ftrong men, but had no cunning, and they would go backe too much in their fight, which was great difgrace unto them. Upon thefe words of difgrace againft Englifhmen, my brother Toby Silver and myfelfe, made challenge againft them both, to Play with them at the Single Rapier, Rapier and Dagger, the Single Dagger, the Single Sword, the Sword and Target, the Sword and Buckler, and two hand Sword, the Staffe, battell Axe, and Morris Pike, to be played at the Bell Savage upon the Scaffold, where he that went in his fight fafter backe then he ought, of Englifhman

lifhman or Italian, fhold be in danger to breake his necke off the Scaffold. We caufed to that effect, five or fix fcore Bils of challenge to be printed, and fet up from Southwarke to the Tower, and from thence through London unto Weftminfter, we were at the Place with all thefe weapons at the time appointed, within a how, fhot of their Fence Skoole: many gentlemen of good accompt, carried manie of the bils of chalenge unto them, telling them that now the Silvers were at the place appointed, with all their weapons, looking for them, and a Multitude of people there to behold the fight, faying unto them, now come and go with us (you fhall take no wrong), or elfe you are fhamed for ever. Do the gentlemen what they could, thefe gallants would not come to the Place of triall. I verily thinke their cowardlly feare to anfwere this chalenge, had utterly fhamed them indeed, had not the Maifters of Defence of London, within two or three daies, after, bene drinking of bottell Ale hard by Vincentios fchoole, in a Hall where the Italians muft of neceffitie paffe through to go to their fchoole: and as they were coming by, the Maifters of Defence did pray them to drinke with them, but the Italians being verie cowardly, were afraide, and prefently drew their Rapiers: there was a pretie wench ftanding by, that loved the Italians, fhe ran with outcrie into the ftreet, helpe, helpe, the Italians are like to be flaine: the People with all fpeede came running into the houfe, and with their Cappes and fuch things as they could get, parted the fraie, for the Englifh Maifters of Defence, meant nothing leffe then to foile their handes upon thefe two faint harted fellows. the next morning after, all the Court was filled, that the Italian teachers of Fence had beaten all the maifters of Defence in London, who fet upon them in a houfe together. This wan the Italian Fencers their credit againe, and thereby got much, ftill continuing their falfe teaching to the end of their lives.

This Vincentio proved himfelfe a ftout man not long before he died, that it might be feene in his life time he had bene a gallant, and therefore no maruaile he tooke upon fo highly to teach Englifhmen to fight, and to fet forth bookes of the fcates of Armes. Upon a time at Wels in Somerfetfhire, as he was in great braverie amongft manie gentlemen of good accompt, with great boldneffe he gave out fpeeches, that he had bene thus manie yeares in England, and fince the time of his firft comming, there was not in it one Englifhman, that could once touch him at the Single Rapier, or Rapier and Dagger. A valiant gentleman being there amongft the reft, his Englifh

hart

hart did rife to heare this proude boafter, fecretly fent a meffenger to one Bartholomew Bramble a friend of his, a verie tall man both of his hands and perfon, who kept a fchoole of Defence in Towne, the Meffenger by the way made the Maifter of Defence acquainted with the mind of the Gentleman that fent for him, and of all what Vincentio had faid, this Maifter of Defence prefently came, and amongft all the Gentlemen with his Cap off, prayed Maifter Vincentio that he would be pleafed to take a quart of wine of him. Vincentio verie fcornefully looking upon him, faid unto him, wherefore fhould you give me a quart of wine? Marie, fir, faid he, becaufe I heare you are a famous man at your weapon. Then prefently faid the Gentleman that fent for the Maifter of Defence; Maifter Vincentio, I pray you bid him welcome, he is a man of your profeffion. My profeffion, faid Vincentio? what is my Profeffion. then faid the gentleman, he is a Maifter of the Noble Science of Defence. Why faid Maifter Vincentio, God make him a good man. but the Maifter of Defence would not thus leave him, but prayed him againe he would be pleafed to take a quart of wine of him. Then faid Vincentio, I have no need of thy wine. Then faid the Maifter of Defence: Sir I have a Schoole of Defence in the Towne, will it pleafe you to go thither. Thy Schoole faid Maifter Vincentio? What fhall I do at thy Skoole? Play with me (faid the Maifter) at the Rapier and Dagger, if it pleafe you. Play with Thee faid Maifter Vincentio? if I Play with thee, I will hit thee, 1, 2, 3, 4, thruftes in the eie together. then faid the Maifter of defence, if you can do fo, it is the better for you, and the worfe for me, but furely I can hardly beleeve that you can hit me: but yet once againe I hartily Pray you good Sir that you will go to my fchoole, and Play with me. Play with Thee faid Maifter Vincentio (very fcornefully!) by God me fcorne to Play with thee. with that word fcorne, the Maifter of Defence was verie much moved, and up with his great Englifh fift, and ftroke Maifter Vincentio fuch a boxe on the eare that he fell over and over, his Legges juft againft a Butterie hatch, whereon ftood a great Blacke Jacke, the Maifter of Defence fearing the worft, againft Vincentio his rifing, catcht the blacke Jacke into his hand, being more then halfe full of beere. Vincentio luftily ftart up, laying his hand on his dagger, and with the other hand pointed with his finger, faying very well: I will caufe to lie in the gaile for this geare, 1, 2, 3, 4, yeares. and well faid the Maifter of Defence, fince you will drinke no wine, will you pledge me in beere? I drinke to all the cowardly knaves in England, and I thinke thee to be the verieft coward of them all: with

R that

that he caſt all the Beere upon him: notwithſtanding Vincentio having nothing but his guilt Rapier, and Dagger about him, and the other for his Defence the blacke Jacke, would not at that time fight it out: but the next day met with the Maiſter of Defence in the Streete, and ſaid unto him, you remember how miſuſed a me yeſterday, you were to blame, me be an excellent man, me teach you how to thruſt two foote further than anie Engliſhman, but firſt come you with me: then he brought him to a Mercer's Shop, and ſaid to the Mercer, let me ſee of your beſt ſilken pointes, the Mercer did preſently ſhew him ſome, of ſeven groates a dozen, then he payeth fourteen groates for two dozen, and ſaid to the Maiſter of Defence, there is one dozen for you, and here is another for me, this was one of the valianteſt Fencers that came from beyond the ſeas, to teach Engliſhmen to fight, and this was one of the manlieſt frayes, that I have heard of, that ever he made in England, wherein he ſhewed himſelfe a fare better man in his life, than in his Profeſſion he was, for he profeſſed armes, but in his life a better Chriſtian. He ſet forth in Print a booke for the uſe of the Rapier and Dagger, the which he called his Practice, I have read it over, and becauſe I finde therein neither true rule for the perfect teaching of true fight, nor true ground of true fight, neither Sence or reaſon for due Proofe thereof, I have thought it frivolous to recite any Part therein contained; Yet that the truth hereof may appeare, let two men being wel experienced in the Rapier and Dagger fight, chooſe any of the beſt branches in the ſame booke, and make tryall with force and agility, without the which the truth betweene the true and falſe fight can not be knowne, and they ſhall find great imperfections therein. And again, for Proofe that there is no truth, neither in his rules, grounds or Rapier fight, let tryall be made in this maner: Set two unſkilfull men together at the Rapier and Dagger, being valiant, and you ſhall ſee, that once in two boutes there ſhall either one or both of them be hurt. Then ſet two ſkilful men together, being valiant at the Rapier and Dagger, and they ſhall do the like. Then ſet a ſkilfull Rapier and Dagger-man the beſt that can be had, and a Valiant man having no ſkill together at Rapier and Dagger, and once in two bouts upon my credit in all the experience I have in fight, the unſkilfull man, do the other what he can for his life to the contrarie, ſhall hurt him, and moſt commonly if it were in continuance of fight, you ſhall ſee the unſkilfull man to have the advantage. And if I ſhould chuſe a valiant man for ſervice of the Prince, or to take part with me or anie friend of mine

Proofes againſt the Rapier fight.

in

in a good quarrell, I would chufe the unfkilfull man, being unencombred with falfe fights, becaufe fuch a man ftandeth free in his valour with ftrength and agilitie of bodie, freely taketh the benefit of nature, fighteth moft brave, by loofing no oportunitie, either foundly to hurt his enemie, or defend himfelfe, but the other ftanding for his Defence, upon his cunning Italian wordes, *Pointoreverfa* the *Imbrocata*, *Stocata*, and being faft tyed unto thefe falfe fightes, ftandeth troubled in his wits, and nature thereby racked through the largenefs or falfe lyings or Spaces, whereby he is in his fight as a man half maimed, loofing the oportunity of times and benefit of nature, and whereas before being Ignorant thefe falfe Rapier fights, ftanding in the free libertie of nature given him by God, he was able in the field with his weapon to anfwere the valianteft man in the world, but now being tied unto that falfe fickle uncertain fight, thereby hath loft in nature his freedome, is now become fcarce halfe a man, and everie boye in that fight is become as good a man as himfelfe.

Jeronimo this gallant was valiant, and would fight indeed, and did, as you fhall heare. He being in a Coch with wench that he loved well, there was one Cheefe, a verie tall man, in his fight naturall Englifh, for he fought with his fword and Dagger, and in Rapier-fight had no fkill at all. This Cheefe having a quarrell to Jeronimo, overtooke him upon the way, himfelfe being on horfebacke, did call to Jeronimo, and bad him come forth of the Coche or he would fetch him, for he was come to fight with him. Jeronimo prefently went forth of the Coch and drew his Rapier and dagger, Put himfelfe into his beft ward or Stocata, which ward was taught by himfelfe and Vincentio, and by them belt allowed of, to be the beft ward to ftand upon in fight for life, either to affault the enemie, or ftand and watch his comming, which ward it fhould feeme he ventured his life upon, but howfoever with all the fine Italianated fkill Jeronimo had, Cheefe with his Sword within two thruftes ran him into the bodie and flue him. Yet the Italian teachers will fay, that an Englifhman cannot thruft ftraight with a fword, becaufe the hilt will not fuffer him to put the forefinger over the Croffe, nor to put the thumbe upon the blade, nor to hold the pummell in the hand, whereby we are of neceffitie to hold fafte the handle in the hand: by reafon whereof we are driven to thruft both compaffe and fhort, whereas with the Rapier they can thruft both ftraight and much further then we can with the fword, becaufe of the hilt: and thefe be the reafons they make againft the fword.

BOTH-

BOTHWELL CASTLE,

IS ſituated on the banks of the River Clyde, from whence this diſtrict, or ſhire, takes the name of Clydeſdale. It ſtands about a mile diſtant from a bridge, called Bothwell Bridge, which was in the reign of Charles the Second, occupied as a poſt by a party of Rebels; they were, however, ſoon diſlodged and defeated by the Duke of Monmouth.

The name of the founder of this noble Pile, magnificent even in ruins, has not been handed down to us, nor is the date of its erection better aſcertained, hiſtory and tradition being equally ſilent as to both theſe particulars.

This Caſtle was frequently the reſidence and burial place of the Earls of Douglas, and has often lent its name to the title of Earl. It is remarked that its poſſeſſors have been peculiarly unfortunate, one family ſeldom continuing long proprietor thereof.

When Edward the Firſt was in Scotland, this was the chief ſtation of his Governour, and after the unfortunate battle of Bannockburne, anno 1314, converted into a priſon for the confinement of the Engliſh taken at that action.

Major ſays, that in 1337, it was taken by the partizans of David Bruce, and levelled to the ground. It is, however, ſuppoſed that this is not to be underſtood literally, but only means to expreſs that it was then totally diſmantled. Indeed the ancient ſtile of its remains juſtifie this conjecture.

Part of the materials of this Caſtle were applied to erecting a new houſe, by the Earl of Norfolk, who therewith built a pretty ſeat, at no great diſtance.

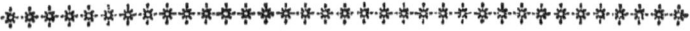

EXTRACT from the WORKS of JOHN TAYLOR, the WATER POET.
Publiſhed Anno 1630.

A VOYAGE in a PAPER BOAT from LONDON to QUINBOROUGH.

I Therefore to conclude this much will note
How I of Paper lately made a Boat;
And how in forme of Paper I did row
From London unto Quinborough, Ile ſhow:

I and

THE ANTIQUARIAN REPERTORY.

I and a Vintner (Roger Bird by Name)
(A Man whom Fortune never yet could tame)
Tooke ſhip upon the Vigill of Saint James,
And boldly ventur'd downe the river *Thames*,
Laving and cutting through each raging billow,
(In ſuch a boat which never had a fellow)
Having no kind of mettall or no wood
To helpe us eyther in our Ebbe or Flood,
For as our boat was paper, ſo our Oares
Were Stock-fiſh, caught neere to the Iſland ſhores.
Stock-fiſhes unbeaten, bound faſt to two canes with packthread.
Thus Oard and Shipt, away we went,
Driving 'twixt *Eſſex* Calves, and ſheepe of *Kent*:
Our Boat a female Veſſel gan to leake,
Being as female Veſſels, moſt weak.
Yet was ſhe able, which did greeve me ſore,
To drown *Hodge Bird*, and I, and forty more.
The water to the paper being got,
In one half houre our boate began to rot:
The Thames (moſt liberall) fill'd her to the halves,
Whilſt Hodge and I ſate liquor'd to the Calves;
In which extremity I thought it fit
To put in uſe a Stratagem of Wit;
Which was, eight bullocks-bladders we had bought,
Puft ſtifly full with wind, bound faſt and tought,
Which in our boat within the Tide we ty'de
Of each ſide foure, upon the outward ſide
The water ſtill roſe higher by degrees,
In three miles going, almoſt to our knees;
Our rotten bottome all to tatters fell,
And left our Boate as bottomleſſe as Hell;
And had not bladders borne us ſtifly up,
We there had taſted of death's fatal cup.
  And now (to make ſome ſport) Ile make it knowne
By whoſe ſtrong breath my bladders all were blown:
One by a cheverell conſcienc'd Uſurer,
Another by a drunken Bag-piper,

The third a Whore, the fourth a Pandar blew,
The fifth a Catpurfe, of the curfed crew,
The fixth, a Poft-knight, that for five groats gaine
Would fweare, and for foure groats forfwear't againe;.
The feventh was an Informer, one that can
By informations beggar any man;
The eighth was blown up by a fwearing Royfter,
That would cut throats as foone as eat an Oyfter.

<small>We had more wind than the Compaffe, for we had eight feverall winds in our bladders, and the 32 of the Compaffe, in all 40.</small>

We being in our watry bufineffe bound,
And with thefe wicked winds encompafs'd round;
For why fuch breaths as thofe it fortunes ever
They end with hanging, but with drowning never;
And fure the bladders bore us up fo tight,
As if they had faid, Gallowes claime thy right;
This was the caufe that made us feeke about,
To find thefe light Tiburnian vapours out.
We could have had of honeft men good ftore,.
As Watermen and Smirhs, and many more,
But that we knew it muft be hanging breath,
That muft preferve us from a drowning death.

<small>Carefully and difcreetly provided.</small>

Yet much we fear'd the graves our end would be
Before we could the towne of Gravefend fee:
Our boate drunke deeply with her dropfie thirft,.
And quaft as if fhe would her bladders burft;
Whilft we, within fix inches of the brim,
(Full of falt-water) downe (halfe funck) did fwim.
Thoufands of people all the fhores did hide,
And thoufands more did meet us in the tide,
With Scullers, Oares, with Ship Boats and with Barges,.
To gaze on us, they put themfelves to charges.

Thus did we drive, and drive the time away,
Till pitchy night had driven away the day:
The fun unto the under world was fled:
The moone was loath to rife, and kept her bed:

The ftarres did twinckle, but the ebon clouds
Their light, our fight, obfcures and overfhrowds.
The tolling billowes made our boat to caper,
Our paper forme fcarce being forme of paper,
The water four mile broad, no oares, to row,
Night darke, and where we were we did not know.
And thus 'twixt doubt and feare, hope and defpaire,
I fell to worke, and *Roger Bird* to prayer;
And as the furges up and downe did heave us,
He cry'd moft fervently, good Lord receive us;
I pray'd as much, but I did worke and pray,
And he did all he could to pray and play.
Thus three houres darkeling I did puzzell and toile
Sows'd and well pickl'd, chafe and muzzell and moile,
Drench'd with the fwolling waves and ftew'd in fweat,
Scarce able with a cone our boat to fet.
At laft (by God's great mercy and his might)
The morning gan to chafe away the night;
Aurora made us foone perceive and fee
We were three miles below the Towne of *Lee*,
And as the morning more and more did cleare,
The fight of *Quinborough* Caftle did appeare:
That was the famous monumental marke,
To which we ftriv'd to bring our rotten barke:
The onely ayme of our intents and fcope,
The anker that brought Roger to the Hope.

<small>He dwelleth now at the Hope on the Bank fide.</small>

Thus we from Saturday, at evening tide,
Till Monday morne did on the water bide,
In rotten paper, and in boyfterous weather,
Darke nights, through wet, and toyled altogether;
But being come to Quinborough and aland,
I took my fellow *Roger* by the hand,
And both of us, ere we two fteps did goe,
Gave thanks to God, that had preferv'd us fo:
Confefling that his mercy us protected,
When, as we leaft deferv'd, and lefs expected,

The Mayor of *Quinborough* in love affords
To entertain us, as we had beene Lords;
It is a yearley feaft kept by the Major,
And thoufand people thither do repaire,
From Townes and Villages that's neere about,
And 'twas our lucke to come in all this rout.
I'th'ftreet, bread, beere and oyfters is their meat,
Which freely, friendly, fhot-free all do eat;
But *Hodge* and I were men of ranck and note,
We to the Major gave our adventurous boat,
The which (to glorifie that Towne of Kent)
He meant to hang up for a Monument.
He to his houfe invited us to dine,
Where we had cheare on cheare, and wine on wine,
And drinke and fill, and drinke, and drinke and fill,
With wellcome upon wellcome, wellcome ftill.
But whilft we at our dinners thus were merry,
The Country people tore our tatter'd wherry
In mammocks peacemeale in a thoufand fcraps,
Wearing the reliques in their hats and caps;
That never traytors corps could more be fcatter'd
By greedy Ravens, then our poore boat was tatter'd,
Which when the Major did know, he prefently
Took patient what he could not remedie.
The next day we with thankes left Quinbroghs coaft,
And heid us home on horfebacke all in poft.
Thus Mafter Birds ftrange voyage was begun,
With greater danger was his money won;
And thofe that do his Coine from him detaine,
(Which he did win with perill and with paine)
Let them not thinke that e'ere 'twill do them good,
But eate their Marrow and confume their Blood.
The worm of confcience gnaw them every day,
That have the meanes, and not the will to pay.
Thofe that are poore, and cannot, let them be
Both from the Debt and Malediction free.

THE

ANTIQUARIAN REPERTORY.

QUEEN's CROSS, NORTHAMPTONSHIRE.

THIS Crofs ftands on an eminence, about three quarters of a mile fouth of the town of Northampton, on the eaft fide of the high road, leading from that town to London.

It was fet up by King Edward I. in memory of Eleanor, of Caftile, his Queen, who died of a fever, November 21, anno 1291, as fome fay, at Grantham, or according to Walfingham, at Herdbye, near Bolingbroke, in Lincolnfhire. Croffes were likewife erected wherever her corpfe refted in the way to London, viz. at Great Grantham, Stamford, Geddington, near Kettering, in Northamptonfhire, Stoney Stratford, Dunftable, St. Albans, Waltham, Cheapfide, in London, and Charing, in Weftminfter. Dr. Stukeley, in his Itiner. Curios. p. 34, adds, Lincoln, Newark and Leicefter. Of all thefe, three only are now ftanding, one at Waltham, much mutilated; another at Geddington, and the fubject of this Plate and Defcription. About the bafe of this Crofs, is a flight of eight fteps, each about one foot broad, and nine inches high. The fhaft of the Crofs is divided into three ftages; the firft is octagonal, fourteen feet in height, and each face of the octagon meafuring four feet. On the fouth and eaft fides are the arms of Ponthieu, in Picardy,
viz.

viz. three bendlets within a bordure, and in another efcutcheon thofe of the kingdom of Caftile and Leon, viz. quarterly, firſt, a caftle triple towered; fecond, a lion rampant; the third as the fecond, and the fourth as the firſt. On the north fide, in two feparate fhields, are the arms of Caftile and Leon, as above, and of England, viz. three lions paffant guardant; on each of thefe, and on the weft fide juſt below the arms, in high relief, is a book open, and lying on a kind of defk. On the north-eaſt fide, in two ef-cutcheons, are the arms of England, and thofe of the county of Ponthieu. The arms on the weft, fouth-weſt, fouth-eaſt, and north-weft fides, are entirely obliterated. The fhaft of the fecond ftage or ftory is of the fame fhape as of that juſt defcribed, but only twelve feet high. In every other face is a niche, in which, under a canopy and pinnacle, fupported by two pillars, ftands a female figure, about fix feet high, crowned, and fuppofed to reprefent the Queen, to whofe honour this Monument was raifed. The figures and ornaments are ftill in good repair.

The upper fhaft is fquare, each fide facing one of the cardinal points of the compafs; its height only eight feet; on each of thefe fides is a fun dial, fet up anno 1712, which when firſt made had the following mottoes upon them. On the eaſt, AB ORTV SOLIS. The fouth LAVDATVR DOMINVS. The weft VSQVE AD OCCASVM. The north AMEN, MDCCXIII. Thefe mottoes were omitted when the dials were repainted in 1762.

The top is mounted with a crofs, which faces the north and fouth points, three feet in height, and added when the whole was repaired by the order of the Bench of Juftices in 1713. On the weftern fide of the lower ftory, and fronting the road, are the royal arms of Great-Britain, carved in ftone, within the garter, and crowned, with the fword and fceptre in faltire behind the fhield, and under it Queen Anne's motto, *Semper eadem*; there is alfo a pair of wings conjoined under the fhield, to which they form a mantleing. Beneath the arms, on a fquare table of white marble, is the following infcription.

In perpetuam Conjugalis Amoris Memoriam
Hoc *Eleanoræ* Reginæ Monumentum
Vetuſtate pene collapfum reftaurari voluit
Honorabilis Jufticiariorum Coetus
Comitatus Northamptoniæ,
MDCCXIII.

Anno

Anno illo feliciffimo
In quo ANNA
Grandæ Britanniæ fuæ Decus
Potentiffima Oppreſſorum Vindex
Pacis Bellique Arbitra
Poſt Germaniam liberatam
Belgiam Præfidiis munitam
Gallos plus vice decima profligatos.
Suis Sociorumque Armis
Vincendi modum ſtatuit
Et Europæ in Libertatem Vindicatæ
Pacem reſtituit.

On the ſouth ſide of the bottom ſtory is fixed a white marble eſcutcheon, charged with this inſcription.

Rurſus emendat, et reſtaurat,
GEORGII III. regis 2 do.
DOMINI. 1762,
N. Baylis.

The ſenſe of which in Engliſh is as follows.
This Monument
Erected to perpetuate the memory
Of the conjugal affection of Queen Eleanor
Being almoſt deſtroyed by Time,
Was repaired by order of
The Honourable Bench of Juſtices
for the County of Northampton,
In the year 1713,
At that auſpicious æra
In which Anne,
The ornament of Britain,
The moſt powerful avenger of the oppreſſed,
And ſovereign arbitreſs of peace and war;
Germany being freed,
Holland ſecured by a ſtrong barrier,

And

And the French more than ten times defeated,
By her arms and thofe of her allies;
Was fatisfied with conqueft,
And after afferting the liberty of Europe,
Reftored peace to it.

Again repaired and beautified
In the year 1762,
Being the fecond year of George III.
N. Baylis.

※※※※※※※※※※※※※※※※※※※※※※※※※※※※※※※※

The Great Eater, *or Part of the admirable Teeth and Stomacks Exploits of* Nicholas Wood, *of Harrifom, in the County of Kent.*

This exceffive Manner of Eating, without Manners, in ftrange and true Manner defcribed by JOHN TAILOR.*

RECORDS and Hiftories doe make memorable mention of diuerfitie of qualities of fundry famous perfons, men and women, in all the countries and regions of the world; how fome are remembered for their Piety and Pitty, fome for Juftice, fome for Seuerity, for Learning, Wifdome, Temperance, Conftancie, Patience, with all the Vertues Divine, and Morall: Some againe have purchafed a memory for Greatneffe and Tolneffe of body; fome for Dwarfifh fmallneffe; fome for beautiful outfides, faire feature and compofition of Limbs and Stature, many have gotten an earthly perpetuity for cruelty and murther, as Nero, Commodus, and others: for leachery, as Heliogabolus: for Drunkenneffe, Tiberius (alias Biberius:) for Effeminacy, as Sardanapulus: for Gluttony, Aulus Vitellius, who at one fupper was ferved with two thoufand forts of fifhes, and feven thoufand fowles, as Suetonius writes in his ninth Booke, and Jofephus in his fifth Booke of the Jewes warres. Caligula was famous for Ambition, for hee would bee ador'd as a God, though he liv'd like a Devill, poyfoning his Unkle, and
Deflowering

* Publifhed about the year 1630.

Deflowering all his Sifters, and in all ages and countries, time hath ftill produced particular perfons, men and women, either for their virtues or their vices, to be remembred, that by meditating on the good, we may bee imitating their goodneffe, and by viewing the bad, we might be efchewing their vices.

To defcend lower to more familiar examples, I have known a great man very expert on the Jewe-harpe, a rich heire excellent at Noddy, a Juftice of the peace fkilful at Quoytes, a Merchant's wife a quicke Gamefter at Irifh (efpecially when fhe came to bearing of Men) that fhe would feldome miffe entring. *Monfieur le Ferr*, a Frenchman, was the firft inventor of the admirable game of Double-hand, Hot-cockles; and *Gregorie Dawfon*, an Englifhman devifed the unmatchable myftery of Blind-man-buffe; fome have the agility to ride Poaft, fome the dexterity to write Poft, and fome the ability to fpeake poafte: For I have heard a fellow make a Hackney of his Tongue, and in a moment he hath Gallop'd a Lye from China to London, without bridle or faddle. Others doe fpeake poaft, in a thick fhuffleing kind of Ambling-trot, and that in fuch fpeede, that one of them fhall talke more in one quarter of an houre, than fhall be underftood in feven yeeres. And as every one hath particular qualities to themfelves, and different from others, fo are the manners of Lives (or livings) of all men and women various one from another, as fome get their living by their tongues, as Interpreters, Lawyers, Oratours, and Flatterers; fome by tayles, as Maquerellaes, Concubines, Curtezanes, or in plaine Englifh, Whores; fome by their feete, as Dancers, Lackeyes, Foot men, and Weavers, and Knights of the Publicke or common Order of the Forke; fome by their braines, as Politicians, Monopolifts, Projectmongers, Suit-joggers, and Stargazers; fome (like Salamander) lived by fire, as the whole Race of Tubalcaine, the Vulcanean Broode of Blackfmiths, Fire men, Colliers, Gunners, Gun-founders, and all Sorts of mettle men; fome like the Cameleon, by the Ayre, and fuch are Poets, Trumpeters, Cornets, Recorders, Pipers, Bag-pipers; and fome by Smoake, as Tobaconifts, Knights of the Vapour, Gentlemen of the Whiffe, Efquires of the Pipe, Gallants in Fumo; fome live by the Water, as Herrings doe, fuch are Brewers, Vintners, Dyers, Mariners, Fifhermen, and Scullers; and many, like Moles, live by the Earth, as griping Vfurers, racking Landlords, toyling Plow men, moyling Labourers, painful Gardners and others.

Amongſt all theſe before mentioned, and many more which I could recite, this Subject of my pen is not (for his qualitie) inferiour to any; and as neare as I can, I will ſtretch my wit upon the Tenters to deſcribe his name and character, his worthy actes ſhall be related after *in due time duly*.

And, be it knowne unto all men, to whom theſe preſents ſhall come, that I *John Tayler*, Waterman, of Saint Saviour's, Southwark, in the Countey of Surrey, the Writer hereof, &c. will write plaine truth, bare and thread-bare, and almoſt ſtarke naked truth, of the deſcriptions, and remarkable, memorable actions of *Nicholas Wood*, of the Pariſhe of *Harriſom* in the County of Kent, Yeoman, for theſe Conſiderations following.

Firſt, I were to blame to write more than truth, becauſe that which is knowne to be true is enough.

Secondly, that which is onely true, is too much.

Thirdly, The Truth will hardly be believed, being ſo much beyond man's reaſon to conceive.

Fourthly, I ſhall runne the hazzard to bee accounted a great lyer, in writing the truth.

Laſtly, I will not lye, on purpoſe to make all thoſe lyers that eſteeme me ſo.

Yet by your leave, Maſter Critick, you muſt give me licence to flouriſh my Phraſes, to embelliſh my Lines, to adorne my Oratory, to embroder my Speeches, to enterlace my words, to draw out my Sayings, and to bombaſte the whole ſuit of the buſineſſe for the time of your wearing. For though truth appeareth beſt bare in matters of Juſtice, yet in this I hold it decent to attire her with ſuch Poore raggs as I have inſtead of Robes.

Firſt then the place of his birth, and names of his parents are to me a meere *Terra incognita*, as far from my knowledge, as content from a Vſurer, or honeſty from a Bawde, but if hee be no Chriſtian, the matter is not much, hee will ſerve well enough for a man of Kent; and if his Education had been as his Feeding, it is evident he had been of moſt mighty breeding; he hath gotten a foule name, but I know not if it came to him by Baptiſme, for it is partly a *Nick*-name, which in the totall is *Nicholas*, I would abate him but a Saint, and call him *Nicholas Shambles*, and were the goodneſſe of his purſe anſwerable to the greatneſs of his appetite, out of all queſtion no man below the Moone would be a better cuſtomer to the Shambles, than he, for though he be chaſt of his body, yet his minde is only upon Fleſh; he is the only Tugmutton, or Muttonmonger betwixt *Dover* and *Dunbarr:* for hee

hath

hath eaten a whole Sheepe of sixteene shillings price, raw, at one meal (pardon me) I think he left the skin, the wool, the hornes and the bones: but why talke I of a Sheepe, when it is apparently knowne, that he hath at one repast, and with one dish, feasted his Carkas with all manner of Meates. All men will confesse that a Hogge will eat any thing, either fish, flesh, fowle, roote, herbe, or excrement; and this same noble *Nick Nicholas*, or *Nicholas Nick*, hath made an end of a Hogge all at once, as if it had been but a Rabbet-sucker, and presently after, for fruit to recreate his palate, he hath swallowed three peckes of Damsons, thus (philosophically) by way of chimicall infusion, as a Hogge will eate all things that are to be eaten, so he in eating the Hogge, did in a manner of Extraction, distill all manner of meates thorow the Limbeck of his Paunch.

But hold a little, I would be loth to cloy my Reader with too much meate and fruite at once, so that after your Sheepe, Hogge and Damsons, I thinke it best to suffer you to pawse and picke your teeth (if you have any) whilst I spend a few words more in paraphrasing upon his Surname. *Wood* is his appellation, denomination, or how you please to tearme it.

Some of the ancienst Philosophers have compared Man to a Tree with the bottome upwardes, whose roote is the braine, the armes, hands, fingers, legges, feete and toes, are the limbs and branches; the comparison is very significant, many Trees do bring forth good fruit, so doe some fewe Men; some stately Trees growe high and fair, yet stand for nothing but shades, and some men growe high and lofty, yet are nothing but shaddowes; some Trees are so malignant, that nothing can prosper under the compasse of their branches; and some Men are so unlucky, that very few can thrive in their service. And as of one part of a Tree a chaire of state may be made, and of another part a carved image, and of a third part a stoole of office; so men being compounded and composed all of one mould and mettle, are different and disconsonant in estates, conditions, and qualities. Too many (like the barren Fig-tree) beare leaves of hypocrisie, but no fruites of Integrity, who serve onely for a flourish in this life, and a flame in that hereafter.

So much for that: now to returne to my Theame of *Wood*; (indeed this last disgression may make my Reader thinke that I could not see Wood for Trees) what Wood he is I know not, but by his face he should be Maple, or Crab-tree, and by his stomache, sure he is heart of *Oake*; some say he is a Meddler, but by his stature, he seems like a low short *Pine*, and certain I

am,

am, that he is *Popular*, a well tymberd piece, or a stone house or belly tymber.

Now, Gentlemen, as I have walked you among the Trees, and thorow the Wood, I pray set downe, and take a taste or two more of this Banquet. What say you to the Leafe or Flecke of Brawne new kild, to be of weight eight pound, and to be eaten hot out of the Bores belly raw? much good doe you Gallants, was it not a glorious dish? and presently after, (in stead of suckets, twelve raw puddings.) I speake not one word of drinke all this while, for indeed he is no drunkard, hee abhorres that swinish vice: Ale-houses nor Tapsters cannot nick this *Nick* with froth, curtoll Cannes, tragicall blacke-pots, and double-dealing bumbasted Jugges, could never cheat him, for one Pinte of Beere or Ale is enough to wash downe a Hog, or water a Sheepe with him.

Two Loynes of Mutton, and one Loyne of Veal were but as three Sprats to him: Once at Sir *Warrham Saint Leigers* house, and at Sir *William Sydleyes*, he shewed himself so valiant of Teeth, and Stomache, that he ate as much as would well have served and suffic'd thirty men, so that his belly was like to turn bankerupt, and breake, but that the serving-men turn'd him to the fire, and anoynted his Paunch with Greace and butter, to make it stretch and hold, and afterwards being lay'd in bed, hee slept eight howres, and fasted all the while: which when the Knight understood, he commanded him to be laid in the stocks, and there to endure as long time as he had lain bedrid with eating.

Pompey the Great, Alexander the Great, Tamberlane the Great, Charlemagne, or Charles the Great, Arthur the Great: all these gat the Title of Great, for conquering kingdomes, and killing of men; and surely eating is not a greater sinne than rapine, theft, manslaughter, and murther. Therefore this noble Eatalian doth well deserve the Tytle of Great: wherefore I instile him *Nicholas* the Great (Eater:) and as these forename Greats have overthrowne and wasted Countreyes, and Hosts of men, with the helpe of their soldiers and followers, so hath *Nick* the Great, (in his own Person) without the helpe or ayde of any man, overcome, conquered, and devoured, in one weeke, as much as would have sufficed a reasonable and sufficient army in a day, for hee hath at one meale made an assault upon seven dozen of good Rabbets at the Lord *Wotton*'s in *Kent*, which in the totall is four-score, which number would have suffic'd a hundred, three-score and eight hungry soldiers, allowing to each of them halfe a Rabbet.

Bell,

THE ANTIQUARIAN REPERTORY.

Bell, the famous Idoll of the Babylonians, was a meere imposture, a juggling toye, and a cheating bable, in comparison of this *Nicholaitan Kentish Tenterbelly*: the high and mighty Duke *All-paunch* was but a fiction to him; Milo the Crotonian, could hardly be his equall: and *Woolner*, of Windsor, was not worthy to be his footman. A quarter of fat Lambe, and threescore Eggs have beene but an easy colation, and three well larded pudding-pyes he hath at one time put to foyle; eighteen yards of black-puddings (London measure) have suddenly been imprisoned in his fowse-tub. A Duck rawe, with guts, feathers and all (except the bill and the long feathers of the wings) hath swomme in the whirlepole or pond of his mawe; and he told me, that three-score pound of Cherries was but a kind of washing meate, and that there was no tacke in them, for hee had tride it at one time. But one *John Dale* was too hard for him at a place called Lennam, for the said Dale had laid a wager that he would fill *Wood*'s belly with good wholesome victuals for 2 Shillings, and a Gentleman that laid the contrary, did wager, that as soon as noble *Nick* had eaten out *Dale*'s 2 shillings, that he should presently enter combate with a Worthy Knight, called *Sir Loyne* of Beefe, and overthrow him; in conclusion, *Dale* bought 6 pots of potent, high and mighty Ale, and twelve new penny white loaves, which hee sop'd in the said Ale, the powerfull fume whereof conquered the conqueror, rob'b him of his reason, bereft him of his wit, violently tooke away his stomache, intoxicated his *Pia mater*, and entered the sconce of his Pericranium, blinde folded him with sleep, setting a *nap* of nine houres for manacles upon his threed-bare eyelids, to the preservation of the rost Beefe, and the unexpected winning of the wager.

This invincible *Ale*, victoriously vanquished the vanquisher, and over our Great Triumpher was triumphant. But there are presidents enow of as potent men as our Nicholas, that have subdued Kings, and Kingdomes, and yet themselves have been captived and conquer'd by drinke; we need recite no more Examples but the Great Alexander, and Holophernes, their ambition was boundlesse, and so is the stomach of my Pens subject, for all the foure Elements cannot cloy him, fish from the deepest ocean, or purest river, fairest pond, foulest ditch, or driest puddle: he hath a receite for fowle of all sorts, from the *Wren* to the *Eagle*, from the *Titmouse* to the Estrich, or *Capawaraway*; his paunch is either a Coope or a Rooste for them: he hath, within himself, a stall for the Oxe, a roome for the Cow, a stye for the Hogge, a parke for the Deere, a warren for Coneies, a storehouse for fruit, a dayery for Milke, Creame, Curds, Whay, Butter-milke, and Cheefe: his mouth is a mill of perpetuall motion, for let the wind or the water rife or fall, yet his teeth will ever bee grinding; his guts are the Rendez-vous or meeting place or Burfe for the beafts of the fields, the fowles of the Ayre, and fifhes of the Sea: and though they be never fo wild, or difagreeing in nature, one to another, yet hee binds or grindes them to the peace, in fuch manners, that they never fall at odds againe.

His eating of a Sheepe, a Hog, and a Duck raw, doth fhew that he is free from the finn of nicenefie or curiofity in his Dyet. (It had been happy for the poore, if their ftomachs had beene of that Conftriution when Sea-coales were fo dear here.) Befides, he never troubles a Larder or Cupboard to lay cold meate in, nor doth he keep any Cats or Traps in his houfe to deftroy vermin, he takes fo good a Courfe, that he layes or fhuts up all fafe within himfelfe; in briefe, give him meate, and he ne'r ftands upon the Cookery, he cares not for the Peacocke of *Samos*, the Woodcock of *Phrygia*, the Cranes of *Malta*, the Pheafants of *England*, the *Caperkelly*, the Heathcocke, and *Termagant* of *Scotland*, the Goate of *Wales*, the Salmon, and Ufquabah of *Ireland*, the Sawfedge of Bolognia, the Skink of Weftphalia, the Spanifh *Potato*, he holds as a bable, and the Italian Figge he efteemes as poyfon.

He is an Englifh-man, and Englifh dyet will ferve his turne; if the *Norfolk Dumplin*, and the *Devonfhire White Pot*, be at variance, he will atone them. The *Bag-puddings* of *Gloucefter*-fhire, the *Blacke puddings* of *Worcefter*-fhire, the *Pan-puddings* of *Shrepfhire*, the White *White puddings* of *Somerfetfhire*, the *Hafty-puddings* of *Hempfhire*, and the *pudding-pyes* of any fhire, all is one to him, nothing comes amifie, a contented mind is worth all, and let any thing come in the fhape of fodder, or eating ftuffe, it is wellcome, whither it bee *Sawfedge*, or *Cuftard*, or *Eg-pye*, or *Cheefe-cake*, or *Flawne*, or *Foole*, or *Froyze*, or *Tanzy*, or *Pancake*, or *Fritter*, or *Flapiacke*, or *Poffet*, or *Galley mawfrey*, *Mackeroone*, *Kickfhow*, or Tantablin, he is no puling Meacocke, nor in all his life time the queafineffe of his ftomache needed any Sawcy fpurre or Switch of fowre *Verjuice*, or acute *Vineger*, his appetite is no ftruggler, nor is it ever to feeke, for he keepes it clofe prifoner, and like a courteous kind Jaylor, he is very tender over it, not fuffering it to want any thing if he can by any meanes procure it: indeede it was never knowne to be fo farre out of reparations, that it needed the affiftance of *Cawdle*, *Alebery*, *Julep*, *Califfe*, *Grewell*, or *Stew'd-broth*, onely a meffe of plaine frugall

Countrey

Countrey *Pottage* was always Sufficient for him, though it was but a *washing-bowle-full* of the Quantity of two pecks, which porrenger of his I my felfe faw at the figne of the White Lyon, at a Village called *Harrifom* in *Kent*, the Hoftefſe of which Howfe did affirme, that he did at once wafh downe that Bowle full of potage, with nine penny loaves of Bread, and three jugges of Beere.

Indeed in my prefence (after he had broken his faft) having (as he faid) eaten one pottle of milke, one pottle of potage, with bread, butter, and cheefe, I then fent for him, to the aforefaid Inne, and after fome accommodated falutations, I afked him if hee could eate any thing? He gave me thankes, and faid, that if he had knowne that any Gentleman would have invited him, that he would have fpared his breakfaft at home (and with that he told me as aforefaid, what he had eaten) yet neverthelefſe (to doe me a courtefie) he would fhew me fome fmall caft of his office, for he had one hole or corner in the profundity of his ftore-houfe into which he would ftow and beftow any thing that the houfe would afford, at his perill and my coft. Whereupon I fummoned my Hoftefſe with three knocks upon the Table, and two Stamps on the floore, with my fift and my foot, at which fhe made her perfonall appearance with a low Curtfie, and an inquifitive What lack ye? I prefently laid the authority of a bold Gueft upon her, commanding that all the Victuals in the Houfe fhould be laid on the Table. She faid fhe was but flenderly provided by reafon goodman *Wood* was there, but what fhe had or could doe, we fhoud prefently have: fo the cloth was difplaid, the falt was advanc'd, fixe penny wheaten loaves were mounted two ftories high like a Rampier, three Six-penny Veale pyes, walled ftiffly about, and well victual'd within, were prefented to the hazzard of the *Scalado*, one pound of fweet-butter (being all fat and no bones) was in a cold fweat at this mighty preparation, one good difh of Thornback, white as Alabafter or the Snow upon the Scythian Mountaines, and in the Reare came up an Inch-thick Slyver of Peck houfe-hold loafe; all which provifion were prefently, in the fpace of an houre, utterly confounded and brought to nothing, by the meere and only valourous dexterity of our unmatchable grand Gurmound. He courageoufly paft the Pikes, and I cleared the Shot, but the houfe yeelded no more, fo that my Gueft arofe unfatisfied, and myfelfe difcontented in being thrifty and faving my money againft my will.

I did there offer him twenty fhillings to bring him up to me to my houfe on the Bank-fide, and there I would have given him as much good meate, as he would eate in tenne dayes, one after another, and five shillings a day every day, and at the renne dayes ende, twenty shillings more to bring him downe againe. I did alfo offer tenne shillings to one *Jeremy Robinson* a Glouer (a man very inward with him) to attend and keepe him company, and two shillings six pence the day, with good dyet and lodging, all which were once accepted, untill *Wood* began to ruminate and examine what fervice he was to doe for thefe large allowances; now my Plot was to have him to the Beare-Garden, and there before a houfe full of people he fhould have eaten a wheele-barrow full of Tripes, and the next Day, as many puddings as fhould reach over the Thames (at a place which I would meafure betwixt *London* and *Richmond*; the third day, I would have allowed him a fat Calfe, or Sheepe of twenty fhillings price; and the fourth day he fhould have had thirty Sheeps Gathers; thus from day to day, he fhould have had wages and dyet with variety: but he fearing that which his merits would amount unto, broke off the match, faying, that perhaps when his Grace (I gueffe who he meant) fhould heare of one that ate fo much, and could worke fo little, he doubted there would come a command to hang him: whereupon our hopefull Beare-garden bufinefs was fhiverd and fhatterd in pieces.

Indeed he made a doubt of his expected performance in his quality, by reafon of his being growne in Yeeres, fo that if his ftomach fhould faile him publickly, and lay his reputation in the mire, it might have been a difcouragement to him for ever, and efpecially in Kent, where he hath long beene famous, hee would be loth to be defamed; but as weake as he was, he faid, that he could make a fhift to deftroy a fat Weather of a pound in two houres, provided that it were tenderly boild, for he hath loft all his teeth (except one) in eating a Quarter of Mutton (bones and all) at *Afhford* in the County aforefaid, yet is he very quicke and nimble in his feeding, and will riddle more eating worke away in two houres, than tenne of the Hungryeft Carters in the Parifh where he dwells. He is furely noble (for his great Stomache) and vertuous, chiefely for his patience in putting *up muche:* moreover he is thrifty or frugall, for when he can get no better meate, he will eat Oxe Livers, or a meffe of warme Ale-graines from a Brew-houfe. He is provident and ftudious where to get more provifion as foone as all is fpent, and yet hee is bountifull or prodigall in fpending all hee hath at once: hee is profitable in keeping bread and meate from mould and maggots, and faving the Charge of Salt, for his appetite will not waite and attend the poudring; his courtefie is manifeft, for he had rather have one *Farewel* than twenty

Godbwyes:

Godbwyes: of all things, hee holds fasting to be a most superstitious branch of Popery, he is a maine enemy to Ember weekes, he hates Lent worse than a Butcher or a Puritan, and the name of Good-Friday affrights him like a Bull-beggar, a long Grace before meate strikes him into a Quotidian Ague; in a word, hee could wish that Christmass would dwell with us all the yeere, or that euery day were metamorphoz'd into Shrouetuesdayes; in briefe, he is a Magazine, a Storehouse, a Receptacle, a Burse or Exchange, a Babel or confusion for all Creatures.

Hee is no Gamester, neither at Dice, or Cards, yet there is not a Man within forty miles of his head, that can play with him at *Maw*; and though his pasture be neuer so good, he is alwayes like one of *Pharaohs* leane Kine; he is swarty, blackish haire, Hawk-nosed (like a Parrot or Roman) hee is wattle-jawde, and his eyes are sunke inward, as if hee looked into the inside of his Intrayles, to note what custom'd or uncustom'd goods he tooke in, whilst his belly (like a Maine-Sayle in a calme) hangs ruffled and wrinkled (in foldes and wreathes) flat to the most of his Empty carkasse, till the storme of aboundance fills it, and violently drives it into the full sea of satisfaction.

   Like as a River to the Ocean bounds,
   Or as a Garden to all Britaines Grounds,
   Or like a Candle to a flaming Linck,
   Or as a Single Ace, unto Sife Cinque,
   So short am I of what *Nick Wood* hath done,
   That having ended I have scarce begun;
   For I have written but a Taste in this
   To shew the Readers where, and what he is.

THE OLD GATE, and BANQUETING HOUSE, WHITEHALL.

THIS plate presents a view of one of the gates, and other parts of the remains of the ancient Palace of Whitehall, with the Banqueting-House, built to form part of a new one intended to have been erected on its site. It also shews the Privy-Garden wall, and the street leading to Charing-Crofs, as they appear when viewed from those houses opposite the end of Downing-street.

The palace of Whitehall was originally built by Hubert de Burgh, Earl of Kent, who in the year 1243, bequeathed it to the Black-Friars, in Chancery-lane, Holbourn, in whose church he was interred Anno 1248; these Friars disposed of it to Walter de Grey, Archbishop of York, who by will left it to his successors for their town manfion, whence it was called York Place; The Royal Palace at Westminster, having suffered much by fire, in the reign of Henry VIIIth, and that Prince taking a likeing to York-House, found no difficulty in prevailing on Cardinal Wolsey to part with it, who accordingly in the year 1530, sold it to him. Henry no sooner became possessed of it, but he made many alterations and additions; among the last was the Gate here seen, the design of which it is said was made by that celebrated painter Hans Holbein; it was adorned on each side with four bustos, with ornamented mouldings, all made of baked clay, in the proper colours, and glazed in the manner of the delft ware. This Gate was taken down a few years ago, in order to widen the street for the passage of the members of both houses of parliament, for which purpose another Gate had been before removed. It is remarkable that the busts abovementioned were when taken down, as entire as when set up, whereas the festoons and other ornaments of stone on the Banqueting-House, are so corroded by the weather as to be scarce intelligible. The materials of this Gate were purchased by the late Duke of Cumberland, and it is said, were set up exactly in their original form somewhere about his lodge at Windsor Great Park.

This Palace is described by Hentzner in his Travels, who says it was a structure truly royal; it continued to be the place of residence of our kings, till the year 1697, when it was destroyed by fire, and has never since been rebuilt, but all the public business is still dated from Whitehall; and many of the great offices are kept in its remains. In the reign of King James the First, that Prince conceived a design of building a new Palace on
the

the fame fpot, when the famous Inigo Jones was employed to prepare a plan, which being done, the prefent Banqueting-Houfe was erected, as a fmall part of the intended work, but after the fire nothing farther was done.

The Banqueting-Houfe was intended for the reception of ambaffadors, and other audiences of ftate. It is a regular and majeftic building, of three ftories.. The loweft has a ruftic wall, with fmall fquare windows, and by its apparent folidity, feems to form a folid bafe for the beautiful fuperftructure; upon this is raifed the ionic ftory, ornamented with columns and pilafters; between the columns are a row of well proportioned windows, with arched and pointed pediments; over thefe is placed the proper entablature, and on this is raifed a fecond ftory, of the corinthian order, like the other confifting of columns and pilafters, column being placed over column, and pilafter over pilafter; from the capitals are carried feftoons, which meet with mafks, and other ornaments in the middle. This ftory is alfo crowned with its proper entablature, on which is raifed the baluftrade, with attic pedeftals between, which crown the work. Every thing in this building is finely proportioned, and as happily executed. The projection of the columns from the wall has a fine effect in the entablature, which being brought forward in the fame proportion, gives that happy diverfity of light and fhade fo effential to fine architecture. The infide of this building is alfo a curiofity in its kind, the ceiling being finely painted by the great Sir Peter Paul Rubens, who was Embaffador here in the time of Charles the firft.. The fubject is an emblematical reprefentation of the entrance, inauguration and coronation of King James the Firft. It is efteemed among his moft capital performances. The Great Apartment is at prefent converted into a Chapel, for the fervice of which certain felect preachers were appointed out of each univerfity by King George the Firft, to preach here every Sunday; for this each is allowed thirty pounds per annum.

For the REPERTORY.

THAT every thing may be had for money, is I am afraid an obfervation no lefs ancient than true. We read of empires, kingdoms and principalities, which have been publickly fold; the fame has been whifpered
respecting

respecting popedoms, bishopricks, and other spiritual dignities; and we have heard (but it is to be hoped without foundation) of venal counties and corrupt boroughs.

Buying and selling the devil, have long been proverbial expressions, but that such a traffic was ever actually negociated will scarcely be credited, nevertheless Blount's Law Dictionary, under the article *Conventio*, gives an instance of such a sale; the story is extracted from the Court Rolls of the Manor of Hatfield, near the Isle of Axholme, in the County of York; where a curious gentleman not long ago searched for and found it regularly entered. A copy of it here follows, together with an English translation, for the benefit of those who do not understand the language, in which the original is written.

'Curia tenta apud Hatfield die Mercurii
Prox post Festum ——— Anno xi^e. Edw. 3^{tii}.

' Robertus de Roderham qui optulit se versus Johannem de Ithon de eo quod non teneat Conventionem inter eos factam & unde queritur quod certo die & anno apud Thorne convenit inter prædictum Robertum & Johannem quod prædictus Johannes vendidit prædicto Roberto Diabolum ligatum in quodam ligamine pro 111^d. ob. & super prædictus Robertus tradidit prædicto Johanni quiddam obolum—earles (i. e. earnest money) per quod proprietas dicti diaboli commoratur in persona dicti Roberti ad habiendum deliberationem dicti Diaboli, infra quartam diem prox. sequent. Ad quam diem idem Robertus venit ad præfatum Johannem & petit deliberationem dicti Diaboli, secundum Conventionem inter eos factam; idem Johannes prædictum Diabolum deliberaro noluit, nec adhuc vult &c. ad grave dampnum ipsius Roberti IX sol. Et inde producit sectam &c. &c. prædictus Johannes venit &c. Et non dedicit Conventionem prædictam. Et quia videtur curiæ quod tale placitum non jacet inter Christianes, ideo partes prædicti adjournantur usque in infernum, ad audiendum Judicium suum, & utraque pars in Misericordia &c. per Willielmum de Scargel Senescallum.'

' Robert de Roderham appeared against John de Ithon, for that he had not kept the agreement made between them, and therefore complains that on a certain day and year at Thorne, there was an agreement between the aforesaid Robert and John, whereby the said John sold to the said Robert, the Devil, bound in a certain bond, for three-pence farthing, and thereupon the said Robert, delivered to the said John, one farthing as earnest money, by which

Curfew

the property of the said Devil rested in the person of the said Robert, to have livery of the said Devil, on the fourth day next following; at which day the said Robert came to the forenamed John, and asked delivery of the said Devil according to the agreement between them made. But the said John refused to deliver the said Devil, nor has he yet done it, &c. to the great damage of the said Robert to the amount of 60 shillings, and he has therefore brought his suit, &c. &c.

'The said John came, &c. and did not deny the said agreement; and because it appeared to the court that such a suit ought not to subsist among christians; the aforesaid parties are therefore adjourned to the infernal regions, there to hear their judgement, and both parties were amerced, &c. by William De Scargell Senefchal.'

To the EDITOR of the ANTIQUARIAN REPERTORY,

SIR,

THE enclosed drawing and letter describe an ancient piece of houshold furniture, which has hitherto escaped the notice of our Antiquaries, or at least has not I believe been before either engraved, or mentioned by them. Perhaps the giving it a place in your Repertory, may induce some of your ingenious correspondents to favour the public with some farther information on the subject.

I am yours, &c. F. G.

THIS utensil is called a Curfew, or Couvre-fen, from its use, which is that of suddenly putting out a fire; the method of applying it was thus,—the wood and embers were raked as close as possible to the back of the hearth, and then the Curfew was put over them, the open part placed close to the back of the chimney; by this contrivance, the air being almost totally excluded, the fire was of course extinguished.

This Curfew is of copper, rivetted together, as solder would have been liable to melt with the heat. It is 10 inches high, 16 inches wide, and 9 inches

ches deep. The Rev. Mr. Goftling, of Canterbury, to whom it belongs, fays it has been in his family for time immemorial, and was always called the Curfew. Some others of this kind are ftill remaining in Kent and Suffex.

Probably Curfews were ufed in the time of William the Conqueror, for the more ready obedience to the laws of that king, who in the firft year of his reign, directed that on the ringing of a certain bell, thence called the Curfew bell, all perfons fhould put out their fires and candles. Whether a bell was ordered to ring exprefly for this purpofe, or whether the fignal was to be taken from the Vefpers bell of the Convents, is a matter in which Antiquaries are not entirely agreed. The Curfew bell is ftill rung in many of our country towns.

The following Letter of Indulgence granted to thofe who fhould con'ribute towards the Reparation and farther Endowment of the Chapel of the Holy Crofs in Colchefter, appears from the Names of feveral of the Bifhops therein mentioned to have been written about the Year 1406. It has feveral Errors in the Chronology, particularly in that Part which places the Vifit of St. Thomas Becket in anno 1200, thirty Years after the Death of that turbulent Prelate. But as this made but a very fmall Part of the Falfities contained in the Whole, it was perhaps thought by the Compofer immaterial, or poffibly it may have been an Error of the Clerk who drew it up. The original Deed, written on Parchment, which has the Appearance of great Antiquity, is in the Library of Thomas Aftle, Efq.

TO all the Children oure Godez holy Churche unto whom thefe p'fent lettrez come Thomas thurgh the fufferaunce of God Archebisfhop of Cannterbury and Primate of all Englond and Legate of the Apoftolyke Seet thurgh the fame fuffraunce of God Archebisfhop of York and Primate of Englond and of the forfaide Seete Legate Robert Bisfhop of London Gye Bisfhop of Seynte Davids Walter of Dyrham Henry of Lincoln Edmonnde of Exetur Henry of Bath and Wells John of Ely Henry of Norwiche Richard of Salyfbury Richard of Worcetur John of Rochefter John of Coventry et Litchefeld Robert of Chicheftur John of Hereford John of Kar-

lill

lill Richard of Bangur Thomas of Landyff and John of Seynte Affe by the Grace of God Bisſhopps ſend Greetyng in evyr Lovis of oure Savioure the Werkis of Mercy by all faithfull people more faynner or gladder to be loved in ſo moche that the Olde ſhall have the Rewarde of God them in the laſte Day of Jugement whereof them Witneffing god hym felf is fpecially accoumpted to be yelde and to all theyme difpifing the faid Werkis of Charite everlafting fere and to all people doying the faide werkis of Charitie the everlafting Kingdom of hevyn muſt be made redy therefore Where as We have underſtanding the free Chappell or hofpitall of the holy Croffe within the Suburbys of the Towne of Colcheftur lying within the Diocefe of London to the Suftentation of power nedy men founded and ordayned for poverte and ympotency of a Wardeyne or keeper and of power Brothers of the fame and alfo for the fmalneffe and Scarffnefs of Londs and rentis of the Chappell or Hofpitall aforfaide is as it were diflate and brought to nought infomoche that the fervice of god therin to the worfhip of god as it was wonnte may not be exerciſed nor the power nedy men may there congruly be fuſteyned but if it be by the mercifull almez of true Chriſten people mercifully be holpyn and fuccourd and alfo it is knowen that the faid Chapell and Hofpitall nedith moche reparation and amendment Therefore We defyrying that the faide Chapell and Hofpitall w^t. due and congrue Worfhippis may be ufed and alfo repayred and alfo that all Chriften people more rather by caufe of Devocion to the faide Chapell and Hofpitall myght come and goo to and the reparacion of the faide Chapell or Hofpital and to the fuftentation of the power nedy men therein put And to theyre reparacion helpyng hands where there thrugh the gyfte of the hevenly King they ſhall fye them felf refreſhed Therfore for the mercy of Almyghti god and of the glorious Virgyn Seynte Mary his Moder and alfo of oure holy patronys and the merits and prayers of all Seyntis trufty to all Chriften Thrugh oure Province Citees and Dioc. abyding and to all other of whom the Diofifanes thefe oure indulgences hath eftablifshed and accept of theire fynnes truly contrite and penitent and confeffed the whiche the forfaide Chapell or Hofpitall by caufe of Devocion or pylgrymage Vifits, And alfo for the tranquli'te and peafe of oure Lorde the King and of the Realme of Englond and for all the Soulis of true Chriften people difleafed feithe there with meke mynde a Pater nofter and an Ave Marie and to the reparacion of the faide Chapell or Hofpitall and alfo to the fuftentation of the power men there of theyre goodis to theyme gevin of goode wilfull helpis of Charite bring or any maner wife Affigne as ofte as evere they doo

the

the forfaide fubfidies and helpis XI dayes of pardon every the of Us mercifully by oure felf oure Lorde grauntith by thefe Pfentis the fm⁴ of all whiche Drawith viij C Dayes of Pardon and xl as oft as eve they foo doo And We Thomas Archbifshop of Canntbury Richard of York Archebiffop Robert of London Gye of Seynte Davies Walter of Durham Henry of Lincoln Edmonnde of Exetur Henry of Bathe and Wells John of Ely Henry of Norwiche Richard of Salyfbury Richard of Worcetur John of Rowcheftur John of Coventre and Lytchefeld Robert of Chichefter Johen of Hereford Johen of Karlill Richard of Bangur Thomas of Landiff and John of Seynt Affe Bifshoppis aforfaide all the indulgence in this Parte lawfully granteth and alfo in tyme comyng to be granted as moche as ev. We may of right We ratify And alfo oure Lorde make fferme and ftedfaft in Witneffe &c. more over in the yere of oure Lorde vi C lxx conftantyne the Sonne of the bleffed and holy woman Seynte Elyn fent his Moder the faid Seynte Elvn unto Jerufalem to enquere of the holy Croffe that oᵣ Savioure Crifte Jehu Died upon lyke wife as it was fhewed to hym by tokyn in the Ayre and alfo by revellacion of the holy gofte Then the holy woman faying the Will of Almighti god Departed oute of the Towne of Colcheftur where fhe was borne there where the faide Hofpitall is founded in the honoure of Almighti ged the holy Croffe and Seynte Elyn and toke her Jorney unto Jerufalem and there by fufferaunce of Almighti God Dyd Wyn the fame Croffe that Crifte Jehu Dyed upon as it was fhewed by myracle at the taking up of the holy Croffe for whiche tyme as the holy Woman hadd everay knowleg where the holy Croffe was leyde She made it to be dygged in the grounde the fpace of xxti fote and there fhe found iij Croffis then fhe having noo verray truft nor knowleg whiche was the very Croffe that Crifte Dyed upon She fet her downe upon her knees and prayed to Almighti god that fhe myght have a veray true knowleg which was the verray Croffe that Crifte died upon and anon as fhe was praying to Almighti god there came a dede Body to the Churche to be buryed, She toke and leyde upon the dede Coorfe on Croffe and then another and the Dede body did lye ftill then fhe laid on the thiyrde Croffe the whiche Crifte Died upon and anon he Rofe from Dethe to lyfe Alfo a Woman that was blynde as it towched her ien fhe fawe her felf, Then the holy Victorious Woman gaf lawde and loving to god and toke on part of the holy Croffe and clofed it wᵗ. golde and fent it to her hofpitall to Colcheftᵣ evemore to be abyding wᵗ. her Ring her gyrdull and her purs wᵗ. other xxiiij curious Reliquis Alfo Seynte Thomas of Cannterbury in the Yere of our Lorde M CC

came

came Riding for by the fame Place infourmed by the holy goofte lighted and halowed the faide Hofpitall and confermed the faide grannte and gaf his Pontifical Ring in tokenying Alfo in the yere of oure lorde m ccccj there came thevis unto the hofpital by nyght and brake up the lokkis where the glorious reliquie that is to fay the holy Croffe that Crifte Dyed on and toke it away and bare it w^h. them away till they came iij Myle oute of the Towne to a Place called Knyfitts Poolis the whiche be of greate Depneffe and then they feying they were lyke to be takyn then they toke the bleffed holy Croffe as it was clofed in golde the weight of xxi ounces and kyft it in to the ponde and when it was in the watur it wold not fynk but flete and ftode above the watur the whiche water was more then iij Yerdis Depe and foo the folkis that did purfue toke it up and brought it home to the place agayne Alfo all thoo that gyve any of theyre goodis to the faid Hofpitall they be Partakers of the Prayers of iij Preeftis a xij beddes and an Ankreffe be fyde eyke folk.

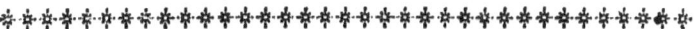

EPITAPH of LAVINIA LADY MANWOOD,

On a fmall Table Monument near the Door of the Church of St. Stephen's, or Hackington, near Canterbury.

GLORY be to God on high our moft Glorious Saviour. Within this Church (the Temple of the ever Living God) lies the body of Levina Lady Manwood in the Valte belonging to my Family Shee was eldeft Daughter to Sr John Ogle, Kn^t. fometime a Collonel in the Netherlands and Governour of Utricht where he was in Martiall affaires, and at home in England both in his life and death juftly preclare. Shee was a moft Indulgent Wife to me from the very howre of our happy and bleffed conjunction in marriage which was on the 11th of December 1627 till the 10th of February 1641 in the Evening of which day between 8 & 9 of the Clock, we were feparated by her diffolution and my recovery out of a dangerous Sicknefs, in the extremity whereof, grief fo pofeffed and pierced through her moft pure heart, that fhee inftantly fickened, and Dyed five days after, in the 36th Year of her Age. Her life was moſt pious, and full of Charity, her Converſation ſweet and moſt ſweetly diſcreet. For ſhe flatterd none, and yet obliged all. Her love to me was moſt ſingularly true and eminent. And as Gods prieſt united us ſacredly in marriage, ſo God himſelf did our hearts and Souls. For we had but one heart, one Soul. Death hath ſeparated our Bodyes, but can never our Souls For her's is praying God in Heaven: and ſo doth mine though my Body is on the Earth. Death and Reſurrection will unite again our Soules and Bodyes eternally to prayſe our God the moſt Glorious Trinity. Which God of his infinite mercy Grant.

If David a Man after Gods own heart thought it ſo great a happineſs, that he had rather be a Door Keeper in the Howſe of the Lord than to dwell in the Tents of Ungodlineſs; how dare I approach thus that am the Miſerableſt of Sinners. Lord Pardon my preſumption.

This Stone with the Inſcription I cauſed to be Erected in a juſt Memory of my Moſt juſtly eſteemed deere Wife: whoſe morall Vertues nether Tongue or Pen can fully expreſs or heart ſufficientlye contemplate her true humilitye, and uprightneſs to God; the 20th of May 1642.

John Manwood.

Anima mea peregrina, et corpus in Mundo.

On a Tomb-ſtone by the Church Porch in the ſame Church Yard.

UNDER this Stone the Body here doth reſt
Of Robt: Mourfield. At the Siege of Breſt
A Soldier, one with Forbeſſer and Drake
That in the Indies made the Spaniard Quake
A Faithful Friend to all that e'er him try'd,
A Loving Neighbour and beloved he died.

February 1, 1629. Aged 74.

For the ANTIQUARIAN REPERTORY.

ON the north fide of the high ftreet of Rochefter in Kent, ftands an Alms Houfe, founded by Richard Watts, Efq. who was a Member of the fecond Parliament in the reign of Queen Elizabeth. It is feemingly an ancient building, and has the following remarkable Infcription.

RICHARD WATTS, Efq'.
by his Will dated 22 Aug. 1579
founded this Charity
for Six Poor Travellers
who not being Rogues, or Proctors
May Receive Gratis for one Night
Lodging, Entertainment
and four pence each
in teftimony of his Munificence
In Honour of his Memory
and Inducement to his Example
NATH^t. HOOD Efq^r. the Prefent Mayor
has caufed this Stone
gratefully to be renewed
and infcribed
A D. 1771.

Although this Infcription in the general fenfe agrees with the ancient one, it differs confiderably from it in the Words and Arrangement, and one caufe of difqualification is totally left out, i. e. being contagiously difeafed.

The Ancient Infcription.
Richard Watts Efq^r. firft devifed
An. 1579. this Relief for Travellers
To be had after the Death of
Marian his wife, which fhe
by the help of Thomas Pagitt
her fecond Hufband, affured
Anno. 1586 and Died 31^{ft} of Decem. 1598.

Juſt over the Door.

Six Poor Travelling
Men not contagiouſly
Diſeaſed, Rogues, nor
Proctors may have
Lodging here one Night
Freely, and every one four
Pence in the Morning

On the Right Hand.

The Mayor and Citizens of
This City, and Dean and Chap
ter of the Cathedral
Church, and Wardens, and
Commonalty of the Bridge are
To ſee this executed for
Ever.

On the Left Hand, on each Side of the Arms of Paggit and Somers.

Thomas Paggit ſecond Huſband
Of Marian Daughter of Thomas
Somers of Halſto Widow of Richard
Watts deceaſed there. An. 1599.

The common reaſon aſſigned for Mr. Watts's great diſlike to Proctors is, that being once dangerouſly ill, he employed a Proctor to make his will, and on his recovery found that honeſt Lawyer had conſtituted himſelf heir to all his eſtates. Others think the word Proctor here meant is derived from Procurator, a kind of itinerant Prieſt, who had a diſpenſation from the Pope to abſolve the ſubjects of this realm from their oath of allegiance made to Queen Elizabeth, on account of her adherence to the Proteſtant Religion.

The READER is deſired to put *Forfar* inſtead of *Norfolk* in the Account of Bothwell-Caſtle in the laſt Number.

THE

ANTIQUARIAN REPERTORY.

The WATER-FALL of LODORE, on KESWICK LAKE, CUMBERLAND.

THE Waterfall of Lodore, or Lochdore, is one of the moſt romantic ſpots or points of view, on the ſo much boaſted Lake of Keſwick. This Lake, like many other beautiful objects, has ſuffered much by the exaggerated praiſes of its panegyriſts, whoſe deſcriptions favour more of the wild and enthuſiaſtic flights of the Poet, than the ſober judgment of the Topographer, which by making travellers expect too much, frequently renders them inſenſible to real excellencies.

The *Coup D'Oeil* of the whole ſcene, though undoubtedly beautiful and pictureſque, by conſiſting of a great number of nearly equal mountains, whoſe tops might be connected by a right line parallel to the horizon, wants that ſimplicity and contraſt ſo neceſſary to the ſublime; and the number of ſmall catching lights on the different objects diſtract the eye, and too much divide the maſſes of light and ſhade.

The two Water-falls too have been as much over-rated, as may be ſeen by conſidering this View, which was taken after a very rainy ſeaſon. As to the other, with reſpect to the quantity of water, it is frequently more than equalled in London at Fleet-bridge and Holborn-hill.

But

THE ANTIQUARIAN REPERTORY.

But although this Lake viewed altogether does not form fo ftriking a fcene as its hiftorians delineate, its parts confidered diftinctly afford many noble objects for the pencil, foremoft among which is that here exhibited, which has thus been defcribed by two different writers. In profe by the author of the Excurfion to the Lakes. The verfe by Dr. Dalton, and publifhed in Dodfley's Collection.

"———— We were landed on a plain of meadow ground, which de-
" fcended to the edge of the water, over which we paffed to an adjoining
" wood at the foot of the rocks, behind Lodore-houfe—After winding
" through feveral paffes in thefe groves and thickets, we gained a fituation
" where we were delighted with the noble objects which prefented them-
" felves to our view.

" Around us was fpread a grove, formed of tall young oaks, afh, and
" birch-trees, which gave an agreeable coolnefs and fhade; above the trees,
" with uplifted looks, to the right we viewed a mountain of rock, called
" Shepherd's Crag, forming a rude circular mafs, fhelving from the foot
" towards its crown in a fpiral form, on every plane of which, and every
" ftep that hung upon its fides, herbage and fhrubs grew fantaftically, whilft
" the very fummit wore a verdant cap of grafs.—To the left there arofe a
" perpendicular grey cliff, faid to be a thoufand feet in height from the
" Lake, rent into innumerable fiffures, and ftanding like maffive columns
" in rude arrangements, to fupport the feeming ruins of a fhattered tower,
" grown white with ftorms, and overlooking Shepherd's Crag fome hundred
" feet.—In the opening between thefe ftupendous rocks, the river pours its
" whole ftream, forming a grand cafcade near 200 perpendicular feet high;
" as the channel is rugged, the water makes a fheet of foam, and roars among
" the caverns and the cliffs, fo that you are deprived of hearing any thing
" befides its tumult;—reaching the wood where the defcent is lefs precipi-
" tate, it winds amongft the trees, fometimes fhewing itfelf, and at others
" totally concealed, whilft it ferpentines towards the Lake.——The fpray
" which is dafhed around the rocks, and carried upon the breeze, wherever
" it meets the rays of the fun, through the openings of the cliffs, takes the
" colours of the rainbow."

———— " To nature's pridé,
" Sweet Kefwick's Vale, the mufe will guide;

" The

" The mufe who trod th' enchanted ground,
" Who fail'd the wond'rous lake around;
" With you will hafte, once more to hail
" The beauteous brook of Borrodale.

" From favage parent, gentle ftream
" Be thou the mufes favourite theme;
" O foft infinuating glide
" Silent along the meadow's fide;
" Smooth o'er the fandy bottom pafs,
" Refplendent all through fluid glafs,
" Unlefs upon thy yielding breaft
" Their heads the painted lillies reft,
" To where, in deep capacious bed,
" The widely liquid Lake is fpread.

" Let other ftreams rejoice to roar
" Down the rough rocks of dread Lodore,
" Rufh roving on with boift'rous fweep,
" And foaming rend the frighted deep;
" Thy gentle genius fhrinks away
" From fuch a rude unequal fray;

" Through thine own native Dale, where rife
" Tremendous rocks amid the fkies,
" Thy waves with patience flowly wind,
" Till they the fmootheft channel find;
" Soften the horrors of the fcene,
" And through confufion flow ferene.

" Horrors like thefe at firft alarm,
" But foon with favage grandeur charm,
" And raife to nobleft thoughts your mind;
" Thus by thy Fall, Lodore, reclin'd
" The cragged cliff, impending wood,
" Whofe fhadows mix o'er half the flood,
" The gloomy clouds with folemn fail, ⎫
" Scarce lifted by the languid gale, ⎬
" O'er the capp'd hill and darken'd vale, ⎭

The

" The ravening kite, and bird of Jove,
" Which round th' aërial ocean move,
" And, floating on the billowy fky,
" With full expanded pinions fly,
" Their flutt'ring or their bleating prey
" Thence with death-dooming eye furvey;

" Channels by rocky torrents torn;
" Rocks to the Lake in thunder borne,
" Or fuch as o'er our heads appear,
" Sufpended in the mid career,
" To ftart again at his command
" Who rules fire, water, air, and land;
" I view with wonder and delight
" A pleafing, though an awful fight;
" For feen with them, the verdant ifles
" Soften with more delicious fmiles;
" More tempting twine their opening bowers,
" More lively blow the purple flowers;
" More fmoothly flopes the border gay,
" In fairer circle bends the bay;
" And laft to fix our wand'ring eyes,
" Thy roofs, O Kefwick, brighter rife;
" The Lake and lofty hills between,
" Where giant Skiddow fhuts the fcene.

" Supreme of mountains, Skiddow, hail
" To whom all Britain finks a Vale!
" Lo his imperial brow I fee
" From foul ufurping vapours free!
" 'Twere glorious now his fide to climb,
" Boldly to fcale his top fublime."

Curious Masques *performed before* Robert Sutton, *alias* Dudlie, *Earl of* Leicester, *at the Towns of* Donhage *and* Leidon, *in* Holland, *Anno Christi*, 1585.

(From *Hollingshed's Chronicle.*)

IN the euening the earle by cresset light, torches, and deuises of fire worke verie strange, entred into the towne of Donhage with a verie princelie traine of our Englishmen, with an hundred and fiftie of his gard, besides all or most of the states of Rotherodam and Delph, with those of Donhage that met him on the water with musket shot verie manie, and great triumphing. At the entrance of my lord by water on the riuer met him certeine fishermen, which represented Peter, James, and John at their herbour: by them Christ walking on the water, who commanded them to cast out their nets the second time (according to that of saint Matthew) they drew in abundance, wherewith they made shew of presentment to the erle, for the which with thanks he passed by. Further on the riuer sat the representation of Mars and Bellona, who uttered speeches unto him as he passed, at that present.

At his landing met him a troope of horssemen, furnished and trapped antikelie in colours, before whome hauing fetcht manie courses, becaufe the street waxed narrow, they rode awaie. At the entrance of the fairest street, being also somewhat narrow, there was on ech side of the same gallorie, raised a mans height, ech against other, all hung with blacke baies, on both which gallories on ech side stood fifteene virgins all clad in white, with branches of palme or box wreathed about wax candles light in their hands, euerie of which did reuerence unto the earle; these stood a speares length distant ech from other. Betwixt euerie one hwng a looking glasse, and betwixt euerie glasse upon a pretie antike pearch stood a wax candle burning, and at ech end of the gallorie stood a champion and a blacke Moore, the one supporting the armes of England, and the other the armes of Holland. This shew was verie proper, but these had no speeches. All the waie as the earle passed through, were artificiallie made gates raised of ragged staues, and upon euerie snag stood a small wax candle burning, by which hwng the armes of diuerse craftsmen of the towne. The street all the waie was hwng with broad clothes, upon the which were placed store of red roses on sheetes of paper painted. At the next turning he was interteined with this shew.

Ouer a gate upon a verie high fcaffold was a conceiued battell fought betweene the Englifh foldiors and the Spaniards, the Englifh men ftill preuailing, under the which was written thus much in effect: furthermore, thefe lines in the Latine twng, alluding to England, ancientlie called Britaine, were written in open fight as followeth:

> Such be our fortune, as this dooth forefhoo,
> To vs freedome, to England fame alfo.

> *Maris terrarúmque fidus,*
> *Aequa Romanorum olim imperio,*
> *Luxit falus, affulfit Conftantinus,*
> *Qui adfertor libertatis, inftaurator*
> *Chriftianæ pietatis:*
> *Da & nobis fidam vicinámque dextram.*
> *Faxit Deus optimus maximus,*
> *Vt reginæ aufpicijs, Dudlæi ductibus,*
> *Militis tui viribus,*
> *Iugo feruitutis excuffo, belli nimbis difcufsis,*
> *Ex infælicifsimis fælicifsimi Belgæ fimus,*
> *Sacro tecum arctóque vinclo iuncti!*

Paffing ftill forward, was a loftie fcaffold verie faire builded, with hir maiefties armes at large placed, on the top ftood feauen virgins, reprefenting the feuen prouinces, euerie virgin holding a fpeare, and the armes at large emblafoned, which prouince fhe did fignifie; in the middeft of whom ftood Minerua armed, incompaffed about the bodie with the armes of England, vpon whome all the reft feemed to relie, as moft euidentlie appeared by their verfe:

> *Adfis ô noftrúmque leues regina laborem.*

All which were reprefented vnto hir maieftie by Neceffitie an old champion. The next was on the like fcaffold, feuen perfons prefented the feauen liberall fciences in their kinds, yeelded to the earle by defert: out of euerie window hoong lanthorns and candles, and euerie ftreet was furnifhed with creffets, torches, and links light: one deuife that hoong in the middeft of the ftreet conteined eight and thirtie lanthorns, and feuerall lights comelie burning: a verie pretie fight. Befides this, againft my lords gate, a barbar had on a wall placed three fcore or more bafons of bright copper, and in the middeft middeſt of euerie one a wax candle burning was placed, in the middeſt of all was painted a roſe and crowne: this made a faire ſhew, and was a pretie deuiſe. Under the red roſe was written theſe verſes following:

> *Floreat hæc ſemper roſa, cuius odore renixit*
> *Belgia langueſcens, regina dite potita.*

Ouer the entrance of the court gate, was placed aloft upon a ſcaffold, as if it had beene in a cloud or ſkie, Arthur of Britaine, whome they compared to the earle; within were hoboies, cornets, and diuers kindes of muſike. And thus they brought him to his lodging triumphantlie, and after he was entred in a great hall of that houſe, they diſcharged ſuch volees of ſhot as was wonderfull to heare. In the night they vſed fireworks of rockets, ſquibs, wheeles, and balles of fire, with a dragon that continued caſting out of fire an houre, wonderfull artificiallie made.

The next daie, on the riuer adjoining to my lords lodging, they deuiſed a running as it were at the tilt in botes, which was thus. From ech end of the river came a bote running with ſix ores, in the ſterne of which on the top ſtood a man armed in a red waſtcote, with a ſtaffe in his reſt, hauing a but end of corke; now ech meeting other with their ſtaues, both fell into the water, where ſpare botes were readie to ſuccour them, for awaie went their horſſes. This ſport with freſh men they continued till the earle was wearie of it, in pitteing the poore caſe of the men.

On the third daie of Januarie the earle with three hundred horſſes in their furniture, verie brauelie with his retinue entred Leidon, where by the waie he was met by the beſt of the towne, firſt by twelue burgomaiſters, clad in long blacke gownes, and on their ſhoulders was the townes name, written in verie large letters of ſiluer: next them followed other twelue of the cheefeſt burgeſſes, and then manie on horſſe backe, all in blacke veluet. At his entrance into the towne, all ouer his head, and downe to the ground on ech ſide; was hanged with ſaie of diuerſe colours to his lodging, which was a great waie; himſelfe with a canopie carried ouer his head was brought to his ſeat, againſt the which was a ſtage, on the which ſtood two men like poets, who preſented theſe ſeuerall ſhews that follow. It is to be noted, that eight yeares before this, they were beſieged, and therefore now preſented their extremities, which at that time they were driuen into. They brought therefore a faire woman on the ſtage verie brauelie apparelled, and ſhe repreſented the towne, hir they aſſalted by Spaniards, with falſe fiers of great and ſmall
ſhot

fhot a long time in order of battell, and then retiring continued their fiege; heere they laie fo long that vittels waxed fcarfe, and then they prefented after the poets of what this fhew had paffed. . Famine attired accordingly then breathed into the woman; after which they prefented men rending dogges and cats aliue in funder, and fed on them, and fouldiors robbing women of their chil'dren.

Sickneffe now poffeffeth hir and peftilence, and this they prefented in abrupt burials of townefmen on heapes; and laftlie with a braue buriall of a capteine, who was borne ouer the ftage with dead matches, howling trumpets, wrapt up ancients, trailed pikes, drawne peeces; and after he was put into the ground, and bid farewell with a volee of great and fmall fhot. The Spaniards pitieng hir, writ and fent letters by diuerfe meffengers, all which fhe read and refufed, without returne of anfwer: now hope poffeffeth hir, and therefore they tooke another waie. Now fhe commanded a light to be fet on the higheft fteeple in the towne, to fignifie vnto the prince of Orange that laie in Delph, how they hoped for fuccor; who againe, by deuife of a doue fent them promife of aid, by which doue they promifed to attend the good houre, and fo the fhew ended.

Now came God's prouidence, vpon whome the towne relied, and fhe leaned: Gods prouidence in the dead of the night ouerthrew a peece of the wall and vawmure of fix and twentie poles. Which the enimie hearing, and fearing the prince and his power to be entred for their aid, they fled, whome when the towne had in purfute, they put all they ouertooke to the fword, the reft efcaped by flight, and fo with the woman, as it were now at libertie that prefented the towne, they marched awaie merilie with great triumph. At the laft they brought in a woman verie braue, armed as the other was, hir they befieged with a Spaniard, intifed with a Frenchman, and flattered with an Italian twife, the Spaniard put by, fhe fled the ftage, and leaping off haftilie hid hir felfe vnder the earls cloke, whom he fhadowed, and the Spaniard threatning marched awaie. The earle led hir to his lodging, whereinto he entred with fhot. On the fcaffold were written thefe verfes, in effect as followeth in Englifh:

> We Flemings being banifhed, now wailing here,
> We are as they in Babilon, by the water clere
> Becaufe we wold not worfhip idols, but Gods word,
> And might not fing our praife vnto the Lord,

Are

Are we driuen out as now dooth appeare,
But our deliuerance is now verie neare,
For God hath looked vpon our miferableneffe,
And fent vs a prince whom he will bleffe,
Which praifed be God as it dooth befeeme,
Who hath deliuered vs from dangerous cafe,
And humbled the hart of fuch a noble queene,
As hath fent vs a gouernor now in this fpace,
Laieng his hand to the warres through his grace
And his arme mightilie, the which vs defend,
Thus praifed may he be world without end,
Which fendeth fuch a prince aboue all that liueth,
And one that gouerns to gods honour he now giueth.

The Politike Conqueft of William *the* Firft,

(*From Hollingfhed's Chronicle.*)

THIS William duke of Normandy, bafe fon of Robert the Sixt duke of Normandy, and nephew unto Edward King of England furnamed the Confeffed, having vanquifhed the Englifh power, and flaine Harold in the field, begins his reigne over England the 15th day of October, being Sunday, in the year after the creation of the World 5033 (as W. Harrifon gathereth) and after the birth of our Saviour 1066, which was in the tenth year of the emperor Henry the 4th, in the fixt of Pope Alexander the fecond, in the fixt of Philip King of France, and about the tenth of Malcolm the third, firnamed Camoir, King of Scotland.

Immediately after he had thus got the victory in a pight-field he firft returned to Haftings, and after fet forward towards London, wafted the countries of Suffex, Kent, Hampfhire, Southerie, Middlefex, and Herefordfhire, burning the towns and fleaing the people, till he came to Beorcham. In the mean time, immediately after the difcomfiture in Suffex, the two earles of Normandy and Mercia, Edwin and Marchar, who had withdrawn themselves from the battel, together with their people came to London, and with all speed sent their sister queene Aldgitha unto the City of Chester, and herewith sought to perswade the Londoners to advance one of them to the kingdom, as Wil. Mal. writeth. But Simon of Durham saith that Aldred Archbishop of York, and the said earles with others would have made Edgar Etheling King. However, whilest manie of the Nobilitie and others prepared to make themselves redie to give a new battel to the Normans (how or whatsoever was the cause) the said earles drew homeward with their powers, to the great discomfort of their friends. Wil. Malm. seemeth to put blame in the bishops, for that the lords went not forward with their purpose in advancing Edgar Etheling to the Crown. For the Bishops, saith he, refused to join with the Lords in that behalf, and so thro' envie and spite which one part bare to another, when they could not agree upon an Englishman they received a stranger, insomuch that upon King William his coming to Beorchan, Aldred archbishop of York, Wolstane bishop of Worcester, and Walter bishop of Hereford, Edgar Etheling, and the aforesaid Earles Edwin and Marchar came and submitted themselves unto him whom he gently received, and incontinentlie made an agreement with them taking their Oth and hostages, as some write, and yet neverthelesse he permitted his people to spoil and burn the countrie.

But now when the feast of Christ's nativitie, commonly called Christmas, was at hand, he approached to the city of London, and coming thither, caused his vauntguard first to enter into the streets, where finding some resistance, he easily subdued the citizens that thus took upon them to withstand him, though not without some bloodshed (as Gemeticen writeth) but as by others it should appear he was received into the city without any resistance at all, and so being in possession thereof he spake many friendly words to the citizens, and promised that he would use them in most liberal and courteous manner.

Not long after when things were brought in order (as was thought requisite) he was crowned king upon Christmas day following by Aldred Archbish. of Yorke, for he woud not receive the crown at the hands of Stigand Archbishop of Canterbury, becaufe he was hated, and furthermore judged to be a verie leud person and a naughtie liver.

At his coronation he caused the bishops and barons of the realme to take their Oth, that they should be his true and loyal subjects (according to the manner in that cafe accustomed.) And being required thereto by the archbishop bifhop of Yorke, he tooke his perfonal Oth before the Altar of St. Peter at Weftminfter, to defend the holie church, and rulers of the fame, to governe the people in juftice as became a King to doo, to ordaine righteous laws and keepe the fame, fo that all manner of bribing, rapine and wrongfull judgments fhould for ever after be abolifhed. After this he tooke order how to keepe the realme in good and quiet government, fortifieing the neceffarie places, and furnifhing them with garrifons. He alfo appointed officers and councellours, fuch as he thought to be wife and difcreet men, and appointed fhips to be in the havens by the coaft for the defence of the land, as he thought moft expedient. After his coronation, or rather before (as by fome authors it fhould feeme) even prefentlie upon obteining of the citie of London, he took his journey towards the Caftel of Dover, to fubdue that and the reft of Kent alffo, which when the archbifhop Stigand and Egelfin the abbot of S. Auguftines (being as it were the chiefeft lords and governors of all Kent) did perceive, and confidered that the whole realme was in an evil ftate; and that whereas in this realme of England, before the coming in of the aforefaid duke William, there were no bondman: now all as well the nobilitie as the commonaltie were without refpect made fubject to the intolerable bondage of the Normans, taking an occafion by the perill and danger that their neighbours were in, to provide for the fafegard of themfelves and their countrie. They caufed all the people of the countie of Kent to affemble at Canterbury, and declared to them the perils and dangers imminent, the miferie that their neighbours were come into, the pride and infolencie of the Normans, and the hardneffe and grief of bondage and fervile eftate, whereupon all the people rather choofing to end their unfortunate life than to fubmit themfelves to an unaccuftomed yoke of fervitude and bondage, with a common confent determined to meet duke William, and to fight with him for the laws of their countrey.

Alfo, the aforefaid Stigand the archbifhop and the abbot Egelfin choofing rather to die in battell, than to fee their nation in fo evil an eftate, being encouraged by the examples of the holy Maccabees, became captains of the army. And at a day appointed all the people met at Swannefcombe, and being hidden in the woods laie privily in wait for the coming of the aforefaid duke William. Now becaufe it cannot hurt to take great heed and be very várie in fuch cafes, they agreed before hand, that when the duke was come and the paffages on every fide ftopped to the end he fhould be no way able to efcape, every one of them as well horfeman as footmen fhould bear

boughs

boughs in their hands. The next day after when the duke was come into the fields and territories near unto Swanescombe, and saw all the countrie set and placed about him, as it had been a stirring and moving wood, and that with a mean pace they approached and drew near unto him, with great discomfort of mind he wondred at that sight. And assoone as the captains of the Kentish men saw that duke William was inclosed in the midst of their army, they caused their trumpets to be sounded, their banners to be displayed, and threw down their boughs, and with their bows bent, their swords drawne, and their spears and other kind of weapons stretched forth, they shewed themselves ready to fight. Duke William and they that were with him stood (as no marvel it was) sorely astonished and amazed: so that he which thought he had already all England fast in his fist, did now despaire of his own life. Therefore on behalfe of the Kentishmen, were sent unto duke William, the archbishop Stigand, and Egelsin abbot of S. Augustin, who told him their message in this sort. My lord duke, behold the people of Kent come forth to meet you, and to receive you as their liege lord, requiring at your hands the things which pertain to peace, and that under this condition, that all the people of Kent enjoy for ever their ancient liberties, and may for evermore use the lawes and customes of their countrie: otherwise they are ready presently to bid battel to you, and them that be with you, and are minded rather to die here altogether than to depart from the laws and customes of their countrie, and to submit themselves to bondage whereof as yet they never had experience.

    The duke seeing himself to be driven to such an exigent and narrow pinch, consulted a while with them that came with him, prudentlie considering, that if he should take any repulse or displeasure at the hands of these people, which be the Key of England, all that he had done before should be disannulled and made of none effect, and all his hope and safety should stand in danger and jeopardy: not so willingly as wisely he granted the people of Kent their request. Now when the covenant was established, and pledges given on both sides, the Kentish men being joyful, conducted the Normans (who also were glad) unto Rochester, and yeelded up to the duke the earledome of Kent, and the noble castel of Dover. Thus the ancient liberties of England, and the lawes and customes of the countrie, which before the coming of duke William out of Normandie were equallie kept throughout all England, doo (through this industrie and earnest travell of the archbishop Stigand, and Egelsin abbott of S. Augustines) remain inviolablie observed untill this day within that countie of Kent.

CLUER

THE ANTIQUARIAN REPERTORY.

CLUER WALL, or CLEAR WELL,

THE Seat of Charles Windham, Esq; takes its name from the village wherein it stands, which is about two miles south of Newland.—It was built by the father of the present proprietor, about forty years ago. It is founded on a solid lime stone rock, and stands chiefly on arches.—Its walls nearly equal in thickness those of the ancient Gothic Castles.—It contains many convenient and spacious apartments, has a noble hall and library. Its offices are well contrived, and though the stile of Architecture gives it a sort of gloomy solemnity, it is on the whole a very desirable Mansion. The park and grounds about it are beautifully situated, they are also kept in very good order, and well laid out.

A Collection of Indulgences, as they were printed in the Hours after the Use of Sarum. *

TO all them that be in a state of grace, that daily say devoutly this prayer [folio 38.] before this blessed Lady of Pity, she will shew them her blessed visage, and warn them the day and the hour of death; and in their last end, the angels of God shall yield their souls to heaven; and he shall obtain 500 years, and so many *lents* of pardon, granted by five holy fathers, Popes of Rome.

Our holy father Sixtus the 4th, Pope, hath granted to all them that devoutly say this prayer [folio 42.] before the image of our Lady, the sum of 11000 years of pardon.

Our holy father the Pope, Sixtus, hath granted, at the instance of the high-most and excellent princess Elizabeth, late queen of England, and wife to our sovereign liege lord king Henry the 7th, (God have mercy on her

* 'The Prayers are in Latin, and the Folios refer to them as in Edition of *Horæ B. Mariæ Virg. ad Uf. Sarum,* printed at Paris 1526.

her sweet soul, and all Christian souls) that every day in the morning, after three tollings of the Ave-bell, say three times the whole salutation of our Lady, *Ave Maria Gratia*; that is to say, at six of the clock in the morning three *Ave Maries*; at twelve of the clock at noon three *Ave Maries*; and at six of the clock at even; for every time so doing, is granted of the spiritual treasure of holy church, 300 days of pardon, *toties quoties*.. And also our holy father, the archbishop of Canterbury and York, with other nine bishops of this realm, have granted, three times in the day, forty days of pardon to all them that be in the state of grace, able to receive pardon; the which began the 26th day of March, anno 1492. *Anno Henrici* 7. and the sum of the indulgence and pardon for every *Ave Maria*, 860 days, *toties quoties*. This prayer [folio 44.] shall be said at the tolling of the Ave-bell.

Our holy father the Pope Boniface, hath granted to all them that devoutly say this lamentable contemplation of our blessed Lady, standing under the cross weeping, and having compassion with her sweet son Jesus, seven years of pardon, and forty Lents. And also Pope John the 22d hath granted 300 days of pardon. [folio 47.]

These be the fifteen *Do's*, the which the holy virgin S. Bridget was wont to say daily before the holy rood in S. Paul's church at Rome; whoso says this [folio 50.] a whole year, shall deliver fifteen souls out of purgatory of his next kindred, and convert other fifteen sinners to good life; and other fifteen righteous men of his kind shall persevere in good life; and what ye desire of God ye shall have it, if it be to the salvation of your souls.

To all them that before this image of pity devoutly say five *Pater Nosters*, and five *Ave Maries*, and a *Credo*, piteously beholding those arms of Christ's passion, are granted 32755 years of pardon; and Sixtus the 4th Pope of Rome, hath made the fourth and the fifth prayer, and hath doubled his foresaid pardon. [folio 54.]

This epistle of our Saviour, sendeth our holy father Pope Leo, to the emperor *Carolo Magno*; of the which we find written, Who that beareth this blessing upon him, and saith it once a day, shall obtain forty years of pardon, and eighty Lentings, and he shall not perish with sudden death. [folio 56.]

This prayer [folio 57.] made by S. Austin, affirming who that says it daily kneeling, shall not die in sin; and after this life shall go to the everlasting joy and bliss.

Our holy father the Pope, John 22d, hath granted to all them that devoutly say this prayer [folio 58.] after the elevation of our Lord Jesus Christ; 3000 days of pardon for deadly sins.

Our holy father the Pope, Bonifacius the Sixth, hath granted to all them that devoutly say this prayer [*Ibid.*] following, between the elevation of our Lord, and the three *Agnus Dei*, 10000 years of pardon.

Our holy father Sixtus the 4th, hath granted to all them that be in the state of grace, saying this prayer [folio 61.] following immediately after the elevation of the body of our Lord, clean remission of all their sins perpetually enduring. And also John the Third, Pope of Rome, at the request of the queen of England, hath granted to all them that devoutly say this prayer before the image of our Lord crucified, as many days of pardon, as there were wounds in the body of our Lord in the time of his bitter passion, the which were 5465.

These five petitions and prayers made S. Gregory, and hath granted unto all them that devoutly say these five prayers [folio 65.] with five *Pater Nosters*, five *Ave Maries*, and a *Credo*, 500 years of pardon.

These three prayers [folio 66.] be written in the chapel of the Holy Cross in Rome, otherwise called, *Sacellum Sanctæ Crucis septem Romanorum*, who that devoutly say them, they shall obtain ten hundred thousand years of pardon for deadly sins, granted of our holy father John, 22d Pope of Rome.

Who that devoutly beholdeth these arms of our Lord Jesus Christ, shall obtain 6000 years of pardon of our holy father S. Peter, the first Pope of Rome, and of thirty other Popes of the church of Rome, successors after him. And our holy father, Pope John the 22d, hath granted unto all them very contrite and truly confessed, that say these devout prayers [folio 68.] following, in the commemoration of the bitter passion of our Lord Jesus Christ, 3000 years of pardon for deadly sins, and other 3000 for venial sins, and say first a *Pater Noster* and *Ave Maria*.

Our holy father, Pope Innocentius the Second, hath granted to all them that say this prayer [folio 71.] devoutly, in the worship of the wound that our Lord had in his blessed side, when he was dead, hanging in the cross, 4000 days of pardon.

This most devout prayer, [folio 72.] said the holy father S. Bernard, daily kneeling in the worship of the most holy name Jesus. And it is well to believe, that through the invocation of the most excellent name of Jesu, S. Bernard

THE ANTIQUARIAN REPERTORY.

Bernard obtained a fingular ward of perpetual confolation of our Lord Jefu Chrift. And thefe prayers written in a table that hanged at Rome in S. Peter's church, nigh to the high altar there, as our holy father the Pope evely is wont to fay the office of the mafs; and who that devoutly, with a contrite heart, daily fay this orifon, if he be that day in the ftate of eternal damnation, then his eternal pain fhall be changed him in temporal pain of purgatory; then if he hath deferved the pain of purgatory, it fhall be forgotten and forgiven through the infinite mercy of God.

EXPLANATION of the MISCELLANEOUS PLATE.

NO. I. A Fragment of the Monument of Strongbowe, Earl of Pembroke, preferved in Tintern Abbey, Monmouthfhire.

No. II. The Cradle in which Edward the IId. was nurfed at Monmouth Caftle.

No. III. The Buck Stone, near Newland, Gloucefterfhire. This Stone has fome appearance of a piece of Druidical Remains, though at the fame time it muft be confeffed its extraordinary pofition may have been caufed by fome great fhower of rain, or rather by the repeated efforts of many fhowers, which by wafhing away the earth from about the rock, left it then ftanding on its point.

It ftands on the weftern fide of a fteep woody hill, about two miles weft of Newland; a large piece of naked rock, of which there are many fticking out of the fides of the hill, ferves for a kind of pedeftal. The figure of which is an irregular fquare, whofe dimenfions are as follows: fouth-eaft fide twelve feet, north fide fourteen feet nine inches, weft fide twenty-one feet five inches. South fide 14 feet.

The Stone itfelf appears entirely feparated from the rock on which it ftands, and is of that fort of which mill-ftones are made, being gritt interfperfed with fmall pebbles. It is nearly in figure an irregular fquare pyramid, poifed on its point, which where it touches the pedeftal is not above two feet fquare, and is faid to be moveable. Its height is about ten feet, its

fouth-eaft

south-east side measures nineteen feet five inches, north side seventeen feet, south-west eight feet, and south-side twelve feet. A small distance east of it is a rock, scooped into a kind of bason, with a channel seemingly intended to let out the water after it is filled to a certain height. Whether this is the work of Art or Nature seems doubtful.

The Form of bidding Prayer before the Reformation.

[*Out of the Festival printed Anno* 1509.]

The Bedes on the Sunday.

YE shall kneel down on your knees, and lift up your hearts, making your prayers to Almighty God, for the good state and peace of all-holy church, that God maintain, save, and keep it. For our holy father the Pope, with all his true college of cardinals, that God for his mercy them maintain and keep in the right belief, and it hold and increase, and all misbelief and heresy be less and destroyed. Also ye shall pray for the holy land, and for the holy cross, that Jesus Christ died on for the redemption of mens souls, that it may come into the power of Christian men the more to be honoured for our prayers. Also ye shall pray for all archbishops and bishops; and especially for the archbishop of Canterbury our Metropolitane, and for the bishop of N. our Diocesan, that God of his mercy give to them grace so to govern and rule holy church, that it may be to the honour and worship of him, and salvation of our souls. Also ye shall pray for abbots, priors, monks, canons, friers, and for all men and women of religion, in what order, estate, or degree that they stand in, from the highest estate unto the lowest degree. Also ye shall pray for all them that have charge and cure of Christian mens souls, as curats and parsons, vicars, priests and clarks; and in especial for the parson and curat of this church, and for all the priests and ministers that serve therein, or have served therein; and for all them that have taken any order, that Almighty God give them grace of continuance well for to keep and observe it to the honour and health of their souls. Also ye shall pray for the unity and peace of all Christian realms,

and in especial for the good estate, peace and tranquillity, of this realm of England, for our liege lord the King, that God for his great mercy send him grace so to govern and rule this realm, that God be pleased and worshipped, and to the profit and salvation of this land. Also ye shall pray for our liege lady the Queen, my Lord Prince, and all the noble progeny of them; for all dukes, earls, barons, knights, and esquires, and other lords of the King's council, which have any rule and governance in this land, that God give them grace so to council, rule, and govern, that God be pleased, the land defended, and to the profit and salvation of all the realm. Also ye shall pray for the peace, both on land and on the water; that God grant love and charity among all Christian people. Also ye shall pray for all our parishes, where that they be, on land or on water, that God save them from all manner of perils; and for all the good men of this parish, for their wives, children, and men, that God them maintain, save and keep. Also ye shall pray for all true tithers, that God multiply their goods and encrease; for all true tillers that labour for our sustenance, that till the earth; and also for the grains and fruits that be sown, set, or done on the earth, or shall be done, that God send such weather that they may grow, encrease, and multiply, to the help and profit of all mankind. Also ye shall pray for all true shipmen and merchants, wheresoever that they be, on land or on water, that God keep them from all perils, and bring them home in safety, with their goods, ships, and merchandises, to the help, comfort, and profit of this realm. Also ye shall pray for them that find any light in this church, or give any behests, book, bell, chalice, or vestment, surplice, water-cloath, or towel, lands, rents, lamp or light, or any other adornments, whereby God's service is the better served, sustained and maintained in reading and singing, and for all them that thereto have counselled, that God reward and yield it them at their most need. Also ye shall pray for all true pilgrims and palmers, that have taken their way to Rome, to Jerusalem, to St. Katherines, or St. James, or to any other place, that God of his grace give them time and space, well for to go and to come, to the profit of their lives and souls. Also ye shall pray for all them that be sick or diseased of this parish, that God send to them health, the rather for our prayers; for all the women which be in our lady's bands, and with child, in this parish, or in any other, that God send to them fair deliverance, to their children right shape, name, and Christendom, and to the mothers, purification; and for all them that would be here, and may not, for sickness or travail, or any other lawful occupation, that
they

they may have part of all the good deeds that shall be done here in this place, or in any other. And ye shall pray for all them that be in good life, that good them hold long therein; and for them that be in debt, or deadly sin, that Jesus Christ bring them out thereof, the rather for our prayers. Also ye shall pray for him or her that this day gave the holy bread, and for him that first began, and longest holdeth on, that God reward it him at the day of doom; and for all them that do well, or say you good, that God yield it them at their need, and for them that otherwise would that Jesus Christ amend them: For all those, and for all Christian men and women, ye shall say a *Pater Noster*; *Ave Maria*; *Deus misereatur nostri*; *Gloria Patri*; *Kyrie Eleison*; *Christe Eleison*; *Kyrie Eleison*; *Pater Noster*; *Et ne nos*; *Sed libera*; *Versus*; *Ostende nobis*; *Sacerdotes*; *Domine salvum fac Regem*; *Salvum fac Populum*; *Domine fiat Pax*; *Domine exaudi*; *Dominus vobiscum*; *Oremus*; *Ecclesiæ tuæ quæsumus*; *Deus in cujus manu*; *Deus a quo sancta*, *&c*. Furthermore, ye shall pray for all Christian souls, for archbishops and bishops souls; and in especial, for all that have been bishops of this diocess; and for all curats, parsons and vicar's souls, and in especial, for them that have been curats of this church, and for the souls that have served in this church. Also ye shall pray for the souls of all Christian Kings and Queens, and in especial for the souls of them that have been Kings of this realm of England; and for all those souls that to this church have given book, bell, chalice, or vestment, or any other thing, by the which the service of God is better done, and holy church worshipped. Ye shall also pray for your father's soul, for your mother's soul; for your godfathers souls, for your godmothers souls; for your brethren and sisters souls, and for your kindreds souls, and for your friends souls, and for all the souls we be bound to pray for; and for all the souls that be in the pains of purgatory, there abiding the mercy of Almighty God; and in especial for them that have most need and least help, that God of his endless mercy lessen and minish their pains by the means of our prayers, and bring them to his everlasting bliss in heaven. And also of the soul *N*. or of them that upon such a day this week we shall have the anniversary; and for all Christian souls ye shall devoutly say a *Pater Noster* and *Ave Maria*; *Psalmus de profundis*, *&c*. with this Collect, *Oremus*; *Absolve quæsumus Domine animas famulorum tuorum Pontificum, Regum, Sacerdotum, Parentum, Parochianorum, Amicorum, Benefactorum Nostrorum, & omnium fidelium defunctorum, ab omni vinculo delictorum; ut in Resurrectionis Gloria inter sanitos & electos tuos refuscitati respirent, per Iesum Christum Dominum nostrum.* Amen.

Description of the Trial by Combate, as in Queen Elizabeth's *Reign.*
Anno 1571.

THE 18 of June, in Trinity Tearme, there was a combate appointed to have beene fought for a certaine Manour and demaine lands belonging thereunto, in the Isle of Harty, adioyning to the Isle of Sheppey in Kent: Simon Low and John Kyme were Plaintifes, and had brought a writ of right against T. Paramore, who offered to defend his right by Battell, whereunto the Plaintifes aforesaid, accepted to answere his Chalenge, offering likewise to defend their right to the same Manour and lands, and to prove by Battell that Paramore had no right, nor no good title to have the same.

Hereupon the said Tho. Paramore brought before the Judges of the common place at Westminster, one George Thorne, a bigge, broad, strong set fellow: and the Plaintifes, brought Hen. Nailor, Master of Defence, and seruant to the right honourable the Earle of Leicester, a proper slender man, and not so tall as the other: Thorne cast down a Gauntlet, which Nailor tooke up. Upon the Sonday before the battell should be tried, on the next morrow, the matter was stayed, and the parties agreed, that Paramore being in possession should have the land, and was bound in 500. pound to consider the plaintifs, as upon hearing the matter the Judges should award. The Q. Maiesty was the taker up of the matter, in this wise. It was thought good, that for Paramores assurance, the order should be kept touching the combat, and that the plaintiffs Low and Kyme should make default of appearance, but that yet such as were sureties of Nailor, their champions appearance, should bring him in, and likewise those that were sureties for Thorne, should bring in the same Thorne in discharge of their band, and that the court should sit in Tuthill fields, where was prepared one plot of ground one and twenty yardes square, double railed for the combate, without the West square, a stage being set up for the Judges, representing the Court of the common pleas. All the compasse without the lists, was set with scaffolds one above another, for people to stand and behold. There were behinde the square where the Judges sate, two Tents, the one for Nailor, the other for Thorne. Thorne was there in the morning timely. Nailor about seuen of the clocke came through London, apparelled in a doublet and galey-gascoigne breeches, all of crimsin sattin cut and raced,

a Hat

a Hat of black velvet, with a red feather and band, before him Drums and Fifes playing: the Gauntlet that was caſt downe by George Thorne, was borne before the ſaid Nailor upon a ſwords point, and his Baſton (a ſtaffe of an ell long, made Taper-wiſe, tipt with horne) with his ſhield of hard leather, was borne after him, by Askam a yeoman of the Queenes gard: he came into the Pallace of Weſtminſter, and ſtaying not long before the Hall doore, came backe into the kings ſtreete, and ſo along through the Sanctuary, and Tuthill ſtreete, into the field, where he ſtayed till paſt nine of the clocke, and then Sir Jerome Bowes brought him to his tent. Thorne being in the tent with Sir Henry Cheiney long before. About ten of the clocke, the Court of common pleas removed, and came to the place prepared: when the Lord chiefe Juſtice with two other his aſſociates were ſet, then Low was called ſolemnely to come in, or elſe hee to loſe his writ of right. Then after a certaine time the ſureties of Henry Nailor were called to bring in the ſaid Nailor, Champion for Simon Low, and ſhortly thereupon Sir Jerome Bowes leading Nailor by the hand, entreth with him the Liſts, bringing him downe that ſquare by which hee entred, being on the left hand of the Judges, and ſo about till hee came to the next ſquare juſt againſt the Judges, and there making curteſie, firſt with one leg, and then with the other, paſſed forth till he came to the middle of the place, and then made the like obeyſance, and ſo paſſing till they came to the barre, there hee made the like curteſie, and his ſhield was held up aloft ouer his head: Nailor put off his neather ſtockes, and ſo bare-feete and bare-legged, ſave his ſtauilonions to the ancles, and his doublet ſleeves tyed up above the elbow, and bare headed, came in as is aforeſaid. Then were the ſureties of George Thorne called to bring the ſame Thorne, and immediately Sir Henry Cheiney entring at the upper end on the right hand of the Judges, uſed the like order in comming about by his ſide, as Nailor had before on that other ſide, and ſo comming to the barre with like obeyſance, held up his ſhield, proclamation was made in forme as followeth: The Juſtices commaund in the Queenes Maieſties name, that no perſon of what eſtate, degree, or condition that he be, being preſent, to be ſo hardy to give any token or ſigne, by countenance, ſpeech, or language, either to the prouer or to the defender, whereby the one of them may take advantage of the other: and no perſon remoove, but ſtill keepe his place; and that every perſon and perſons keep their ſtaves and their weapons to themſelves: and ſuffer neither the ſaid proouer nor defender to take any of their weapons, or any other thing, that may ſtand either to the ſaid proover or defender any

auails,

auails, upon paine of forfeiture of lands, tenements, goods, chattels, and imprifonment of their bodies, and making fine and ranfome at the Queenes pleafure.

Then was the proover to be fworne in forme as followeth: This heare, you Juftices, that I have this day neither eate, drunke, nor have upon me either bone, ftone, nor glaffe, or any inchantment, forcerie, or witchcraft, where, through the power of the word of God might be inleafed or diminifhed, and the devils power encreafed: and that my appeale is true, fo helpe me GOD and his Saints, and by this booke.

After this folemne order was finifhed, the Lord chiefe Juftice rehearfing the manner of bringing the writ of right by Simon Low, of the anfwere made thereunto by Paramore, of the proceeding therein, and how Paramore had chalenged to defend his right to the land by battell, by his champion George Thorne, and of the accepting the triall that was by Lowe, with his champion Henry Nailor, and then for default in appearance in Lowe, he adiudged the land to Paramore, and difmiffed the champions, acquitting the fureties of their bands. He alfo willed Henry Nailor to render againe to George Thorne his gauntlet, whereunto the faid Nailor anfwered, that his Lordfhi, might command him any thing, but willingly he would not render the faid gauntlet to Thorne except he would win it: and further, he chalenged the faid Thorne to play with him halfe a fcore blowes, to fhew fome paftime to the Lord chiefe Juftice, and the other there affembled: but Thorne anfwered, that hee came to fight, and would not play. Then the Lord chiefe Juftice commending Nailor for his valiant courage, commanded them both quietly to depart the field, &c.

For the ANTIQUARIAN REPERTORY.

The Form of an old Deed of gifte.

I Kyng Athelftane gyves to Paullane, Odhiam and Rodhiam, als guid and als fayre, als ever yay mine wayre, and yarto witneffe Malde my wife.

The Form of the Surrender of the Warden and Freers of the Houſe of Saynt Francis in Coventrie of their Lands, &c. to King Henry 8th.*

FOR as moche as We the Warden and Freers of the Houſe of Saynt Francis in Coventrie, in the county of Warwick, commonly callyd the Grey Freers in Coventre, doo profoundly confider, that the perfection of Chriſtian livinge dothe not confiſt in dume ceremonies, werynge of a grey coot, difgeafing our felfe aftur ſtraunge faſſions, dokynge, noddynge, and beckynge, in gurdyng our felves wythe a gurdle fulle of knotts, and other like Papiſtical ceremonies, wherein we hade ben moofte principally practyfed and myſlyd in times paſte; but the very tru waye to plefe God, and to live a tru Chriſtian mon, witheout all ypocrifie, and fayned difeymulation, is fincerely declared unto us by our Maifter Chriſte, his Evangeliſtes, and Apoſteles: Being myndyd hereaftur to followe the fame, conformynge our felfe unto the will and plefure of our fupreme Hedde, under Gode on erthe, the Kynges Majeſtie, and not to followe henfeforth the fuperſtitius traditions of ony Forinfecall Potentate, or Peere; with mutual affent and confent, doo furrendre and yelde up into the hondes of the fame, all our feide houſe of Saynt Francis, in the city of Coventre, commonly callyd the Grey Freers in Coventre, wythe all the londes, tenements, gardens, medowes, waters, pondiards, fedynges, paſtures, commens, rents, reverfions, and alle other our intereſt, ryghts, or titles, appertaining unto the fame. Moofte humbly befeechinge his moſt noble Grace to difpofe of us, and of the fame, as befte fhall ftonde wythe his moofte gracious plefure: And further frely to graunte unto every one of us, his licenfe, under wretynge and feeale, to chaunge our habitts into fecular faſſion, and to receive fuche maner of livinges as other fecular prieſts commonly be preferred unto. And We alle faithfully fhall pray unto Almighty Gode long to preferve his moofte noble Grace wythe increfe of moche felicitie and honor. And, in witneſs of alle and fingular the premiſſes, We the feide Warden and Convent of the Grey Freers in Coventre, to thes prefences have putte our Covent Seealle,

the

---

* The fame Form *(mutatis mutandis)* was fubfcribed by the Carmelites and others on the fame occafion.

the fivithe day of October, in the thirtythe yeare of the raynge of our moofte foveraynge Lord King Henry the Eyghte: or *Anno* 1539.

John Stafford, Gardian.

Thomas Maller.	Thomas Aucock.
Thomas Sanderfon.	Mathew Walker.
John Abell.	Robart Walker.
John Woode.	Thomas Bangfit.
Roger Lilly.	William Gofnelle.

Defcription of two Men of extraordinary Stature.

[*From* Stow's *Chronicle.*]

IN the yeare 1581 were to be feene in London, two Dutchmen of ftrange ftatures, the one in height feuen foot and feuen inches, in breadth betwixt the fhoulders three quarters of a yard, and an inch, the compaffe of his breaft one yard and halfe, and two inches: and about the waft one yard, quarter, and one inch, the length of his arme to the hand, a full yard: a comely man of perfon but lame of his legges (for he had broken them with lifting of a barrel of beere.) The other was in height but three foote, had neuer a good foote, nor any knee at all, and yet could hee daunce a Galliard, hee had no arme, but a ftumpe to the elbow, or little more on the right fide, on the which finging, hee would daunce a cup, and after toffe it aboue three or foure times, and euery time receiue the fame on the faid ftumpe: he would fhoote an arrow neere to the marke, flourifh with a rapire, throw a bowle, beat with a hammer, hew with an axe, found a trumpet, and drink euery day ten quarts of the beft beere if he could get it. I my felfe on the 17 of July, faw the taller man fitting on a bench bareheaded, and the leffer ftanding on the fame bench, and hauing on his head a hat with a feather, was yet the lower. Alfo the taller man ftanding on his feet, the leffer (with his hat and feather on his head) went vpright between his legs, and touched him not.

THE

ANTIQUARIAN REPERTORY.

WINDSOR CASTLE.

THE public are here prefented with an Engraving from an original and very capital Drawing of Sir Peter Lely, the property of Paul Sandby, Efq. In the fore ground is reprefented King Charles the Second going to take the diverfion of fhooting, attended by his proper officers and fervants, with led horfes. The King is fufficiently pointed out by being the only perfon in the groupe who is covered.

In the back ground is a view of Windfor Caftle, which is fo well known, that a defcription of it would be unneceffary; a few words therefore refpecting its builders will fuffice.

A Caftle was built here by William the Conqueror foon after his acceffion to the Crown, and afterwards greatly enlarged by Henry the Firft, who furrounded it with a ftrong wall. King Edward the Third caufed the ancient buildings to be taken down, and rebuilt the whole, employing for Architect William of Wickham, afterwards Bifhop of Winchefter, who thereby fo far gained his Mafter's favour, that he caufed in memory thereof this fentence to be cut on one of the towers: THIS MADE WICKHAM; which fome bufy tell-tale reporting to the King, as if Wickham meant thereby to aſſume the honour of building that Tower at his own expence, that Monarch was at firſt angry, but was both appeaſed and pleaſed by the Biſhop's explanation, which was this: That building the Caſtle, HAD MADE HIM, by procuring him the Royal favour, to which he owed his preſent greatneſs.

Great additions were in ſucceeding times made to this Caſtle by ſeveral of our Kings, particularly Edward the Fourth, Henry the Seventh, Henry the Eighth, Elizabeth, and Charles the Second. By the laſt it was entirely repaired, having been much injured during the troubles in his father's and his time, and ſuffered to run to ruin. As he uſually kept his court here during the ſummer ſeaſon, he ſpared no expence in rendering it convenient and magnificent. Some farther additions and decorations were done in the two ſucceeding reigns of James the Second and William the Third. The whole of this edifice, which confiſts of two wards, ſtands on near twelve acres of ground.

Windſor Caſtle is confidered by foreigners as one of the moſt beautiful ſpots in England, and the air is remarkably clear and wholeſome. For theſe reaſons, as well as for its ſtrength, natural as well as artificial, it has been the reſidence of many of our Kings and Queens.

Here are preſerved many valuable Paintings of moſt of the Italian and Flemiſh maſters, as likewiſe the Portraits of moſt of the celebrated Beauties who adorned the court of Charles the Second.

Here likewiſe is a Portrait of the Countefs of Deſmond, who is ſaid to have lived to within a few days of 150 years. It is related of her that ſhe danced at Court with Richard the Third, whom ſhe declared to have been as goodly a man as ever her eyes beheld, not crooked, but very properly ſhaped.

St. George's Chapel, where the ceremony of inſtalling the Knights of the Garter is performed, ſtands within the precinéts of this Caſtle. It was built by King Edward the Third, and greatly enlarged by Edward the Fourth and Henry the Seventh. Sir Reginald Bray contributed towards compleating the roof and ornamenting the Chapel. The whole of this Building is eſteemed an elegant ſpecimen of Gothic Architecture.

To the Editor of the ANTIQUARIAN REPERTORY.

SIR, *Portsmouth, Sept.* 20th, 1775.

THE era of an invention so useful as the Mariner's Compass, would, one might imagine, be as positively ascertained as any fact in history, and its inventor handed down as an universal benefactor to mankind; but such is the absurdity in our distributions of honour, that whilst his name is forgotten who enabled us to direct our way over the face of the pathless ocean, with precision and safety, the most trifling actions of those scourges of humanity, an Alexander or Louis the Fourteenth, are recording with a minute exactness.

Diverse countries, it is true, claim the honour of this invention, as several cities of Greece contend for being the birth place of Homer. But had either this discovery been considered as important, when first made, or Homer regarded whilst living, no such dispute could have arisen.

The loadstone, and its power of attracting iron, was well known to the ancients, and is mentioned by Plato, who calls it the Herculean stone; also by Plutarch, Lucretius, and diverse others; but they seem to have been totally ignorant of its polarity or constant inclination towards the North. It has indeed been said by Albertus Magnus, that this property is mentioned by Aristotle, in a book treating of stones; but the authenticity of this part is doubted by most of the criticks. Two passages in Plautus are likewise pointed out, one in the Merchant, Act 5th, Scene 2d; the other in the Three Pieces of Money, Act 4th, Scene 3d; where the Compass is (as it is pretended) meant by the name of " Vorsariam;" but it is generally agreed the Vorsoria or Versoria, though now sometimes used for the Compass, and even Rudder, originally meant only a Cord fastened to the sail, serving to turn it to the windward side, and in that sense the words " Cape Vorsoriam" may be translated, Put about.

Some attribute this invention to the Chinese, who it is said, pretend the Emperor Chiningus, a celebrated Astrologer, had the knowledge of it 1120 years before Christ. The Chinese only divide their Compass into 24 points; at first they used to float it in a vessel of water by means of a piece of cork. Du Halde, in his History of that people, says, it is still a very clumsy machine; that they constantly burn perfumed pastils before it, and likewise offer up burnt facrifices to it, but are fo ignorant of its properties that their magazine for nails is near it in the binnacle, which fhews that if they were the difcoverers, it muft have been by fome accident, and not by any feries of experiments. Their Needle has a Fleur de Lis at one end, and a trident at the other.

Marcus Paulus, a Venetian, is faid to have brought it from China in the year 1260, when it was at firft ufed in Europe, in the manner of the Chinefe, fwimming in a veffel of water.

Flavio de Amalfi, or Flavio Gioia, a Neopolitan, is likewife named as the inventor of this ufeful machine; and it is pretended that the arms of the territory of Principato, in that kingdom, which is a Compafs, was affumed in memory of that invention.

The French too put in their claim to the honour of having the Compafs many years before either of thefe laft named periods. Fauchet, in fupport of it, quotes the following verfes written by Guyot de Provence, who lived in France about the year 1200, which, if genuine, inconteftibly prove the affertion. It is there called the Marinette.

> Icelle eftoile ne fe muet
> Un art font qui mentir ne puet
> Par vertu de la Marinette
> Une pierre laide & Noirette
> Ou li fer volontiers fe joint.

The fenfe of which is,—This ftar is immoveable; a rule is formed which cannot deceive, by virtue of the Compafs, an ugly black ftone, to which iron voluntarily joins itfelf.

From thefe verfes it appears, the Stone itfelf was firft ufed inftead of a Steel Needle touched with it.

The French endeavour farther to ftrengthen their title by obferving, that the Fleur de Lis, the arms of France, is ufed by every nation to diftinguifh the North point.

Doctor Wallis feebly puts in for the honour in behalf of the Englifh, for which he brings no better reafon, than that the word Compafs, the name whereby it is univerfally called in every language, is of Englifh origin, and in many parts of England fignifies a circle.

Ludi Vertomanus, who was in the Eaft-Indies about the year 1500, fays, he faw a Compafs like thofe commonly ufed. And Mr. Barlow, in his Navigator's gator's Supply, anno 1597, fays, that in a perfonal conference with two Eaft Indians they affirmed, that inftead of our Compafs they ufed a Magnetical Needle of fix inches and longer, upon a pin in a difh of white China earth filled with water, in the bottom whereof they had two crofs lines for the principal winds, the reft of their divifions being left to the fkill of their pilots.

I have here thrown together every thing material I have met with in the courfe of my reading refpecting this fubject. If any of your correfpondents can give a more fatisfactory account, I wifh they would favour the world with it through the channel of your Repertory.

I am, Sir, your's, &c.

A SAILOR.

The LYFE of SAYNT WENEFREDE;

From the Golden Legend, publifhed by Wynkyn de Worde, 1512.

AFTER that holy man Beuno hadde do make many chyrches, and had ordeyned the Servyce of God devoutly to be fayd in them, he came to a place of a worfhypfull man named Jenythe: the whiche was the fon of a noble fenatour called Elynde. And defyred y[t] he wolde gyve hym as moche grounde as he myght buylde a Chirche on in the honour of God. Than he granted hym his afkynge with good wyll, and than dyde do buylde thereon a fayr chyrche to the whiche this worfhypfull man, his wyfe, and his doughter Wenefryde reforted dayely for to here therin divine fervice. And than Wenefryde was fette to fcole to this holy man Beuno, and he taught her full dilygently and enformed her parfyghtly in the fayth of Jhefu Cryft. And this holy mayde Wenefryde gave credence to his wordes and was fo enflambed with his holy doctryne, y[t] fhe purpofed to forfake all worldly pleafaunces and to ferve almyghty God in mekenes & in chaftyte. And than it fortuned

fortuned upon a Sondaye fhe was difeafed and fhe abode at home & kept her faders hous whyle they were at Chyrche. To who there came a younge man for to defoule her, who was named Cradoche the fon of a kynge named Alane, whiche yonge man brened in the concupyfcence of her, by the entyfynge of the fende whiche had envye at this holy virgyn Wenefryde. And fhe demanded the caufe of his coming, and when fhe underftood his corrupte entente fhe excufed her and put him of all that fhe myght. And he alwaye abydynge in his foule purpofe wolde in no wife be anfwered. Than fhe confyderynge his foule defyre, & ferynge left he wolde oppreffe her, fayned her as fhe wolde have confented and fayd fhe wolde goo into the chambre for to araye herfelf for to pleafe hym the better. And when he had agreed to her, fhe clofed fafte the chamber dore, & fledde pryvely by another dore towarde the chyrche. And whan this yonge man had efpyed her he folowed her w^t his fwerde drawen lyke a wood man : & whan he had overtaken her, he fayd to her thefe wordes. Sometyme I loved the and defyred the to have the unto my wyfe. But one thynge tell now to me fhortly, eyther confente to me to accomplyfhe my pleafure, or elfe I fhall flee the w^t this fwerde. Than this bleffed Virgin Wenefryde thought fermerly y^t fhe wolde not forfake ye fone of ye everlaftynge kynge, for to pleafe the fone of a temporall kynge, and fayd to him in this maner. I will in no wyfe confente to thy foule and corrupte defyre, for I am joyned to my fpoufe Jhefu Cryfte, whiche preferveth & keepeth my virgynyte. And truft thou verely that I wyll not forfake him for all thy menaces and thretynges. And whan fhe had fayd thus this curfed tyraunt full of malyce fmote of her heed. And in the fame place where as the heed fell to the grounde, there fprange up a fayre well gyvynge out haboundantly fayre clere water, where our Lord God yet dayly fheweth many myracles. And many feke people havynge dyverfe dyfeafes have there ben cured and heled wyth the merytes of this bleffed virgyne faynt Wenefryde, and in the faid well appeareth yet ftones befprynƈte and fpercled as it were w^t blood, which cannot be had away by no meane. And the moffe y^t groweth on the ftones is of a mervyllous fwete odour & that endureth unto this daye. And when the fader and moder knew of their doughter they made grete lamentacyon for her deth, bycaufe they had no mo chyldern, but her onely. And when this holy man Beuno underftode the dethe of Wenefryde and faw the hevynes of her fader and moder, he comforted them goodly and brought them to the place where as fhe laye deed. And there he made a fermon to the people declarynge her virgynyte.

And

And howe fhe hadde avowed to be a relygyous woman. And after toke up the heed in his hondes, and fette it into the place where it was cutte of, and defyred to all tha people that there were prefente to knele downe, and pray devoutly unto Almighty God, that it might pleafe hym to reyfe her agayne unto lyfe, and not only for the comfort of fader and moder, but for to accomplyfhe the vowe of relygyon. And when they arofe from prayer, thys holy vyrgyne arofe with them alfoo made by myracle alive agayn by the power of Almighty God: wherefore all the people gave lawde and prafynge to hys holy name for this grete myracle. And ever as long as fhe lived after there appeyered about her necke a rednes round about lyke to a reed threde of fylke in fygne and token of her martyrdome. And whan this yonge man that had thus flayne her, hadde wyped his fwerde on the grafs, and ftode ftylle there befiyde, and had noo power to remove away, ne to repente hym of that curfed deed. And than this holy man Beuno reproved him, not only of the homycyde, but alfo becaufe he reverenced not the Sondaye, and dredde not the grete power of God there fhewed upon this holy vyrgyne and fayd to him, Why haft thou not contricyon for thy myfdede, but fyth thou repenteth not, I befeche Almighty God to reward the after thy defervynge. And than he fell downe deed to the grounde, and his body was all blacke, and fodeynly borne awaye with fendes. Than after this holy made Wenefryde was veyled and confecrate into relygyon by the hondes of this holy man Beuno, and he commanded her the habyte in the fame churche, that he had do make there, by the fpace of feven yere. And there to affemble to her vyrgynes of honeft and holy converfacyon whom he fholde enforme in the lawes of God. And after the feven yere to go to fome holy place of relygyon, and there to abyde the refidue of her lyfe. And whan this holy man fholde departe from her and go into Irlonde, fhe folowed hym tyll fhe came to the forefayd well, where they ftode talkyng alonge whyle of hevenly thynges and whane they fholde departe this holy man fayd. It is the wyll of our Lorde that they fend to me every yere, fome token whiche thou fhalt put into the ftreme of the welle and fro thens it fhall by the ftreme be brought into the fee, and fo by the purveyance of God it fhall be brought over the fee the fpace of fyfty myle to the place where I fhall dwelle, and after they were departed, fhe with her vyrgynes made a chefyble of fylke werke, and the nexte yere folowynge, fhe wrapped it in a whyte mantell, and layd it upon the ftreme of the fayd welle, and frō thens it was brought unto this holy man Beuno thrugh the waves of the fee, by the purveaūce of our Lorde Jhefu Cryfte.

After

After this the bleſſed virgine Wenefryde encreaſed fro daye to daye in grete vertue and goodnes, and ſpecyally in holy contemplacyons with her ſyſters moeuynge them in grete devocion and love of Almyghty God. And whan ſhe had abyden there vii. yere ſhe departed thence and went to the monaſterye, called Wythcrachus, in whiche were bothe men and women of vertuous and holy converſation, and whan ſhe had confeſſed, and tolde her lyfe unto the holy Abbot Eleryus, he receyved her honourably and brought her to his moder Theodnye a bleſſed woman, whiche had the rule and charge of all the ſyſters of that place, and whan Theodonye was deceaſed out of this worlde, this holy Abbot Eleryus delyvered to this holy virgine Wenefryde the charge of the ſiſters, but ſhe refuſed it, as longe as ſhe might. But by conſtreynte ſhe toke the charge and lyved afterwarde a vertuous life and more ſtrayte and harder than ſhe dyd before, in gyvynge good example to all ſyſters, and whan ſhe had contynued there in the ſervyce of God eyght yere ſhe yelded up her ſpiryte to her Maker. To whom let us praye to be a ſpeciall interceſſour for us. Amen.

✤✤✤✤✤✤✤✤✤✤✤✤✤✤✤✤✤✤✤✤✤✤✤✤✤✤✤✤✤✤✤✤✤✤

The Charter of King William the Firſt, granted unto the Citie of London, at the Special Sute of William then Biſhop of the ſame Citie, Anno 1067.

(From *Hollingſhed's Chronicle.*)

WILLIEM Kyng grets Williem Biſccop and Godfred Porterefan, & ealle ya Burghwarn binnen Lōdon Frenciſce, & Engliſce frendlice, & Ic kiden coy, yeet Ic wille yeet git ben ealra weera lagayweord, ye get weeran on Eadwerds daege kings, and Ic will yeet aelc child by his fader yrfnume, aefter his faders daege. And Ic nelle ge wolian, yeet aenigman eoy aenis wrang beode. God eoy heald.

———

Wilhelmus rex ſalutat Wilhelmum Epiſcopum, & Goffridũ Portegreſiũ & omnẽ Burghware infra London Franſ. & Angl. amicabiliter. Et vobis notũ facio, quòd ego volo, quòd vos ſitis omni lege illa digni qua fuiſtis Edwardi diebus regis. Et volo quòd omnis puer ſit patris ſui hæres poſt diem patris ſui. Et ego nolo pati quod aliquis homo aliquam inſuriam vobis inferat. Deus vos ſaluet.

TINTERN

TINTERN ABBEY, MONMOUTHSHIRE,

WHETHER confidered as a pleafing object, or a venerable piece of Antiquity, is well deferving the obfervation of the curious. Indeed fuch is its reputation, as always to make a vifit to it part of the excurfion from Bath, to Chepftow, Pearcefield, and its environs.

It ftands on the banks of the Wye, about five miles from Chepftow; nothing can exceed the beauty of its fituation, which feems by nature formed for monaftic retirement. To the South, Eaft, and Weft, it is environed by woody hills, which rifing in different directions, hang over it, and feem to form a barrier excluding the reft of the world. On the North it is bounded by the Wye, and fenced from the cold blafts by a high mountain, which as if for that purpofe towers up almoft perpendicularly on the Gloucefterfhire fide of the River.

As a work of Art it exhibits a moft elegant fpecimen of Gothic Architecture, and its carvings fhew that at the time of its erection the Arts were not at that low ebb, it is ufually imagined. His Grace the Duke of Beaufort, to whom it belongs, merits the public thanks for the care with which he caufes it to be kept, as well as feveral other Monuments of Antiquity, which are his property, and which may be confidered as national ornaments. This Abbey is moreover ftill applied to a fort of religious ufe, the keeping of it being intrufted to a poor widow, who by fhewing it, gains a comfortable livelihood.

Tintern Abbey was founded anno 1131, by Walter de Clare, brother to Gilbert Strongbowe, Earl of Pembroke. Several of the Strongbowe's are faid to be buried here. A broken figure of a Knight in a coat of mail, is fhewn as part of one of their Monuments. At the diffolution the eftates of this Abbey were valued at 192l. 1s. 4d. as Dugdale has it. Speed fays, 256l. 11s. 6d. The fite was granted the 28th of Henry the Eighth to Henry Earl of Worcefter. About that time here was only thirteen Monks.

The Plate here annexed fhews the infide of the building, as viewed from a ftation a little to the northward of the entrance. In a future Number fhall be given a Drawing fhewing the fine Weft Window.

To the EDITOR of the ANTIQUARIAN REPERTORY.

SIR,

THE following extract is taken from the Northumberland-Houfe Book, being one of the Explanatory Notes written by the ingenious Doctor Percy. As this book was printed at the expence of his Grace the Duke of Northumberland, and only a few copies taken off to give away, it is extremely rare, and therefore worthy a place in your Repertory.

The ufe of forks at table, did not prevail in England till the reign of James the Firft, as we learn from a remarkable paffage in Coryat, the infertion of which may be pardoned among the petty collections here raked together. The reader will laugh at the folemn manner in which this important difcovery or innovation is related.

" HERE I will mention a thing that might have been fpoken of before
" in difcourfe of the firft Italian towne. I obferved a cuftom in all thofe
" Italian Cities and Townes through the which I paffed, that is not ufed in
" any other country that I faw in my Travels, neither do I thinke that
" any other nation of Chriftendome doth ufe it, but only Italy. The
" Italian and alfo moft ftrangers that are commonant in Italy, doe always at
" their meals ufe a Little Forke when they eat their meate; for while with
" their Knife which they hold in one hand, they cut the meate out of the
" difh, they faften the Fork which they hold in the other Hand, upon the
" fame difh, fo that whatfoever he be that fitting in the company of any
" others at Meale fhould unadvifedly touch the difh of meat with his fingers
" from which all the table doe cut, he will give occafion of offence unto the
" Company as having tranfgreffed the lawes of good manners, in fo much
" that for his Error he fhall be at leaft brow-beaten, if not reprehended in
" wordes. This form of feeding I underftand is generally ufed in all places
" of Italy, their Forks being for the moft part made of yronn, fteele, and
" fome of filver, but thofe are ufed only by Gentlemen. The Reafon of
" this their Curiofity is, becaufe the Italian cannot by any means indure to
" have his difh touched with fingers, feeing all mens fingers are not alike
" cleane. Hereupon I myfelf thought good to imitate the Italian Fafhion
" by this forked cutting of meate, not only while I was in Italy, but alfo
" in

" in Germany, and often times in England since I came home: being once
" quipped for that frequently using my Forke, by a certain learned Gen-
" tleman a familiar friend of mine, Mr. Lawrence Whitaker; who in his
" merry humour doubted not to call me at table *Furcifer*, only for using a
" Forke at feeding, but for no other cause."

Coryat's Crudities, p. 90, 91. 40 London 1611.

Even when Heylin published his Cosmography (1652) Forks were still a novelty, see his 3d book, where having spoke of the Ivory Sticks used by the Chinese, he adds, " The use of Silver Forks with us by some of our
" spruce Gallants taken up *of late* came from hence into Italy, and from
" thence into England."

From the Popish Courant, *a periodical Work first published Anno* 1678, *and continued to* 1681.

> *Vive, vale bone BOS, tibi & altera & altera supplex*
> *Si qua cupit, nec quit; Matris cognoscere Nomen*
> *Frondentes Ramos & amœnas porriget Herbas.*

IN the foregoing historical part, having had occasion to relate a desperate squabble between the *Monks* and *Towns-folk* of St. Edmund's Bury, it puts me in mind of a pleasant custom formerly promoted and practised by the religious Fathers of that Monastery, and having had the fortune to obtain copies of the authentic evidences thereof, lest the memory of so notable a Pope's ceremony should be swallowed by oblivion, we think fit to recommend the same to the public and posterity.

The Monks of Bury had heretofore, to bring grist to their mill, spread an opinion, that if any married woman were barren, and had no children, if she would but come with a white bull to the bier of St. Edmund, (whence that town derives its name) and make her offerings and vows, she should presently
after

after conceive with child; the manner whereof was thus: A white bull was provided, curiously adorned with garlands of flowers between his horns, ribbons, &c. who being led by one of the Monks, the lady or woman followed him, often ſtroaking him, and the reſt of the religious crew attending her, as in a proceſſion. They commonly ſet forth from the ſouth gate, and ſo (to be more publicly ſeen) paſſed through Church-ſtreet, Guildhall-ſtreet, and Cook-row, down to the great gate of the Abbey, whence the woman proceeded to St. Edmund's ſhrine, ſaid her prayers, made her offerings, and returned with full aſſurance of a ſpeedy conception.

This ridiculous wheadle of the crafty Abbey-lubbers had got ſuch credit, that not only diverſe eminent women of England frequented it, but even from beyond the ſeas ladies cauſed it to be done; and that a white bull for this ſacred uſe might not be wanting, the tenants of the Abbey lands were obliged to find one always in readineſs, as appears by ſeveral of their leaſes, as follow.

Hæc Indentura teſtatur, &c. In Engliſh thus: This Indenture witneſſes, that Mr. John Swaffham, Sacriſt of the Monaſtery of St. Edmund of Bury, with the aſſent and will of the Prior; and convent of that place, has granted and to farm let to Simons Lolepeke of Bury aforeſaid yeoman, the mannor called Habyrdon in Bury aforeſaid, &c. to hold, &c. for the term of ſeven years, &c. Yielding therefore yearly, &c. And the ſaid Simon, his executors and aſſigns, ſhall find or cauſe to be found one white bull every year of his ſaid term, as oft as it ſhall happen that any gentlewoman or any other woman out of devotion or vow by them made, ſhall come to the bier of the glorious King and Martyr St. Edmund, to make their oblations of the white bull. In witneſs whereof, &c. Dated 4 June in the 2 year of K. Henry 7th.

2^d. This Indenture made the 12th of Sepr. in the 11th year of King Henry the 8th. between John Eye, Sacriſt of the Monaſtery of St. Edmund of Bury, and Richard Skinner, of Bury aforeſaid, huſbandman, witneſſes that the ſaid John by the aſſent, &c. hath granted and to farm letten to the ſaid Richard the mannor of Habyrdon, &c. for the term of 10 years, &c. and the ſaid Richard ſhall find one white bull as often as it happen, &c. as in the former deed.

3^d. This Indenture witneſſes, that John, by divine permiſſion, Abbot of the Monaſtery of St. Edmund of Bury, by the aſſent, &c. hath letten to Robert

THE ANTIQUARIAN REPERTORY.

Robert Right, glazier, and John Anable, pewterer, of Bury aforefaid, our mannor of Habyrdon, with the appurtenances for 20 years, yielding, &c. And that the faid Robert and John fhall find yearly one white bull as often (as above.) In witnefs, &c. Dated 28 April in the 25 year of Henry the 8th Anno Dom. 1533.

4. To all faithful Chriftian people that fhall infpect thefe prefents, John Swaffham, Sacrift of the Monaftery of St. Edmund of Bury, an exempt jurifdiction appertaining immediately to the apoftolick fee, and Arch Deacon of the fame place, Health, on the Author of Health: We made known to you all by thefe prefents that Father Peter Minnebode Licentiate in Holy Theology and Father Peter Brune, together with Father Cornelius a lay brother of the order of Carmelites, of the city of Gaunt, on the fecond day of the month of June in the year of our Lord 1474, did in the prefence of many credible perfons offer at the bier of the Glorious King, Virgin and Martyr St. Edmund at Bury aforefaid, one White Bull, according to the antient cuftom, to the honour of God, and the faid Glorious Martyr, in relief of the defire of a certain *Noble Lady*. Sealed with the feal of our office; Dated the day place and year abovefaid.

The firft and laft of thefe deeds were within thefe fifty years extant, and the originals to be feen in the hands of one Mr. James Copin, a Publick Notary and Proctor in the Ecclefiaftical Court; the fecond in the hands of Mr. John Maloffe, an Attorney of the Court of Common Pleas; the third in the cuftody of Mr. John Hill, an Attorney of the King's Bench, all three perfons of repute and unqueftionable credit, and at the fame time of St. Edmund's Bury; and no doubt thofe originals are yet remaining in the poffeffion of fome of the heirs or fuccedents of thofe refpective gentlemen. However we are affured a tranfcript of the third of them under feal remains on record in the Augmentation Office.

We publifh this to fhew how grofsly the Monks heretofore bubbled our anceftors, and withal cannot but remark that this conceit feems ftolen (like many other Popifh ceremonies) from the Heathen; who had feftivals called *Lupercalia*, at which time goats being killed, of their fkins were made whips, wherewith boys (almoft naked) ran through the ftreets, and therewith fcourged the women they met, who offered themfelves to thofe lafhes, as fancying the fame would promote conception. See Ovid's Faftorum in February, and Plutarch, both in Romulus and Caius Cæfar.

The ANTIQUARIAN REPERTORY.

The fcope of this cheat is apparent, for as at firft fome offerings muft be made, fo if any woman (by ftrength of imagination, and the affiftance of a kind friend, not excluding a lufty young Monk upon occafion) happened fhortly after to prove with child, the fuperftitious reverence to St. Edmund was not only advanced, but new prefents in grateful acknowledgement muft be brought to his fhrine.

MISCELLANEOUS PLATE.

THIS Plate fhews fome of the Roman Utenfils found at Lidney Park in Gloucefterfhire, the feat of Thomas Bathurft, Efq; a fpot as remarkable for its beauty as refpectable for the many Roman Antiquities with which it abounds, and which would afford an ample harveft to the refearches of an able Antiquarian. The above Utenfils, with many curious coins found there, are in the poffeffion of Mrs. Bathurft.

No. 1. and 2. Roman Soldiers, chafed on pieces of thin iron plate; by fome pitchy matter at the back they feem to have been ftuck upon fome other furface; they are nearly of the fize here reprefented.

No. 3. An ornament of the Necklace or Bracelet kind; feveral of them feem intended to be ftrung together, the holes feen at the top running quite through them. The front and back fide are here fhewn; it is made of a dark brownifh wood, and is of the fame fize as here delineated.

No. 4. A Brafs Ornament, probably a kind of broch.

No. 5. A Fibula of Brafs.

No. 6. An Animal in Brafs, fuppofed to be a Wolf.

No. 7. A fmall Lamp. N. B. No. 4. 5. 6. and 7. are all of the fame fize as here depicted, as are all the following, No. 8. excepted.

No. 8. A Roman Veffel of baked earth, ufed in facrifices. Its diameter is three inches, and depth two.

No. 9. An Iron Spoon.

No. 10. An Ivory Pin.

No. 11. A Piece of ornamented Brafs, fuppofed to have been a handle to fome utenfil.

To

To the Editor of the Antiquarian Repertory.

SIR,

AMONG the many superstitious opinions of our forefathers, none have been more deservedly ridiculed, than their great credulity in the articles of witchcraft and walking spirits. The belief of which was not only inculcated by the writings of many divines and graduated members of both universities, but even defended by King James himself. Many of their histories in support of these notions are truly laughable.

Foremost in this rank, stands the following story, told in Doctor Henry More's collection of philosophical writings, which is a striking instance how far credulity may be extended. Dr. More took it from the relation of Mortinus Weinrichius, a Silesian physician.

Johannes Cuntius, a citizen of Pertsch in Silesia, near sixty years of age, and one of the aldermen of the town, very fair in his carriage, and unblameable, to men's thinking, in the whole course of his life, having been sent for to the mayor's house, (as being a very understanding man, and dexterous at the dispatch of businesses) to end some controversies concerning certain wagoners, and a merchant of Pannonia, having made an end of those affairs, is invited by the mayor to supper: he gets leave first to go home to order some businesses, leaving this sentence behind him, *It's good to be merry while we may, for mischiefs grow up fast enough daily.*

This Cuntius kept five lusty geldings in his stable, one whereof he commanded to be brought out, and his shoe being loose, had him tied to the next post: his master, with a servant, busied themselves to take up his leg to look on his hoof; the horse being mad and mettlesome, struck them both down; but Cuntius received the greatest share of the blow: one that stood next by helped them both up again. Cuntius no sooner was up and come to himself, but cryed out, *Woe is me, how do I burn and am all on a fire!* which he often repeated. But the parts he complained of most, the women being put out of the room, when they were searched, no appearance of any stroke or hurt was found upon them. To be short, he fell downright sick, and grievously afflicted in mind, loudly complaining, that his sins were such that they were utterly unpardonable, and that the least part of them were bigger than all the sins of the world besides; but would have no divine come to him, nor did particularly

ticularly confefs them to any. Several rumours, indeed there were that once he fold one of his fons, but when and to whom it was uncertain, and that he had made a contract with the devil, and the like. But it was obferved, and known for certain, that he had grown beyond all expectation rich, and that four days before this mifchance, he being witnefs to a child, faid, that that was the laft he fhould be ever witnefs to.

The night he died, his eldeft fon watched with him; he gave up the ghoft about the third hour of the night, at what time a black cat opening the cafement with her nails, (for it was fhut) ran to his bed, and did fo violently fcratch his face and the bolfter, as if fhe endeavoured, by force, to remove him out of the place where he lay. But the cat afterwards fuddenly was gone; and fhe was no fooner gone, but he breathed his laft. A fair tale was made to the paftor of the parifh, and the magiftracy of the town allowed it; he was buried on the right fide of the altar, his friends paying well for it. No fooner Cuntius was dead, but a great tempeft arofe, which raged moft at his very funeral, there being fuch impetuous ftorms of wind, with fnow, that it made men's bodies quake, and their teeth chatter in their heads; but as foon as he was interred, of a fudden all was calm.

He had not been dead a day or two, but feveral rumours were fpread in the town, of a Spiritus Incubus or Ephialtes, in the fhape of Cuntius, that would have forced a woman. This hapened before he was buried; after his burial the fame fpectre awakened one that was fleeping in his dining-room, faying, " I can fcarce withhold myfelf from beating thee to death." The voice was the voice of Cuntius. The watchmen of the town, alfo affirmed, that they heard, every night, great ftirs in Cuntius's houfe; the falling and throwing of things about; and that they did fee the gates ftand wide open betimes in the morning, though they were never fo diligently fhut o're night; that his horfes were very unquiet in the ftable, as if they kicked and bit one another; befides unufual barkings and howlings of dogs, all over the town: but thefe were but preludious fufpicions to further evidence, which I will run over as briefly as I may.

A maid fervant of one of the citizens of Pertfch (while thefe tragedies and ftirs were fo frequent in the town) heard, together with fome others lying in their beds, the noife and tramplings of one riding about the houfe, who at laft ran againft the walls with that violence, that the whole houfe fhaked again, as if it would fall, and the windows were all filled with flafhings of light. The mafter of the houfe being informed of it, went out of doors in the morning to

fee

see what the matter was, and he beheld, in the snow, the impressions of strange feet, such as were like neither horses, nor cows, nor hogs, nor any creature that he knew.

Another time, about eleven of the clock in the night, Cuntius appears to one of his friends, that was a witness to a child of his, he speaks unto him and bids him be of good courage, for he came only to communicate to him a matter of great importance. *I have left behind me,* said he, *my youngest son* James, to whom you are god-father. *Now there is at my eldest son* Steven's, *a citizen of* Iegerdorf, *a certain chest wherein I have put four hundred florins :* This *I tell you, that your god-son may not be defrauded of any of them, and it is your duty to look after it, which, if you neglect, woe be to you.* Having said *this,* the spectre departed, and went up into the upper rooms of the house, where he walked so stoutly, that all rattled again, and the roof swagged with his heavy stampings. This Cuntius, his friend, told to the parson of the parish, a day or two after for a certain truth.

But there are also other several notorious passages of this Cuntius. As his often speaking to the maid that lay with her mistress, his widow, to give him place, for it was his right; and if she would not give it him, he would writhe her neck behind her.

His galloping up and down, like a wanton horse, in the court of his house. His being divers times seen to ride, not only in the streets, but along the valleys of the field, and on the mountains, with so strong a trot, that he made the very ground flash with fire under him.

His bruising of the body of a child of a certain smith's, and making his very bones so soft, that you might wrap the corps on heaps like a glove.

His miserably tugging all night with a Jew that had taken up his inne in the towne, and tossing him up and down in the lodging where he lay.

His dreadful accosting of a wagoner, an old acquaintance of his, while he was busie in the stable, vomiting out fire against him to terrifie him, and biting of him so cruelly by the foot, that he made him lame. What follows, as I above intimated, concerns the relator himself, who was the parson of the parish, whom this fury so squeezed and pressed when he was asleep, that wakening he found himself utterly spent, and his strength quite gone, but could not imagine the reason. But while he lay musing with himself what the matter might be, this spectre returns again to him, and holding him all over so fast, that he could not wag a finger, rowled him in his bed backwards and forwards a good many times together. The same hapned also to his wife

wife another time, whom Cuntius coming through the cafement in the fhape of a little dwarf, and running to her bedfide, fo wrang and pulled as if he would have torn her throat out had not her daughters come in to help her.

He preffed the lips together of one of this theologer's fons fo, that they could fcarce get them afunder.

His houfe was fo generally difturbed with this unruly ghoft, that the fervants were fain to keep together anights in one room, lying upon ftraw, and watching the approaches of this troublefome fiend. But a maid of the houfe, being more couragious than the reft, would needs, one night, goe to bed, and forfake her company; whereupon Cuntius finding her alone, prefently affaults her, pulls away the bedding, and would have carried her away with him; but fhe hardly efcaping, fled to the reft of the family, where fhe efpied him ftanding by the candle, and ftraightway after vanifhing.

Another time, he came into her mafter's chamber, making a noife like a hog that eat grains, fmacking and grunting very fonoroufly. They could not chafe him away by fpeaking to him, but ever as they lighted a candle he would vanifh.

One other time, about evening, when this theologer was fitting with his wife and children about him, exercifing himfelf in mufick, according to his ufual manner, a moft grievous ftink arofe fuddenly, which, by degrees, fpread itfelf to every corner of the room, hereupon he commends himfelf and his family to God by prayer. The fmell, neverthelefs, increafed, and became,. above all meafure, peftilently noifome, infomuch that he was forced to go up to: his chamber. He and his wife had not been in bed a quarter of an hour, but they find the fame ftink in the bed-chamber; of which, while they are complaining one to another, out fteps the fpectre from the wall, and, creeping to his bed-fide, breathes upon him an exceeding cold breath, of fo intolerable ftinking and malignant a fent, as is beyond all imagination and expreffion. Hereupon the *theologer*, good foul, grew very ill, and was fain to keep his bed, his face, belly and guts fwelling, as if he had been poifoned; whence he was alfo troubled with a difficulty of breathing, and with a putrid inflamation of his eyes, fo that he could not well ufe them of a long time after.

But taking leave of the fick divine, if we fhould goe back and recount what we have omitted, it would exceed the number of what we have already recounted. As for example, the trembling and fweating of Cuntius's gelding, from which he was not free night nor day. The burning blue of the candles at the approach of Cuntius's ghoft. His drinking up the milk in the milk bowls,

bowls, his flinging dung into them, or turning the milk into blood: his pulling up posts deep set in the ground, and so heavy that two lusty porters could not deal with them. His difcourfing with feveral men he met concerning the affairs of the wagoners: His ftrangling of old men: His holding faft the cradles of children, or taking them out of them: His frequent endeavouring to force women: His defiling the water in the font, and fouling the cloth on the altar on that fide that did hang towards his grave, with dirty bloody fpots: His catching up dogs in the ftreets, and knocking out their brains againft the ground: His fucking dry the cows, and tying their tails like the tail of a horfe: His devouring of poultry, and his flinging of goats bound into the racks: His tying of an horfe to an empty oat-tub in the ftable to clatter up and down with it, and the hind foot of an other to his own headftall: His looking out of the window of a low tower, and then fuddenly changing himfelf into the form of a long ftaff: His chiding of a matron for fuffering her fervant to wafh difhes on a Thurfday, at what time he laid his hands upon her, and fhe faid it felt more cold than ice: His pelting one of the women that wafhed his corps, fo forcibly, that the prints of the clods he flung were to be feen upon the wall: His attempting to ravifh another, who excufing herfelf and faying, *My Cantius, thou feeft how old, wrinckled and deformed I am, and how unfit for thofe kinds of fports*, he fuddenly fet up a loud laughter and vanifhed.

But we muft not infift upon thefe things, only we will add one paffage more that is not a little remarkable. His grave-ftone was turned of one fide, fhelving, and there were feveral holes in the earth, about the bignefs of moufe-holes, that went down to his very coffin, which however they were filled up with earth, and all made plain over night, yet they would be fure to be laid open the next morning.

It would be a tedious bufinefs to recite all thefe things at large, and profecute the ftory in all its particular circumftances. To conclude, therefore, their calamity was fuch, from the frequent occafions of this reftlefs fury, that there was none but either pitied them or defpifed them; none would lodge in their town, trading was decayed, and the citizens impoverifhed by the continual ftirs and tumults of this unquiet ghoft.

And though the *Atheift* may perhaps laugh at them as men undone by their own melancholy and vain imaginations, or by the waggery of fome ill neighbours: yet if he ferioufly confider what has been already related,

there,

there are many paſſages that are by no means to be reſolved into any ſuch principles: but what I ſhall now declare, will make it altogether unlikely that any of them are.

To be ſhort therefore, finding no reſt, nor being able to excogitate any better remedy, they dig up Cuntius his body, with ſeveral others buried both before and after him; but thoſe both after and before were ſo putrefied and rotten, their ſculls broken, and the ſutures of them gaping, that they were not to be known by their ſhape at all, having become in a manner but a rude maſs of earth and dirt, but it was quite otherwiſe in Cuntius: his ſkin was tender and florid, his joints not at all ſtiff, but limber and moveable, and a ſtaff being put into his hand, he graſped it with his fingers very faſt; his eyes alſo of themſelves would be at one time open, and another time ſhut; they opened a vein in his leg, and the blood ſprang out as freſh as in the living; his noſe was entire and full, not ſharp, as in thoſe that are ghaſtly ſick or quite dead: and yet Cuntius his body had lain in the grave from February 8th, to July 20th, which is almoſt half a year.

It was eaſily diſcernible where the fault lay; however nothing was done raſhly, but judges being conſtituted, ſentence was pronounced upon Cuntius his carcaſe, which (being animated thereto from ſucceſs in the like caſe ſome few years before in this very province of Sileſia, I ſuppoſe he means at Breſlaw, where the ſhoe-maker's body was burnt) they adjudged to the fire.

Wherefore there were maſons provided to make a hole in the wall near the altar to get the body through, which being pulled at with a rope, it was ſo exceeding heavy that the rope brake, and they could ſcarce ſtir him. But when they had pulled him through and gotten him on a cart without, which Cuntius his horſe that ſtruck him (which was a luſty-bodied jade) was to draw; yet it put him to it ſo, that he was ready to fall down ever and anon, and was quite out of breath with ſtriving to draw ſo intollerable a load, who notwithſtanding could run away with two men in the ſame cart preſently after, their weight was ſo inconſiderable to his ſtrength.

His body when it was brought to the fire, proved as unwilling to be burnt as before to be drawn, ſo that the executioner was fain with hooks to pull him out, and cut him in pieces to make him burn, which while he did, the blood was found ſo pure and ſpiritous, that it ſpurted into his face as he cut him; but at laſt, not without the expence of two hundred and ſixteen great billets,

billets, all was turned into afhes, which they carefully fweeping up together, as in the foregoing ftory, and cafting them into the river, the *fpectre* never more appeared.

I muft confefs I am fo flow witted myfelf that I cannot fo much as imagine what the Atheift will excogitate for a fubterfuge or hiding place from fo plain and evident convictions.

For the ANTIQUARIAN REPERTORY.

IT is an obfervation no lefs common than true, that no character is completely confiftent, the beft not being entirely free from vice, and the worft not totally deftitute of virtue.

A ftriking inftance of this occurs in an anecdote related of Judge Jefferys, which I believe never before appeared in print. That Judge, though in general fo inimical to every effort in fupport of the liberty of the fubject, yet once, at leaft, not only approved of, but rewarded in the nobleft manner, the fpirited behaviour of one acting in its defence, an exertion wherein he himfelf was the fufferer.

At a contefted election for a Member to ferve in Parliament for the Town of Arundel, in Suffex, Government ftrenuoufly interfered, and that fo openly as to fend down Jefferys, then Lord Chancellor, with inftructions to ufe every method to procure the return of the Court Candidate.

On the day of election, in order to intimidate the Electors, he placed himfelf on the huftings clofe by the Returning Officer, the Mayor, who had been an Attorney, but was retired from bufinefs, with an ample fortune and fair character; he well knew the Chancellor, but for prudential reafons acted as if he was a ftranger both to his perfon and rank.

In the courfe of the poll, that Magiftrate, who fcrutinized every man before he admitted him to vote, rejected one of the Court party, at which Jefferys rifing in a heat, after feveral indecent reflections declared the man fhould poll, adding, " I am the Lord Chancellor of this realm." The Mayor, regarding him with a look of the higheft contempt, replied in thefe words,

words, " Your ungentlemanlike behaviour convinces me, it is impoffible you fhould be the perfon you pretend; was you the Chancellor, you would know that you have nothing to do here, where I alone prefide;" then turning to the Crier, " Officer," faid he, " turn that fellow out of court;" his commands were obeyed without hefitation, and the Chancellor retired to his inn, in great confufion, and the election terminated in favour of the popular candidate.

In the evening the Mayor, to his great furprife, received a meffage from Jefferys, defiring the favour of his company at the inn, which he declining, the Chancellor came to his houfe, and being introduced to him made the following compliment: " Sir, notwithftanding we are in different interefts, I cannot help revering one who fo well knows, and dares fo nobly execute the law; and though I myfelf was fomewhat degraded thereby, you did but your duty. You, as I have learned, are independent, but you may have fome relation who is not fo well provided for; if you have, let me have the pleafure of prefenting him with a confiderable place in my gift, juft now vacant." Such an offer, and fo handfomely made, could not fail of drawing the acknowledgements of the party to whom it was made, he having a nephew in no very affluent circumftances, named him to the Chancellor, who immediately figned the neceffary inftrument for his appointment to a very lucrative and honourable employment.

Order for the Apprehenfion of the Templers, in the Reign of Edward the Second.
(From *Hollingfhed's Chronicle.*)

ON Wednefday after the Epiphany, the Knightes Templers in England were apprehended all in one day by the King's commandment, upon fufpicion of haynous crimes and great enormities by them practifed, contrary to the articles of the Chriftian fayth. The order of their apprehenfion was on this wife, the King directed hys writtes vnto al and euery the Sherifes of counties within ye realm, y^t they fhuld giue fummonance to a certain number of fubftanciall perfons Knightes or other men of good accompt, to be afore them at certayne places within their gouernementes, named in the fame writtes, on the Sunday the morrowe after the Epiphanie then nexte enfuing, and that the fayde Sherifes fayle not to be there the fame daye in their owne perfons, to execute that whiche in other writtes to them directed, and after

to

to be fent, fhould be conteyned. The date of this writte was the fiftenth of December.

The fecond writ was fent by certaine chaplaynes, in which the fherifs were commaunded upon the opening of the fame, forthwith to receyue an othe in prefence of the fayde chaplaynes, to put in execution all that was therein contayned; and not to difclofe the contents to any man, till they had executed the fame with all expedition, and therewith to take the like othe of thofe perfons, whome by vertue of the firft writte, they had fummoned to appeare afore them. An other writte there was alfo framed and fente by the fame chaplaines, by the which, the faid fheriffs wer cōmanded to attach by their bodies, al the templers within the precinct of their gouernemēts, and to feife al their lands and goodes into the kings hāds, togither with their writings, charters, dedes and miniments,, and to make thereof a true inuentorie and indenture, in prefence of the warden of the place, whether he were brother of that order, or any other, in prefence of honeft men being neyghbors, of which indēture, one part to remain in the cuftody of the fayd warden, and the other with the fherife, under feale, that fhould fo make feafure of the fayd goodes: and further, that the fayde goodes and chatels fhould be put in fafe cuftody, and that the quicke goodes and cattaile, fhould be kept and found of the premiffes as fhould feeme moft expediente, and that their lands and poffefiōs fhould be manured and tilled to the moft cōmoditie.

Further, that the perfons of the fayde templers being attached in manner as before is fayde, fhoulde bee fafely kepte in fome competent place out of theyr owne houfes, but not in ftraighte prifon, but in fuch order, as the fherifs might bee fure of them to bring them forth when he fhould be cōmanded, to be found in the meane time according to their eftate of their owne goodes fo feifed, and hereof to make a true certificate unto the treaforer and barōs of the efcheker, what they had done cōcerning the premiffes, declaring how many of the faid tēplers they had attached with their names, and what lands and goodes they had feafed by vertue of this precept: the date of thefe two laft writtes was from Biffet the xx. of December, and the returne thereof to be made unto the exchequer, was the morrow after the purification. There were writtes alfo directed into Ireland, as we haue there made mētion, and likewife unto John de Brytaine Earle of Richmonde, Lorde Warden of Scotlanne, and to Euftace de Cotefbache, Chamberlane of Scotlande, to Walter de Peberton Juftice of Weft Wales, and to Pugh Aldighle, *alias* Audley, Juftice of North Wales, to Robert Hollande, Juftice of Chefter, under like fourme and maner as in Irelande wee haue expreffed.

A Defcription

A Defcription of a Fifh, like to a Man, that was taken by Fifhers, at Oreford in Suffolk, in the Sixth Year of King John's Reign.
From *Hollingfhed's Chronicle.*)

IN this fixt yeare of King John's raigne, at Oreford in Suffolk, as Fabian hath (although I think I thinke he be deceiued in the time) a fifh was taken by fifhers in their nettes as they were at fea, refembling in fhape a wilde or fauage man, who they prefented unto Sir Batholmew de Glanuille, knight, that had then the keeping of the caftell of Oreford in Suffolke. Naked he was, and in all his limmes and members refembling the right proportion of a man. He had heares alfo in the ufual parts of his body, albeit that on the crown of his head he was balde: his beard was fide and rugged, and his breaft verie hearie. The knight caufed him to be kept certaine dayes and nightes from the fea. Meate fet afore him he greedily deuoured, and eate fifh both raw and fodde. Thofe that were rawe he preffed in his hande tyll he had thruft out all the moyfture, and fo then he did eate them. Hee would not, or could not utter any fpeeche, although to trye him they hung him uppe by the heeles, and myferably tormented him. He woulde get him to his couche at the fetting of the funne, and ryfe agayne when it rofe.

One day they brought him to the hauen, and fuffered him to go into the fea, but to be fure hee fhould not efcape from them, they fet three ranks of mightie ftrong nettes before him, fo to catche him againe at their pleafure (as they ymagined) but he ftreyght wayes dyuing down to the bottome of the water, gotte paft all the nettes, and comming uppe fhewed himfelfe to them againe, that ftoode wayting for him, and dowking dyuerfe tymes under water and coming up agayne, hee behelde them on the fhore that ftoode ftill looking at him, who feemed as it were to mocke them, for that he had deceived them, and gotte paft theyr nettes. At length, after hee had thus played him a great while in the water, and that there was no more hope of hys returne, he came to them againe of his owne accorde, fwimming through the water, and remayned wyth them two monethes after. But finally, when he was negligently looked to, and nowe feemed not to be regarded, hee fledde fecretelye to the fea, and was neuer after feene nor heard of.

Erratum in the laft Number.

The Reader is defired to correct a Miftake made by the Printer in the Article of the Cradle.—Henry the Fifth, inftead of Edward the Second, was the Prince to whom it belonged.

THE

ANTIQUARIAN REPERTORY.

The GREAT GATE *of St.* Auguſtine's Monaſtery, Canterbury.

THIS Gate is univerſally eſteemed one of the moſt elegant ſpecimens of Gothic Architecture now remaining in England; the View here given ſhews the inſide of it, together with part of the dwelling houſe and other offices of the Monaſtery, as they appear when viewed from the South Eaſt.

This Monaſtery was firſt founded by St. Auguſtine, about the year 605, and dedicated to St. Peter and St. Paul; to theſe Archbiſhop Dunſtan, anno 987, aſſociated St. Auguſtine, and it has ever ſince been beſt known by the name of St. Auguſtine's Monaſtery. It was a mitred Abbey, and enjoyed every privilege and immunity which the ſuperſtition of thoſe times commonly allowed to Religious Houſes, among which was a permiſſion to coin money.

The buildings of this Houſe were conſtructed at very different periods, ſome are ſaid to have been extant before Chriſtianity was eſtabliſhed in that part of England, whilſt others are as late as the days of Henry the Seventh. At what time this Gate was built is not known.

At the Diffolution, 31ft of July, in the 30th of Henry the Eighth, its annual revenues were eftimated at 1412l. 4s. 7d. The deed of refignation was figned by John Effex, the Lord Abbot, and thirty of the Monks, being one half of the eftablifhment of that Houfe.
It is now the property of Sir Edward Hales, Baronet.

The Maffacre at Stonehenge, *by* Hengift, *and his Souldiers; and fome Account of* Merlin.

From the Ancient Hiftory of Great-Britain.

HENGIST (a fubtle and malicious man) upon retorn of this embaffy, under color of peace, devifed the fubverfion of al the nobility of Britain, and chofe out, to com to this affembly, his faithfulleft and hardieft men, commaunding every one of them to hide, under his garment, a long knif (or, as the Britifh hiftory is, in their britches) as long as their thies; with which, when he fhould give the watchword, nymyd ywr fexys, he commaunded that every one fhould kil the Briton next him. Both fides met upon the day appointed, and treating earneftly upon the matter, Hengift fodenly gave the watchword, and fodenly caught Vortiger by the coler; and the Saxons, with their long knives, violently murdred the innocent and unarmed Britons, none of them having on him fo much as a knif. At what tyme ther were thus treacheroufly murdred, of earles and noblemen of the Britons, 460. and neverthelefs ther were many Saxons then flain by the Britons, with ftones ther taken up; wher Aldol, earle of Gloucefter, or Caergloin, gote into his hand a ftake, and flew therwith 70 Saxons, and then efcaped home to his own city. Herupon Hengift detained Vortiger in prifon, in irons, until, for his ranfom, he delivered four of his chiefeft cities, and chiefeft forts, *(viz.)* London, York, Lincoln and Winchefter. Wherupon they miferably wafted the provinces belonging to thos cities. And Hengift, from thensfurth, made Kent the feat of his kingdom. And Vortiger (as Sigebert faieth) departed into Wales, *A. D.* 439. And Eugethufius deriveth the name of Saxons, of knives, faieing,

Quippe

THE ANTIQUARIAN REPERTORY. 147

Quippe brevis gladius apud illos faxa vocatur,
Unde fibi Saxo nomen traxiffe putatur.

And Jodocus Badius noteth, that the Britons, in the Tyme of Peace, wear no weapons. Vortiger, who alone was the caufe of al thes evels which happened to him and his people, wherof it greatly repented him, being no way able to remedy it, like a man in defpair, retired himfelf into Cymbri (afterwards cauled Wales); wher he was altogether directed by the counfel of his magicians and fouthfaiers, demaunding of them, What was beft to be don? who anfwered him, That it was beft for him to build a ftrong caftle or fort, in fom defenfible place; for which purpos a place was thought fiteft in the mountains of Yriri in Caernarfonfhyre, in Northwales, wher, it femeth, that Vortiger was born; for Taliefin cauleth him Gwrtheirn Gwyned, curfing him for bringing in the Britons into bondag, faieing, Pell bwynt hychmyn y wrtheyrn Gwyned, efgyrawt Allmyn y allituted. Vortiger laieing a fundation for to build a ftrong caftle, the fame would not ftand, for default in the fundation; and Vortiger demaunding of his magiciens the caus therof, they could not tel it: yet, to excufe their ignorance, wheras ther was one Merdyn, cauled in Laten Ambrofius Merlinus, a yong man, yet greatly lerned, fpecialy in the mathematicks, and having the fpirit of prophefy; thes magicians greatly maligned this Merdyn, for his lerning and knowledge, and thought it now a fit tyme to work his diftruction; that wheras he was the fon of a nun, the daughter of the king of Northwales, and his father was not knowen, but the fame went, that he was the fon of an Incubus (yet fom fay that he anfwered the king, That his father was *unus de Confulibus Romanæ gentis*) thes magiciens, knowing that, tould the king, that the fundation of his caftle would not ftand, til the morter therof were mingled with the blood of a man that had no father, hoping therby to move the king to kyl Merdin: wherupon Merdin was fent for, and brought before the king; to whom the king demaunded, How he was called? he anfwered Ambreis guletic, i. e. I am cauled Ambros (which is not al one with Emreis Wledic). Merdin behaved himfelf fo wifly before the king, manifefting to the king the defect, why the fundation ftood not, by a pole of water that was under the fundation, that he grew fo greatly in the king's favour, that the king gave him (as Ninius affirmeth) a caftle, with the kingdom of Weft wales, being the inheritaunce of his grandfather; and demaunding of him fome queftions, touching his eftate,

Merdin

Merdin byd him avoid the fire of the fons of Conftantine, who (he faied) would be his diftruction. And of his prophefies I will fpeke no further, nor of his byrth, *ex Incubo*, though I had writen (out of many lerned fathers, and other lerned men, Chriftians and pagans) a fpecial treatife of the Incubi and Fairies, and of children begotten by them, and of their qualities comon with fpirites, as great alacrity of fence, velocity of motion, penetrability, and invifibility; for which caus, lerned men have cauled them fpirites, and Saxo Grammaticus mortal fpirites. And of their qualities, comon with men, to have bodies of flefh, bloud, and bone; to live by meat, drink, and fleap; to be fubject to difeafes, as agues, impoftumations, and the like, for which they are forced to feke phyfick; and in the end differing from fpirites, and men, they dy as a beaft, for that they have no foules, nor are fpirites. And of the difference betwixt them and fpirites and fpecters; which treatife I thought to have fuppreffed for three caufes; the firft, left I fhould offend God, in fearching further into his fecrets, then may ftand with his holy wil: the fecond, in dedicating my boke to the king's majeftie, left he might note me of great prefumption, to offer to his highnefs any thing that might fmel of ftrang doctrine. The third, left the reader fhould judg me humourous or fingular in my own confceit, and to offend in furquidry, in feming to know that precifely, wherof no man (but Theophraftus Paracelfus) who have writen therof, have treated but doubtingly; yet I am overruled to let it pas.

Vortiger, giving over his building in Yriri, cam into the fouth part of Wales, into a country cauled Gunneffi; and ther, as Ninius faieth, he built a city (or caftle) which of his name he cauled Caer Guororthigin (or Caerg-worthigyrn).

Extract

Extract from Blount's Antient Tenures.

TUTBURY.

HENRICUS Sextus dei Gratia Rex Angliæ et Franciæ & Dominus Hiberniæ, omnibus ad quos præsentes Literæ pervenerint salutem. Inspeximus Literas patentes Johannis nuper Regis Castellæ & Legionis ducis Lancastriæ proavi nostri factos in hæc verba.—*Johan par le grace de dieu Roy de Castille & de Leon Duke de Lancastre a tous ceux qui cestes nos Letres verront ou orront Saluz. Saches nous avoir ordinez constitut, & assignez nostre bien ame* ——*le Roy de* Minstraulx *deins nostre Honor de* Tutbury *quore est, ou qui par le temps serra,* par prendre & *arrester touts les* Minstraulx *deins mesmes nostre* Honeur & Franchise, queux refuront de faire lour services & Ministralcie as eux appurtenants a *fair de ancient temps a* Tuttebury *suisdit annualement les jours del* Assumption *de nostre dame, Donants & grantants audit Roy de* Minstralx *pur le temps esteant plein poyer & mandement des les fair reasonablement justifier et constrener de fair lour services & Minstralcies en manere come appeint & come illonques ad este use & de ancient temps accustome. Et en festimoigniance de quel chose nous avous fait faire cestes noz Letres patent, don souz nostre privie Seale a nostre Chastel de* Tuttebury *le xxij jour de August le an de regne nostre tres dulce le Roy* Richard, *quart.*

Nos autem Literas prædictas ad requisitionem dilecti nobis in Christo Thomas Gedney, Priori de Tuttebury, duximus examplicandos per præsentes, in cujus rei testimonium has Literas nostras fieri fecimus patentes. Datum sub Sigillo nostri ducatus *Lancast.* apud Palatium nostrum de Westm. 22 die Febr. anno regni nostri vicesimo primo.

Item est ibidem quædam consuetudo quod Histriones venientes ad Matutinas in festo Assumptionis beatæ Mariæ habebunt. unam taurum de Priore de Tuttebury si ipsum capere possunt citra aquam Dove, propinquiorem Tuttebury, vel Prior dabit eis xl d pro qua quidem Consuetudine dabuntur domino ad dictum Festum annuatim xxd.

IN ENGLISH.

Henry the Sixth by the Grace of God, King of England & France & Lord of Ireland, to all to whom these Letters shall come greeting. We have perused the Letters patent of our Ancestor John late King of Castile & Leon

Leon and Duke of Lancaſter, expreſſed in theſe words. John by the Grace of God, King of Caſtile and Leon, Duke of Lancaſter, to all who ſhall ſee or hear theſe our Letters greeting. Know ye that we have ordained, conſtituted, and aſſigned our well-beloved ———— the King of the Minſtrels in our Honour of Tutbury, who is or for the time ſhall be, to ſeize and arreſt all Minſtrels in that our Honor and Franchiſe who ſhall refuſe to perform their Services and Minſtrelcy, which from ancient time they were bound annually to do on the days of the Aſſumption of our Lady. Giving and granting to the ſaid King of the Minſtrels for the time being full power and authority to make them reaſonably juſtifie themſelves, and to conſtrain them to perform their Services and Minſtrelcy in the manner appointed, and as has been uſual, and of ancient times the cuſtom. And in teſtimony whereof we have cauſed theſe our Letters to be made patent, given under our Privy Seal the 22d day of Auguſt, and in the fourth year of the reign of our very dear Lord King Richard.

Now We at the requeſt of our dearly beloved in Chriſt Thomas Gedney, Prior of Tutebury, have thought proper to exemplify the ſaid Letters by theſe preſents, in teſtimony of which we have cauſed theſe our Letters to be made patent. Given under our Seal of the Dutchy of Lancaſter at our Palace of Weſtminſter 22 day of February in the 21ſt year of our reign.

There is alſo at the ſame place a certain cuſtom that the Minſtrels coming to Matins at the feaſt of the Aſſumption of the Bleſſed Mary, ſhall have a Bull from the Prior of Tutbury if they are able to ſeize him on the ſide of the River Dove next Tuttebury, or in lieu thereof the Prior ſhall give them xl^d. for which cuſtom 20^d. ſhall be given annually at the ſaid feaſt by the Lord of the Manor.

Out of the Coucker-Booke of the Honour of Tutburye, Cap. de Libertatibus.

THE Prior* of Tutburye ſhall have yerely, one oure Ladye day the Aſſumption, a Bukke delivered him of Seyſſone by the Wood Maſter and Keepers of Nedewoode: and the Wood maſter and keepers of Needwoode ſhall every yere mete at a Lodgge in Nedewoode called Birkeley Lodgge by one of the cloke at afternone one Seynt Laurence dey, at which dey and place a woodmote ſhall be kept, and every keper making deffalte ſhall looſe

xii^d.

* The Erle of Devonſhire is now Prior, ab. H. 8.

xii^d. to the Kynge and there the Wood mafter and Kepers fhall chofe 2 of the Kepers yerely as itt cometh to their turne to be Stewards for to prepare the dyner at Tutburye Caftell one our Ladye dey the Affumption for the Wood mafter & kepers and Officers within the Chafe, and there they fhall appoint in lykewife where Bukke fhall be kylled for the Prior ageynfte the faide Ladye dey; and alfo where the Bukke fhall be kylde for the Kepers dyner ageynft the fame dey: and on the faide feafte of Affumption the Woodmafter or his Lyvetenant and the Kepers and their Deputies fhall be at Tutburye, and every man one Horfebake and foo ryde in order two and two together from the Gate called the Lyde at goinge into the common felde unto the High Croffe in the Towne; and the Keper in whofe office the Seynt Marye Bukke was kylled fhall beire the Bukks Heade garnifhed aboute with a rye of peafe & the Bukks Heede muft be * cabaged with the hole face and yeeres beinge one the Sengill of the Bukke with two peces of fatte one either fide of the Sengill muft be faftened upon the broo ankelers of the fame heed, and every keeper muft have a grene boghe in his hand: and every keper that is abfent that dey being noder fikke nor in the King's fervice fhall lofe xii^d. and foo the kepers fhall ridde two and two together tyll they come to the faid Croffe in the Towne; and all the Minftrells fhall goe afore them one foote two and two together; and the Woodmafter or in his abfence his Lyvetenant fhall ride hindermoft after all the kepers; and at the faid Croffe in the Towne, the formaft keper fhall blow a *Seeke*, and all the other kepers fhall anfwer him in blowinge the fame, and when they come to the cornell ageynft the nue hall the formoft keper fhall blowe *a Recheate* and all the other kepers fhall anfwere hyme in blowinge of the fame; and fo they fhall ride ftill tyll they come into the Church Yorde and then light and goo into the Churche in lyke arrey, and all the Minftrells fhall pley one their Inftruments duringe the offeringe tyme, and the Woodmafter or in his abfence his Livetenant fhall offer up the Bukks head moyd in Silver, and every keper fhall offer a peny, and as foone as the Bukks head is offered uppe all the Kepers fhall blow a *Morte* three tymes: and then all the kepers goo into a Chappell and fhall there have one of the Monks redye to fey them Maffe: and when Maffe is done, all the kepers goo in lyke arrey uppe to the Caftell to dynner, and when dynner is done the Stewards goo to the Prior of Tutburye, and he fhall give them yerely xxx^s. towards the charges of ther dynner:

* Caboffed Ears Single or Toyle Brow Antlers.

ner: and if the dynner come to more the kepers shall beire it amongst them: and one the morrow after the Assumption there is a court kept of the Minstrells, at which Court the Woodmaster or his Lyvetenant shall be: and shall oversee that every Minstrell dwelling within the Honor and makinge defaulte shall be amerceyed: whiche amercement the kynge of the Minstrells shall have: and after the Courte done the Pryor shall deliver the Minstrells a Bull or xviii'. of Money: and shall turne hyme loose amongs them, and if he escape from them over the Dove river the Bull is the priours owne ageyne: and if the Minstrells can take the Bull ore he gett over Dove then the Bull is their owne.

The Modern Usage.

UPON the morrow after the Assumption of the Blessed Virgin, being the 26th of August, all the Musicians within the Honour are to repair to the Bailiff's House in Tutbury, where the Steward * of the Court (who is usually a Nobleman) and the Woodmaster or his Lieutenant are to meet them, from whence they go to the church in this order; first, two wind Musicians as trumpets or long pipes, then four string Musicians, two and two, all playing: then the Steward of the Court or his Deputy, and the Bailiff of the Manor, deputed by the Earl of Devon, the King of Musick going between them: after whom the four Stewards of Musick, each with a white wand in his hand, and the rest of the company follow in order.

At the church the Vicar of Tutbury for the time being reads the service of the day, for which every Musician pays him a penny; then all go from the Church to the Castle in manner as before, where the Steward takes his place upon the bench in Court, assisted with the Bailiff and Woodmaster, the King of Musick sitting between them, to see that every Minstrel within the Honor, being called and making default, be presented and amerced by the Jury, which amercements are collected by the Stewards of Musick, who accompt the one moiety to his Majesty's Auditor, the other they retain to themselves for their pains in collecting them.

When the King's Steward and the rest are so sate, the Steward commands an oyez to be made three times by one of the Musicians, as Crier of the Court, that all the Minstrels within the Honor, residing in the counties of
Stafford,

* The present Steward is the Duke of Ormond, and Mr. Edward Foden his Deputy. The Earl of Devon is Prior.

Stafford, Derby, Nottingham, Leicefter or Warwick, do appear to do their fuit and fervice, on fuch pain and peril as the Court fhall inflict for their default. Effoynes neverthelefs are allowed, in excufe of defaulters, upon good reafon fhewed.

After which all the faid Minftrels are called by a fute roll, as fuitors are in a Court Leet, and then two Juries are impanelled of the chief Minftrells by the Stewards of Mufick, each Jury confifting of twelve, which are returned into the Court, where the Steward fwears them; the form of their oath is the fame which is given in a Court Leet, only in a Leet the Jury fwear to keep the King's Counfel, their fellows and their own; in this to keep the King of Mufick's Counfel, their fellows and their own.

The better to inform the Jurors of their duty, the Steward gives them a charge, in commendation of the antient Science of Mufick, fhewing what admirable effects it has produced, what Kings and noble perfons have been Profeffors of it, what manner of perfons the Profeffors ought to be, and to admonifh them to choofe fkilful and good men to be Officers for the year enfuing.

The Officers chofen by the Juries are one King and three Stewards of Mufick. The fourth is chofen by the Steward of the Court; the King is chofen one year out of the Minftrells of Staffordfhire, and the next year out of thofe of Derbyfhire.

The Steward of the Court iffues out warrants to the Stewards of Mufick in their feveral diftricts, by virtue whereof they are to diftrain and levy in any city, town corporate, or other place within the *Honor*, all fuch fines and amerciaments as are impofed by the Juries on any Minftrel for offences committed againft the dignity and honor of the profeffion; the one moiety of which fines the Stewards account for at the next audit, the other they retain themfelves.

As foon as the charge is given an Oyez is made, with a Proclamation, that if any perfon can inform the Court of any offence committed by any Minftrel within the faid *Honor*, fince the laft Court, which is againft the honor of his profeffion, let them come forth and they fhall be heard. Then the Juries withdraw to confider of the points of the charge; and the old Stewards of Mufick bring into the Court a treat of wine, ale, and cakes, and at the fame time fome Minftrels are appointed to entertain the company in Court with fome merry airs. After which the Juries prefent one to be

King for the year enfuing, who takes his oath to keep up all the dignities of that noble fcience, &c.

Then the old King arifeth from his place, refigning it and his white wand to the new King, to whom he alfo drinks a glafs of wine, and bids him joy of his honour; and the old Stewards do the like to the new, which done, the Court adjourns to a certain hour after noon, and all return back in the fame order they came to the Caftle, to a place where the old King, at his own coft, prepares a dinner for the new King, Steward of the Court, Bailiff, Stewards of Mufick, and Jurymen.

After dinner all the Minftrels repair to the Priory Gate in *Tutbury*; without any manner of weapons, attending the turning out of the Bull, which the Bailiff of the Manor is obliged to provide, and is there to have the tips of his horns fawed of, his ears and tail cut off, his body fmeared all over with foap, and his nofe blowed full of beaten pepper. Then the Steward caufes Proclamation to be made, that all manner of perfons, except Minftrels, fhall give way to the Bull, and not come within forty foot of him at their own peril, nor hinder the Minftrels in their purfuit of him. After which Proclamation the Prior's Bailiff turns out the Bull among the Minftrels, and if any of them can cut off a piece of his fkin before he runs into Derbyfhire, then he is the King of Mufick's Bull: But if the Bull get into Derbyfhire found and uncut, he is the Lord Prior's again.

If the Bull be taken, and a piece of him cut off, then he is brought to the Bailiff's houfe, and there collared and roped, and fo brought to the bull-ring in the High-ftreet in Tutbury, and there baited with dogs, the firft courfe in honour of the King of Mufick, the fecond in honour of the Prior, the third of the Town, and if more, for divertifement of the Spectators; and after he is baited, the King may difpofe of him as he pleafes.

This ufage is of late perverted, the young men of *Stafford* and Derbyfhires contend with cudgels about a yard long, the one party to drive the Bull into Derbyfhire, the other to keep him in Staffordfhire, in which conteft many heads are often broken.

The King of Mufick and the Bailiff have alfo of late compounded, the Bailiff giving the King five nobles in lieu of his right to the Bull, and then fends him to the Earl of *Devon*'s Manor of Hardwicke to be fed and given to the poor at Chriftmas.

The SCOWLS, *in the Woods of* Thomas Bathurst, *Esq; near his Seat at* Lidney Park, Gloucestershire.

THE Scowls are excavations of the earth, in some places to the depth of 25 or 30 feet, forming a kind of irregular trench, interspersed with solid rocks, some of which are standing, and other huge fragments thrown down, or disjointed in such a manner, as could only be effected by gunpowder, or some violent convulsion of nature. A kind of rude passage runs through the whole, which occupies near an acre of ground, though this is frequently interrupted by great pieces of fallen rock, over which passengers must climb. The grotesque figure of the rock, covered with moss, and entwined with roots of shrubs and trees, the solemn gloominess of the whole, owing to the exclusion of light from a great quantity of wood with which it is surrounded and overshadowed, join in affording a most romantic scene.

Various are the conjectures relative to this place, some supposing it the effects of an earthquake, others deeming it a place of pagan worship; but the most probable opinion is, that it was an ancient mine, made in search of iron ore, of which there is great plenty hereabouts. If this is true, it must be many ages since it was worked, there not being the least tradition of it in the neighbourhood, besides the moss with which the rocks are overgrown; and the large old trees shooting out of many parts of the rock, give their testimony of its antiquity.

As in the adjoining Park of Lidney there was a Roman fort, as is evident from a bath now remaining, diverse Roman utensils, coins, tesserated pavements, and the foundations of many buildings, with several entrenchments, possibly this mine might have been opened by that people, and ever since neglected. For what reason it is called the Scowls does not appear, or from what the word is derived; that appellation is however given to another exhausted mine in Gloucestershire.

The neighbouring rustics have given names to diverse rocks from their appearances, such as the Pillar, the Chapel Window, &c. On the whole, whatever may be its antiquity, as a picturesque object it well deserves the observation of the curious, and may rank with Mother Ludlam's Cave in Surry, Poole's Hole, and the other Derbyshire Caverns.

To

To the EDITOR of the ANTIQUARIAN REPERTORY.

SIR,

THE study of the Antiquities of this country has long been my favourite amusement, and I seldom pass a summer in the country without visiting every place of note in the neighbourhood, and particularly the Churches in search of Inscriptions, Ancient Monuments, and other curiosities.

In the course of these pursuits I have observed, that on most of the engraved brass plates laid over grave stones, where they represent a man and his wife, among the ancient ones the lady takes the right hand of her husband, but in those of more modern date, the husband lies on the right of his wife.

I have some doubt whether this is universally the case; if it is, it may be accounted for, from the high honours paid to the fair sex in the days of chivalry; but when those romantic notions began to go out of fashion, the husbands seized the opportunity to assert their superiority, and their wives were removed from the place of honour, which the male sex for many years maintained. All public addresses to a mixed assembly of both sexes till sixty years ago, commenced Gentlemen and Ladies, at present it is Ladies and Gentlemen.

As the field of my observations is extremely limited, I should be much obliged to any of your correspondents whose knowledge on this head is more extensive, if they would in your Repertory favour me with answers to the following questions.

First, Whether they have observed any particular mode or position respecting the right or left hand in those grave plates representing a married couple which have fallen under their inspection?

Secondly, At what particular periods were they used?

And lastly, Whether there can any reason be given for thus placing them?

I am, Sir, your's, &c.

A LOVER OF ANTIQUITIES.

The Hiftory of King Leyr, and his Three Daughters.

From the Ancient Hiftory of Great-Britain.

LYR, or Leyr, the fon of Bladud, fucceaded him, who raigned fixty years. He builded a cyty upon the ryver Soram, wherin he built a temple to Janus, and ther erected a flamin, and cauled the cyty of his name, Caerlyr (which is Leicefter.) He had no fon, but thre daughters, whos names were Goronilla, Ragan and Cordeila, whom the father much loved, and moft of al he loved the yongeft; and drawing into his ould age, he bethought him how he fhould leave his kingdom and wealth amongeft his daughters, and therfore he thought to trie which of his daugters loved him moft, to the end, to beftow her in marriage with the beft part of his kingdom. Wherupon he cauled to him Goronilla, his eldeft daughter, and afked her, how wel fhe loved him : fhe fware by heaven and earth that fhe loved him better than her owne foule, which he believing, faid unto her ; for as much as thou loveft me fo wel I will give thee to a hufband in Britaine, as thou fhalt chofe, with the third part of my kingdom ; and that faid, he cauled to him his daughter Ragan, his fecond daughter, and demaunded, of her how much fhe loved him, fhe fware by the power of God, that fhe could not declare with her tong, how much fhe loved him; which he believing lykwife willed her to chofe whom fhe would for her hufband, and fhe fhould have the third part of this kingdom. And therupon he cauled to him his yongeft daughter Cordeila, and demanded of her how much fhe loved him, to whom fhe anfwered him, that fhe ever loved him, as becometh her daughter to love her father, and yet doth, adding, Thou fhalt be beloved as thou art worth or worthi ; upon which anfwer he grew colar, and faid unto her ; for as much as thou haft fo much defpifed me, and loveft me not fo much as thy other fifters, thou fhalt never have part with them of my kingdom : and torning his love of her into hate, he faught not to beftow her in marriage : but his two eldeft daughters he beftowed in marriage : Goronilla to Maglawn duke of Scotland, and Ragan to Honwin duke of Cornwall, with half his kingdom betwixt them, in poffeffion, and the whole after his daies. And Aganippus king of France (or as Zirixeus faieth of the third part of Gaule Belgick) hearing of the fame, and great beuty of Cordeila, fent to her father to demaund her in marriage. To whos meſſengers king Leyr anſwered that king Aganippus ſhould willingly have her to wyf, but without doury of his kingdom; for that he had aſſured the ſame to his other two daughters, and their huſbands: which when Aganippus underſtood, and of the beuty of Cordeila, he ſaid that he had wealth enough, and that he ſought but a virtuous and beutiful wyf, to have children of her to inherit his kingdom. And therupon he toke Cordeila to wyf. And afterwards king Lyr living long, in his ould age his two ſones in law thought it long to ſtay for the abſolute kingdom of Britain til after his death, thei made war upon the ould king, who had honorably governed his kingdom, and wan it from him, and divided it betwixt them: and therupon Maglawn duke of Albany toke Lyr to him, with allowance of forty knights to attend him: and after that Lyr had been a certen tyme with Maglawn, his daughter Goronilla did grudge that her father had ſuch great attendance on him, and ſpake to her husband to abridge the nombre, who accordingly abridged the nombre to thirty two, which King Lyr taking in evil part departed thens to his other ſon in law, Henwyn duke of Cornwall, wher at firſt he was honorably entertained, but within a year ther fel ſom ſtrife between the men of Leir and his ſon in law, by color wherof Ragan frowned upon her father, and willed him to put away al his knights but one to ſerve him, which Leir toke very heavily, and was very ſad, and departed thens with his knights back again, to his daughter Goronilla, hoping ther to be entertained again ; and when he cam thether, his daughter Goronilla ſware in wrath by heaven and earth, that if he ſtaid ther, he ſhould have but one knight to attend upon him, which was yenough for an ould man of his age, and not finding better relief at his daughter's hands he put away al his knights but one, and having ſo remained a while, and thinking upon his honorable and proſperous eſtate, and reputation in tymes paſt, he remembred his daughter Cordeila in Gaule, and being weary and aſhamed of the reproachful eſtate he lived in, it cam to his thought to ſeke relief at her hands, notwithſtanding the great unkindneſs and unnatural cours he had ſhewed her: and therupon he toke his journey towardes Gaule, and going on ſhipboard, ſeing his poor attendance, of two ſervants only, he brake out into thes ſpeaches. O deſtiny, how doeſt thou go over the accuſtomed boundes! How haſt thou thrown me down from my long felicity! It is more plain to remember proſperity loſt than never to have had it. I now reſceave more ſorrow and pain in remembring my wealth, honor and reputation loſt ; and the unkindnes of my daughters and ſones-in-law, then al the adverfities which have happened unto me: The multitude of enemies with whom in my profperity I have had to deal withal troubled me, not fo much as the ingratitude of thes men. " O goddes of heaven, and earth, " wil the tyme com wherin I may be reveng'd of thes men! O Cordeila, " my wel beloved daughter, how true were the woordes thou fpakeft unto " me! That I fhould be beloved as much as I was worth: For fo long as I " was in wealth and profperity, and able to live, al men loved me; but in " truth thei loved not me, but my wealth, and as it paffed from me, fo did " their love. And therefore, O daughter Cordeila, how can I for fhame " requeft aid at thy hands, whom I fo wrongfully rejected for thy great " wifdom, and fo unfatherly put thee from me in mariag, rather with dif- " dain then advancement, and like a loft child, never hoping of comfort, " or joy, by thy match, and yet thou now far furmounteth thy fifters in " honor, reputation, vertue and wifdom". And thus lamenting and wailing, he approched the cyty wher his daughter remained, and fent a meffenger unto her, fignifieing unto her of his adverfity, and overthrowen eftate, his want of money, apparel, and other neceffaries, defiring her to have commiferation upon him; which when fhe heard fhe wept, and demanded how many knights attended him: To whom it was aunfwered, but one or two fervants. Whereupon fhe fent him plenty of gould and filver, and willed him to go into another towne, and take on him to be fick, til he had provided him apparel, and forty knights to attend him wel-furnifhed, with hors, armor and apparel; which done, he fhould fend meffengers to king Aganippus and her, to certify them of his coming, which he did accordingly; and fent meffengers to his daughter, and king Aganippus fignifying his coming, and how he was driven out of Britain by his fones-in-law, and that he was com to feke their aid, to be reftored to his kingdom. Which when Aganippus underftood, he and his quene, and al their houfhold cam very honorably to mete with king Leir, according to the worthines of the king of Britain, and refceaved him with joy, and during his abode in Gaule, Aganippus gave Leir the whole rule of his kingdom, to the end he might the eafier levy power ther to recover his kingdom of Britain. Whereupon Aganippus muftred his fubjects, and felected an army of his worthieft fouldiers in aid of king Leir to recover his kingdom. And having al things in a readines, king Leir and his daughter Cordeila, with that army cam into Britain, and fighting with his fones-in-law, gote the victory, and recovered his kingdom again, and al his fubjects yielding unto him, he raigned in peace

three

three yeares afterwardes, and then died, and was buried in a vault or tomb, which he had made under the ryver Saram: And wheras he had builded a temple to Janus in Caerlyr, as is aforefaid, when the day of the folemn feaft of that temple cam, al the artificers and workmen of the cyty and countrey therabouts repaired to that temple, wher they began al things, which they had to do the year folowing. And fhortly after Aganippus died alfo.

   Cordeila fucceaded her father in the kingdom of Britain, who have raigned five yeares in peace, her two nephewes, her fifter's fones, Margan fon of Maglaw, duke of Albany, and Chuneda fon of Henwyn, duke of Cornwal, levied warr againft her, and obtained the victory, and toke her prifoner, and imprifoned her, wher throw forrow for the los of her kingdom, her father, and her hufband, fhe killed her felf, and was buried at Leicefter. Wherupon Margan and Chuneda devided the kingdom betwixt them, by which devifion Margan had al the north beyond Humber, and Chuneda had the reft. But within two yeares after Margan repented him of this partition, for that Chuneda had the better, who was fon of the youngeft fifter; and therfore to undo this partition, Margan levied war againft Chuneda, and entred his countrey with fyre and fword, with whom Chuneda with a great army encountred, and forced him to flie into Wales, wher they fought a bloodie battel, in which Margan was flaine, and of him the countrey toke the name, and fpecially the abby of Margan. And touching the conqueft of Morganwc by Robert Fitzhamon, I refer you to Powel, whos opinion was that the countrey toke the name of Morgan Mwynfawr, great grandfather to Jeftin ap Gyrgan, who brought Robert Fitzhamon into that countrey. Wherof I allow not. For it bare that name in the tyme of Merchiawn Gul. king thereof, above one thoufand yeares paft, as it appeareth by a charter by him made to St. Eltutus, touching the priviledg of his fcole in that countrey. By our antiquities it appeareth that eighteen battels were fought in the quarrel of the tytles of Leyr's three daughters..

Account

Account of the Sweating-Sickness, in the Year 1486.

From Hollingshead's Chronicle.

IN the yeare 1486 a newe kynde of sickneffe invaded sodeynly the people of this lande, paffing thorough the same from the one end to the other. It began about the. xxi. of September, and continued till the latter end of October, beyng so sharpe and deadly, that the lyke was never hearde of to any mannes remembrance before that tyme. For sodeynely a deadely burnyng sweate so assayled theyr bodies, and distempered their bloud wyth a moste ardent heat, that scarse one amongst an hundred that sickned did escape with life: for all in maner as soone as the sweat tooke them, or within a short tyme after yelded up the ghost: besyde the great number which deceassed within the citie of London two Mayres succeffively died within viii. days and vi. Aldermē. At length by the diligent obfervatiō of those that escaped (which marking what thinges had done thē good, and holpen to their deliverance, vsed the lyke agayne: when they fell into the same diseafe, the second or thirde tyme, as to dyuers it chaunced, a remedie was founde for that mortall maladie, which was this: if a man on the day tyme were taken with the sweate, then should he streight lye downe with al his cloathes and garments, and continue in hys sweat. xxiiii. houres, after so moderate a sort as might bee. If in the nyghte hee chaunced to be taken, then shoulde he not ryse out of his bedde for the space of. xxiiii. hours, so castyng the cloathes that he myght in no wyse prouoke the sweate, but so lye temperately, that the water mighte diftyll out softly of the owne accord, and to abstein from all meat if he might so long suffer hunger, and to take no more drinke neyther hot, nor colde, thā wold moderately quench and asfuage his thirftie appetite. And thus with lukewarme drinke, temperate heate, and meafurable clothes manye escaped: fewe whiche vsed this order after it was founde out dyed of that sweat. Mary one point diligētly above all other in this cure is to be obferved, that he neuer put out his hande or feete out of the bed, to refreshe or coole him, which to do is no leffe ieopardie than short and prefent death.

Thus this diseafe comming in the first yeare of king Henries reigne, was iudged (of some) to be a token and figne of a troublous reigne of the same king, as the profe partly afterwards shewed it selfe.

MISCELLANEOUS PLATE.

THIS Plate contains a View, Ground Plan and Section, of a Roman Bath in Lidney Park, Gloucestershire.

It is situated on the westernmost edge of an almost perpendicular precipice, amidst the remains of tesserated pavements, and other vestiges of a Roman fortress.

Although its shape and dimensions are sufficiently explained by the Plan and Section, to save the reader the trouble of measuring them they are here given in words.

The whole length of the Bath measures six yards, one yard and a half of which, at the south end, is taken off for a kind of dressing place, and is elevated a foot and a half above the bottom of the Bath, which gradually sloping towards the north, terminates at the depth of about four feet. Its breadth is three yards.

The whole is lined with a stone wall, which appears to have been plaistered over with a strong cement, seemingly made with brick rubbish; at the ends it still remains pretty perfect, but towards the sides has been peeled off. About a yard from the south end, and in the bottom of the easternmost side, is a hole about three inches square, formed for the passage of water, either into, or from the Bath.

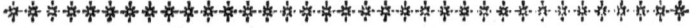

A Discovery by Sea from London to Salisbury.

From the Works of John Taylor, *the* Water Poet.

AS our accounts in Almanacks agree
The yeere cal'd sixteen hundred twenty-three
That Julyes twenty-eight, two houres past dinner
We with our wherry and five men within her
Along the cristal Thames did cut and curry
Betwixt the counties Middlesex and Surry.

Whilst

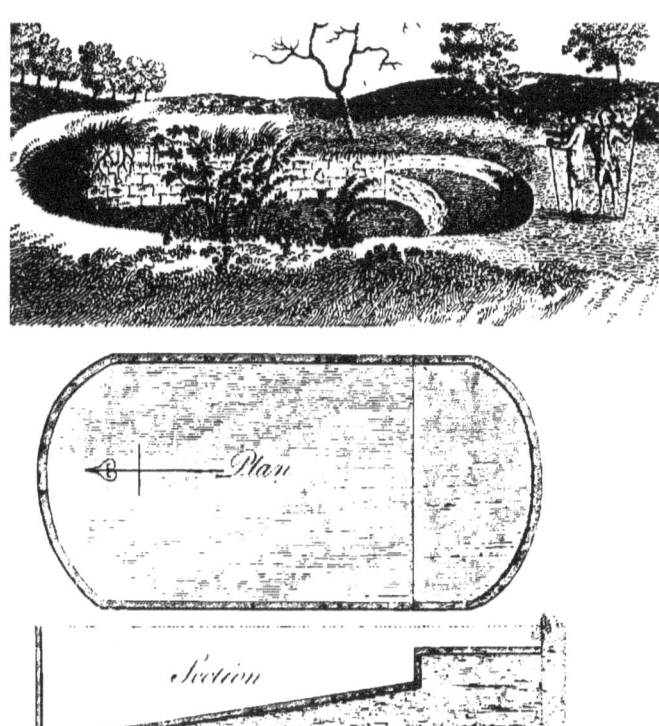

Whilft thoufāds gaz'd we paſt the bridge with wōder
Where fooles and wife men goe aboue and vnder;
We thus our Voyage brauely did begin
Downe by S. Katherines, where the Prieſt fell in,
By Wapping, where as hang'd drown'd Pirates dye,
(Or elfe fuch * Rats, I think as would eat Pye)
And paſſing further, I at firſt obferu'd,
That † Cuckold's Hauen was but badly feru'd;
For there Old Time had fuch confufion wrought,
That of that antient place remained nought;
No monumentall memorable Horne
Or Tree or Poſt, which hath thofe Trophies borne
Was left, whereby Poſterity may know
Where their forefathers Crefts did grow, or fhow.
Which put into a maze my muzing Mufe
Both at the World's neglect, and times abufe,
That that ſtout Pillar, to Obliuion's pit
Should fall, whereon *Plus ultra* might be writ,
That fuch a marke of Reuerend note fhould lye
Forgot, and hid, in blacke obfcurity,
Efpecially when men of euery fort
Of countries, cities, warlike campes or court
Vnto that Tree are plaintiffs or defendants,
Whofe ‡ loues, or fears, are fellows or attendants
Of all eſtates, this Hauen hath fome partakers
By Lot fome Cuckolds, and fome Cuckold-makers,
And can they all fo much forgetfull be
Vnto that ancient, and renowned Tree,
That hath fo many ages ſtood erected,
And by fuch ſtore of Patrons beene protected
And now inglorioufly to lye unfeene
As if it were not, or had never beene?
Is lechery wax'd fcarce, is bawdry fcant,
Is there of Whores, or Cuckolds any want?

Are

* Any Rat that eats Pye is a Pyrat. † When I paſt downe the River, there was not any Poſt or Horne there, but fince it is moſt worthily repaired.
‡ All eſtates or degrees do either loue or fear this Hauen.

Are Whoremafters decaid, are Bawds all dead,
Are Panders, Pimps, and Apple Squires all fled?
No furely, for the Surgeons can declare
That Venus warres, more hot than Marfes are.
Why then, for fhame this worthy Poft maintain,
Let's haue our Tree, and Hornes fet vp again,
That paffengers may fhew obedience to it
In putting off their hats, and homage doe it;
Let not the Cornucopiæs of our land
Vnfightly and vnfeene neglected ftand;
I knowe it were in vaine for me to call
That you fhould rayfe fome famous Hofpitall,
Some Free fchoole, or fome Almfhoufe for the pore,
That might increafe good deeds, & ope heau'ns dore..
'Tis no taxation great, or no collection
Which I doe fpeake of for this great erection,
For if it were, men's goodneffes, I know
Would proue exceeding barren, dull, and flow;
A Poft and Hornes, will build it firme and ftable,
Which charge to beare, there's many a beggar able.
The place is ancient, of refpect moft famous,
The want of due regard to it doth fhame us:
For Cuckold's Hauen, my requeft is ftill,
And fo I leaue the Reader to his will.
But holla Mufe, no longer be offended,
'Tis worthily repaired, and brauely mended,.
For which great meritorious worke, my pen
Shall give the glory unto Greenwitch men,
It was their onely coft, they were the actors,
Without the helpe of other benefactors;.
For which my pen their prayfes here adornes,
As they have beautifi'd the Hau'n with Hornes.
From thence to Debtford we amaine were driuen,
Wheras an anker unto me was given:
With parting pintes, and quarts for our farewell,
We tooke our leaues, and fo to Greenwitch fell,

There

There fhaking hands, adiews, and drinkings ftore,
We tooke our fhip againe, and left the fhore;
The downe to Erith, 'gainft the tide we went
Next London, greateft Maior towne in Kent
Or Chriftendome, and I approue it can,
That there the Maior was a Waterman,
Who gouernes, rules, and reignes fufficiently,
And was the image of authority.
With him we had cheap reck'nings and good cheere,
And nothing but his friendfhip we thougth deere.
But thence we rows'd our felves and caft off fleepe,
Before the day-light did begin to peepe;
The tyde to by Gravefend fwiftly did us bring
Before the mounting lark began to fing;
And e'r we came to Lee with fpeedy pace
The Sun 'gan rife with moft fufpicious face
Of foule foreboding weather, purple, red,
His radiant tincture, Eaft, North-eaft o'erfpread,
And as our oares thus downe the Riuer pull'd,
Oft with a fowling-peece the gulls we gull'd,
For why, * the Mafter Gunner of our fhip
Let no occafion of aduantage flip,
But charg'd, and difcharg'd, fhot and fhot againe,
And fcarce in twenty times fhot once in vaine;
Foule was the weather, yet thus much I'll fay,
Ift had beene faire, fowle was our food that day.
Thus downe alongft the fpacious Coaft of Kent,
By Grane and Sheppies Iflands downe we went,
We paft the Nowre-head, and the fandy fhore,
Vntill we came to th' Eaft end of the Nowre.
At laft Ramfgates Peere we ftiffly rowed,
The winde and tyde againft vs blow'd and flowed,
Till neere vnto the Hauen where Sandwitch ftands
We were enclofed with moft dangerous fands;

* His name is Arthur Bray, a Waterman of Lambeth, and a good Markfman.

There we were fows'd & flabber'd, wafh'd & dafh'd,
And gravell'd, that it made vs * halfe abafh'd,
We look'd and pry'd, and ftared round about
From our apparent perils to get out,
For with a ftaffe, as we the depth did found,
Foure miles from land, we almoft were on ground.
At laft (unlook'd for) on our larboord fide
A thing turmoyling in the fea we fpide,
Like to Meareman; wading as he did
All in the fea his neather parts were hid,
Whofe brawney limbs and rough neglected beard,
And grim afpect, made half of us afeard,
And as he unto us his courfe did make
I courage tooke, and thus to him I fpake:
Man, monfter, fiend or fifh, what-e'er thou be
That trauelft here in Neptune's monarchy,
I charge thee by his dreadfull, three-tin'd mace
Thou hurt not me or mine, in any cafe;
And if thou bee'ft produc'd of mortall kinde,
Shew us fome courfe, how we the way may finde
To deeper water, from thefe fands fo fhallow,
In which thou feeft our fhip thus wafh and wallow.
With that (he fhrugging up his fhoulders ftrong)
Spake (like a Chriftian) in the Kentifh tongue;
Quoth he, kinde fir, I am a fifherman,
Who many yeeres my liuing thus haue wan,
By wading in thefe fandy troublous waters
For fhrimps, wilks, cockles, and fuch vfefull matters;
And I will lead you (with a courfe I'll keepe)
From out thefe dangerous fhallows to the deepe;
Then (by the nofe) along he led our boate
Till (paft the Flats) our barke did brauely floate.
Our fea-horfe, that had drawne vs thus at large,
I gaue two groats vnto, and did difcharge.

            Then

* We were fiue men, and two of us were afraid, two were not afraid, and I was half afraid.

Then in an houre and halfe, or little more,
We throgh the Downs at Deale went safe on shore;
There did our hosteffe dreffe the fowle we kill'd,
With which our hungry ftomacks well we filled.
The morrow being Wednefday (breake of day)
We towards Douer tooke our weary way;
The churlish windes awak'd the Seas high fury,
Which made us glad to land there, I affure yee;
Blind Fortune did fo happily contriue
That we (as found as bells) did fafe ariue
At Douer, where a man did ready ftand
To giue me entertainment by the hand,
A man of mettle, marke and note, long fince
He graced was to lodge a gracious Prince,
And now his fpeeches fum, and fcope and pith
Is Jack and Tom, each one his coufin Smith,
That if with pleafant talke you pleafe to warme ye,
He is an hoft much better then an army,
A goodly man, well fed, and corpulent,
Fill'd like a bag-pudding with good content,
A right good fellow, free of cap and legge,
Of compliment, as full as any egge;
To fpeake of him, I know it is of folly,
He is a mortall foe to melancholy;
Mirth is his life and trade, and I thinke very
That he was got when all the world was merry:
Health vpon health, he doubled and redoubled,
Till his, and mine, and all our braines were troubled;
Vnto our abfent betters there we dranke,
Whom we are bound to loue, they not to thanke.
By vs mine hoft could no great profit reape,
Our meat and lodging was fo good and cheape;
That to his praife thus much I'll truly tell,
He vs'd us kindly euery way and well;
And though my lines before are merry writ,
Where'er I meet him, I'l acknowledge it.

To fee the Caftle there I did defire,
And up the hill I foftly did afpire
Whereas it ftands, impregnable in ftrength,
Large in circumference, height, bredth, and length,
Built on a fertile plat of ground, that they
Haue yeerely growing twenty loads of hay,
Great ordinance ftore, pafture for kine and horfes,
Rampires and walls, t', withftand inuafiue forces;
That it be well with truth and courage man'd,
Munition, victuall'd, then it can withftand
The powers of twenty Tamberlaine's (the Great)
Till in the end with fhame they would retreat.
'Tis gouern'd by a graue and prudent * Lord,
Whofe juftice doth to each their right afford;
Whofe worth (within the Caftle, and without)
The Sinc Ports, and the country all about,
The people with much loue doe ftill recite,
Becaufe he makes the wrongers render right.
The kindneffe I received there was fuch
That my remembrance cannot be too much:
I faw a gun thrice-eight foot length of braffe,
And in a wheele I faw a comely affe
(Dance like a dog) that's turning of a fpit,
And draw it as it were from the infernall pit,
Whofe deepe abiffe is perpendicular,
One hundred fathome (or well neere as farre)
So chriftaline, fo cleere, and coole a water,
That will in fummer make a man's teeth chatter;
And when to fee it vp, I there had ftood
I dranke thereof, and found it fweet and good.
So farewell Caftle, Douer, Douer Peere
Farewell, Oaft Bradfhaw, thanks for my good cheer.

(To be continued.)

* The Right Honourable Lord Zouch, Lord Warden of the Cinque Ports.

THE
ANTIQUARIAN REPERTORY.

EDWARD THE BLACK PRINCE.

THE Public are here prefented with a curious Portrait of Edward the Black Prince, engraved from a Picture in the Poffeffion of the Right Hon. George Onflow. On the Back of which, in the hand of his father the Right Hon. Arthur Onflow, is the following infcription. This original picture of the Black Prince I had from Betchworth Caftle in Surrey, where it had long been. A'. Onflow.

The Hon. Horace Walpole, whofe judgement in thefe matters is univerfally known and acknowledged, in his Anecdotes of Painting, likewife fuppofes this picture to be an original: his words are

"Mr. Onflow, the late Speaker, had a head of the Black Prince, which there is great reafon to believe was painted at the time. It is not very ill done, it reprefents him in black armour, emboffed with gold, and with a golden lion on his breaft. He has a hat on, with a white feather, and a large ruby ftill in the crown. He appears lean and pale, as he was towards the end of his life. This very curious picture come out of Betchworth Caftle in Surrey."

The history of this prince, and his glorious victory of Poictiers, wherein with an army of twelve thousand men only, he defeated and took prisoner the King of France at the head of sixty thousand, are too well known to need mentioning here. Nor was he less famous for his humanity and moderation towards his captives, which, if possible, did him more honour than the victory. He died 8th June, 1375, aged only 46, and was buried at Canterbury, when, according to common tradition, the real armour he usually wore in battle is suspended over his tomb, instead of those fictitious trophies commonly made use of on those occasions.

Mr. Gostling, in his Walk through Canterbury, seems to countenance this opinion.—As his description of the monument of this prince is extremely full and entertaining, and besides contains some particulars not generally known, it is here transcribed at length, and to it is added the epitaph as given in Rapin.

" When we come up hither from the south isle, the first monument we see
" is that of Edward the Black Prince, son of King Edward IIId. very entire
" and very beautiful; his figure, in gilt brass, lies in it compleatly armed,
" except the head, on which is a scull-cap with a coronet round it, once set
" with stones, of which only the collets now remain, and from thence hangs
" a hood of mail down to his breast and shoulders. The head of the figure
" rests on a casque or helmet, pointed to the cap, which supports his crest
" (the lion) formed after the trophies above the monument, where are his
" gauntlets curiously finished and gilt, his coat of arms quilted with fine cot-
" ton, and at least as rich as any of those worn by the officers of arms on
" public occasions (but much disfigured by time and dust) and the scabbard
" of his sword, which could be but a small one; the sword itself is said to have
" been taken away by Oliver Cromwell. His shield hangs on a pillar near the
" head of his tomb, and has had handles to it." This makes it probable it was a real shield, as had it been made only for the funeral, no handles would have been put on. Mr. Gostling continues----" One cannot observe how warriors
" were armed in those days, without wondering how it was possible for them
" to stir under such a load of incumbrances, and particularly how a com-
" mander could look about him, and see what passed, when his head was in-
" closed in a case of iron resting on his shoulders, with only narrow slits at his
" eyes, and a few holes something lower to admit air for breathing; with all
" these helps, his casque is rather stifling to those who have tried it on, though
" not in action, or in a croud."

" No lefs unfit does it feem for giving or receiving orders and intelligence,
" in the noife and confufion of a field of battle; but that this was then the
" fafhion is plain, not only from this particular inftance, but from the broad
" feals of feveral of our Kings and Princes, for many years before and after
" his time.*"

" As the choir and eaftern part of our church are built over vaults, the
" bodies which reft in thefe parts could not be interred in graves, but are in-
" clofed in altar or table monuments raifed above the pavement.

" This of the Black Prince has a long infcription in old French profe and
" verfe, on brafs plates and fillets round the borders of the ftone, on which
" his figure is laid. The fides and ends of it are adorned with efcutcheons,
" alternately placed, one bearing the arms of France and England quarterly,
" with the file of three points for his diftinction, and a label above it, on
" which is written *houmout*; the other his own arms, viz. three oftrich fea-
" thers, the quill end of each in a focket, with a label crofling there, on
" which is his motto, *Ich dien*; a larger label above the efcutcheon, having
" the fame words on that too. Thefe words, perhaps, were defigned to ex-
" prefs the excellent character he bore, *houmout*, in the German language,
" fignifying a *haughty spirit*, might reprefent him as an intrepid warrior, and
" *Ich dien, I ferve* as a dutiful fon.

" There feems to have been an altar oppofite to the tomb, where mafles
" might be faid for his foul, a ftone ftep very much worn, being under a
" window there, and within memory his plumes, and the arms of France and
" England, as on the monument, were in the painted glafs here; the efcut-
" cheon with the feather has long been broken and loft, the other was a few
" years ago taken away to mend a window at another place."

The

* Mr. Sandford, in his *Genealogical Hiftory of the Kings of England*, has given Prints of many of thefe Great Seals, which fhow that from the time of King John, all the head-pieces were made fo clofe as not to fhow the face; that particularly of this Prince refembles this over his mo- nument, except that is has more and larger air-holes. This fafhion continued till the time of King Edward IVth. on whofe feal we find part of his face open to be feen, as are thofe of his fucceffors to King Henry VIII. the firft that difcovers the whole face by means of a vifor to lift up, which feems to be the defign on his feal.

This invention feems therefore of no earlier date than his days, and if fo there is very little reafon to believe that the fuit of armour fhown in the Tower of London for that of the Black Prince, was ever worn by him, or made till above two hundred years after his death.

The inscription, or epitaph, above alluded to, is circumscribed on a fillet of brass, beginning at the head---

Cy gift le noble Prince Monsieur Edward aisnes filz du tres noble Roy Edward tiers, jadis Prince D'Aquitain & de Gales, Duc de Cornwaille & Comte de Cestre, qi morult en la feste de la Trinite; qestoit le viii jour de Juyn, l'an de grace mil trois cenz septante sisine, L'alme de qi Dieu eit mercy Amen.—

On the South Side of the Tomb. *At the Foot of the Tomb.* *On the North Side of the Tomb.*

Tu qi passez oue bouche close	Mes ore su jeo poures & chetiffs	Moult est estroit ma meson;
Par la ou ce corps repose,	Perfond en la tre gris.	En moy na li verite non.
Entent ce qe ce dirai,	Ma grand beaute est tout alee	Et si ore me veillez
Sy come te dire le say.	Ma char est tout gastee.	Je ne quide pas qi vous deissez,
Tiel come tu es au tiel fu,		Qa je eusse onques home este
Tu feras tiel come ie su.		Si su je ore de tant changee.
De la morte ne pensai je mye,		Pour dieu priez au celestien Roy,
Tant come javoi la vie:		Qe mercy ait de l'ame de Moy.
En tre avoi grand richesse;		Tous ceulx qi pur moy prieront
Dont je y fis grand noblesse.		Ou a dieu macorderont.
Terre, Mesons, grand tresor,		Dieu les mette en son Paradis
Draps, chivaux, argent & or.		Ou nul ne poet estre chetiffs.

To a person skilled in Painting, this Portrait will seem both much out of Drawing, and extremely flat; these faults the Engraver could easily have corrected, but in Pictures of this kind, the exactness of the copy even in defects constitute the greatest value of the Piece. Ancient Portraits serve not only to hand down some resemblance of the person represented, but also the state of the Arts at the time of their execution. Amendments would undoubtedly frustrate information in both these articles.

M. S.

M. S. Dodfworth in Bibliothecâ Bodleiana Oxon, Vol. 147, *Fol* 79.

Communicated by T. ASTLE, Efq:

Noverint prefentes et futuri.

WETES all that be heere
  Or that fhall be lief and deer
That I *Jefus* of *Nazareth*
For mankind have fuffer'd death
Upon the Crofs with Woundes five
Whilft that I was man alive—

Dedi et Conceffi.

I have given and do grant
To all that afke in Faith repentant,
Heavens Bliffe without ending
So long as I am their King.

Reddendo et Solvendo.

Keep I no more for all my fmarte
But the true love of thy Hearte
And that thou be in Charitee
And love thy Neighbour, as I love thee.

Warrantizo.

If any man dare fay
That I did not his Debts pay
Rather than Man fhall be forlorn
Yet would I eft be all to Torn.

Hiis Teſtibus.

Witneſs the Day that turn'd to night
And the clear Sun that loſt his Light
Witneſs the Earth that then did quake
And Stonis great that in ſunder brake
Witneſs the Veil that then did rend
And Gravis which ther Tenants forth did ſend
Witneſs my Moder and Saint John
And By-Standers many a one.

In cujus Rei Teſtimonium.

For further Witneſs who liſt to appeal
To my here under hanged Seel
For the more ſtable ſureneſſe
Thy Wound in my Hearte the Seale is.

Datum.

Yeoven at Mount Calvarie
The fyrſt Daye of y' great Mercie.

N.B. The 5. points in the Heart or Seal are to repreſent the 5. Wounds.

C·H·S  I·H·S·

Seal'd and deliv'd in the preſence of,   *Ita fidem faciunt*
Mary Moder of God, Mary Cleo-   *Matthewe* ⎫
phiæ, Mary Jacobi, John the Diſ-   *Marke*   ⎬ Notarii
ciple, Longinus y' Centurion.   *Luke*   ⎭ Publici.
                                                               John

In Greek above the Seal, the Text of 2d Tim. Chap. 2. v. 19.—Under the Seal, upon a Label,

Cor Chartæ appenſum Roſei vice cernè Sigillum—Spreta morte tui ſolus id egit amor.

From

From the Cuftomhall of the Cinque Ports, corrected and amended in the Reigns of Henry the 7th & 8th.

DOVER. AND when any fhall flee into the Church or Churchyard for Felony, claiming thereof the priviledge for any Action of his Life, the head Officer of the fame Liberty where the faid Church or Church-yard is, with his Fellow Jurats or Coroners of the fame Liberty, fhall come to him and fhall afk him the caufe of being there, and if he will not confefs Felony, he fhall be had out of the faid Sanctuary; and if he will confefs Felony immediately, it fhall be entered in Record, and his Goods and Chattles fhall be forfeited, and he fhall tarry there 40 days, or before if he will he fhall make his Abjuration in Form following before the head Officer, who fhall affign to him the Port of his Paffage; and after his Abjuration there fhall be delivered unto him by the head Officer or his Affignees, a Crofs, and Proclamation fhall be made, that while he be going by the Highway towards the Port to him affigned, He fhall go in the King's Peace; and that no Man fhall grieve him in fo doing, on pain to forfeit his Goods and Chattles. And the faid Felon fhall lay his right hand on the Book & fwear this. You hear Mr. Coroner

" That I A. B. a Thief, have ftolen fuch a Thing, or have killed fuch a
" Woman or Man, or a Child, and am the Kings Felon, and for that I have
" done many Evil Deeds and Felonys in this fame his Land, I do Abjure and
" Forfwear the Lands of the Kings of England, and that I fhall hafte myfelf
" to the Port of DO, which you have given or affigned me; and that I fhall
" not go out of the Highway, and if I do I will that I fhall be taken as a
" Thief and the King's Felon, and at the fame place I fhall tarry but one
" Ebb and Flood, if I may have paffage, and if I cannot have paffage in
" the fame place, I fhall go every Day into the Sea to my knees and above,
" crying Paffage for the Love of God and King N his fake, and if I may
" not within 40 days together I fhall get me again into the Church as the
" Kings Felon.

" So God me help and by this Book according to your Judgement."

And if a Clerk flying to the Church for Felony, affirming himfelf to be a Clerk, He fhall not Abjure the Realm, but yeilding himfelf to the Laws of the Realm, fhall enjoy the Libertys of the Church, and fhall be delivered to the Ordinary, to be fafe kept to the Convict Prifon according to the Laudable Cuftom of the Realm of England.

Extracts

Extracts from an old Churchwardens Book belonging to the Parish of Basingborne in Cambridgeshire.

MEMORANDUM. Received at the Play held on St. Margarets-day A. D. MDXI in Basingborn of the holy Martyr St. George.

Received of the Township of Royston xii^s Tharfield vi^s, viii^d Melton v^s, iiii^d, Lillington x^s. vi^d Whaddon iv^s, iiii^d Steeplemenden iiii^s Barly iv. i. Ashwell iiii^s, Abingdon iii^s, iv^d. Orwell iii^s, Wendy ii^s ix^d. Wimpole ii^s. vii^d Meldreth ii^s. iv^d Arrington ii^s, iv^d Shepreth ii^s, iv^d. Kelsey ii^s, v^d Willington i^s x d Fulmer i^s, viii^d Gilden Morden i^s Tadlow i^s Croydon i^s i^d Hattey x^d Wratlingworth ix^d Hastingfield ix^d Barkney viii^d Foxten iv^d Kneesworth vi^d.

Item received of the Town of Basingborn on the Monday and Friday after the play together with other comers on the Monday xiv^s, v^d

Item received on the Wednesday after the play with a pot of ale at Knees-worth all costs deducted i^s vii^d

Expences of the said play

First paid to the Garnement Man for Garnements and Propyrts and play-books xx^s

To a Mynstrel and three Waits of Cambridge for the Wednesday, Saturday and Monday Two of them the first day and Three the other days vs xid

Item in expences on the Players, when the Play was shewed, in bread and ale and for other Vittails at Royston for those Players iii s ii d

Item in expences on the playday for the bodies of vi Sheep xxii d each ix s ii d

Item for three Calves and half a Lamb viii s ii d

Item paid five days board of one Pyke Propyrte making for himself and his Servant one day and for his horses pasture vi days is iv d

Item paid to Turners of Spits and for Salt ix d

Item for iv Chickens for the Gentlemen iv d

Item for fish and bread and setting up the Stages iv d

Item to John Becher for painting of three Fanchoms and four Tormentors

Item to Giles Ashwell for easement of his Croft to play in is

Item to John Hobarde Brotherhood Priest for the playbook ii s viii d

From

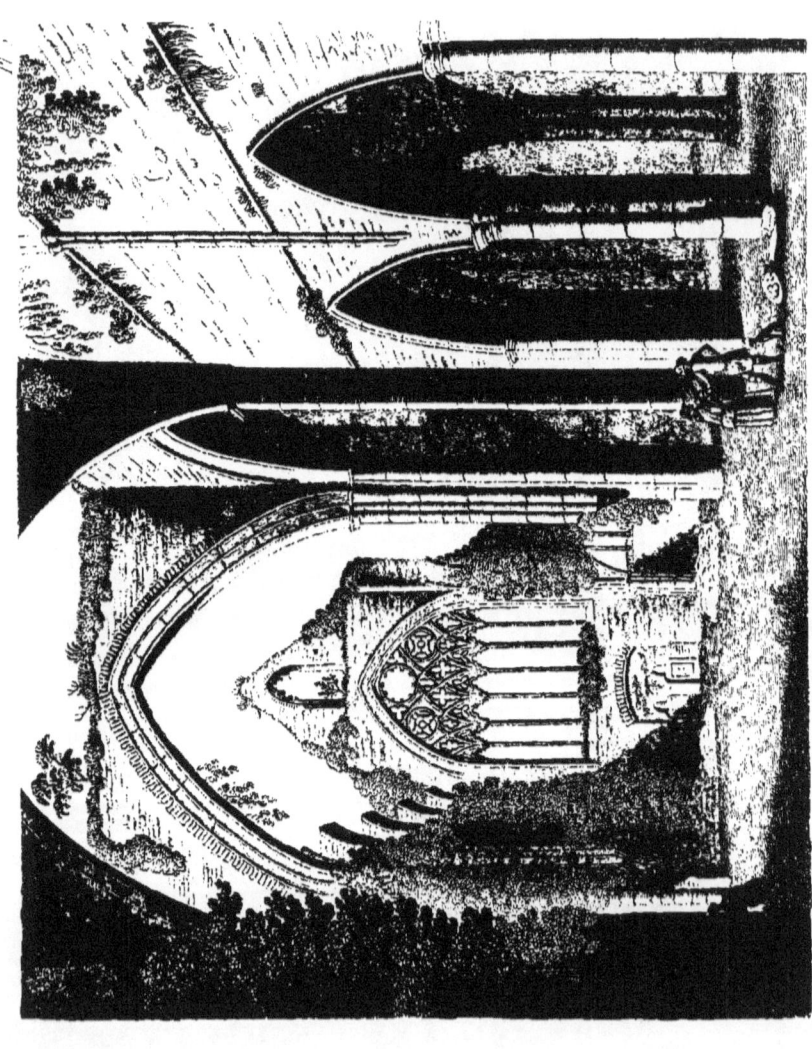

For the ANTIQUARIAN REPERTORY.

To the Writers on Antiquities,

The HUMBLE PETITION of the Words PERHAPS and PROBABLY.

Shewing,

THAT your petitioners have for a long time been moſt unmercifully made uſe of on every occaſion, by writers on ſubjects of Antiquity, to ſupport diverſe contradictory ſyſtems and opinions, inſomuch that they have been more uſed and employed, than any other words in the Engliſh language, oftentimes to their great diſcredit and impeachment, both as to veracity and conſiſtency.

Your petitioners therefore moſt reſpectfully ſolicit, that like veteran ſoldiers, who have performed their duty, they may be ſuffered at length to enjoy that repoſe to which their many labours ſo amply entitle them. And this their prayer may be eaſily complied with, if the Students in Antiquity will pleaſe to deal more in matter of fact, and leſs in conjecture, a meaſure which will greatly tend to encreaſe their own honour and credibility, as well as the repoſe of your petitioners.

Your petitioners are well aware that by withdrawing themſelves, the Antiquarian will be deprived of two of his moſt eſſential ſervants; but they beg leave in their ſtead to ſuggeſt the ancient words, *It ſembleth,* and *Peradventure;* words, which have enjoyed a reſt of many years, and may therefore now, in their turn, well ſupply the place of your petitioners.

But if this indulgence cannot be obtained, your petitioners beg that when ever they are uſed, they may appear in capitals, whereby their great importance and indiſpenſible utility may be rendered conſpicuous.

And your Petitioners ſhall ever pray.

TINTERN ABBEY, MONMOUTHSHIRE.

THE Grand Weſt Window of the Church is here delineated, as it appears from a ſtation almoſt diametrically oppoſite to that from whence the former View of this Building was drawn.

Y y   Nothing

Nothing could have been more magnificent than this Window, when entire and filled with painted glafs; the defign of its tracery is elegant, and well conceived, but its proportions, according to fome criticks in Architecture, are defective, it being, as they fay, too broad for its height. That objection, however, if juft, lies againft the Window only, the remainder of the Building affording as elegant a fpecimen of Gothic proportions as is to be found in any edifice of that ftile; and when it was covered over with a roof, and the glare of light mitigated by paffing through the coloured glafs, it might not perhaps be deficient in folemnity, the want of which has been objected to it.

In a word, with all its faults about it, Tintern Abbey is an object well worthy the obfervation of all curious travellers, who are either fond of Antiquities or delight in feeing picturefque and romantic Profpects; thefe venerable Ruins yielding an ample treat of the one, and the river Wye, and the adjacent country, an almoft inexhauftible variety of the other.

To the EDITOR of the ANTIQUARIAN REPERTORY.

SIR,

ALTHOUGH your Work bears the title of the Antiquarian Repertory, I obferve you fometimes admit Defcriptions of Modern Curiofities; this has induced me to offer you fome abfurd Epitaphs, which I have tranfcribed from tombftones in different church-yards. I hope their very extraordinary ftile and compofition will compenfate for their want of Antiquity, and that they will divert your readers as much as they did

Your humble fervant,

E. L.

In Wimbleton Church-yard, Surry.

Sweet Saviour Jesus, give me wings
Of Peace and perfect Love
As I may move from Earthly Things
To rest with thee above.
For Sins and Sorrows overflow
All Earthly things so High.
That I can't find no rest below
Till up to thee I Fly.

In East-Grinstead Church-yard, Sussex.

I was as Grafs that did grow up
And wither'd before it grew
As Snails do waste within their Shells
So the number of my days were few.

In West-Grinstead Church-yard, Sussex.

Vast Strong was I, but yet did dye
And in my Grave a sleep I Lye
My Grave is Steaned all round about
Yet I hope the Lord will find me out.

In Chidingstone Church-yard, Kent.

Here Lyeth the Body of Honest Hanah Knight wife of
James Knight who stay'd at home
and lived very near, by her Childrens side she
Doth lie, because she loved her Husband & her
Children Dear. who died Decem. ye 6th. 1759
Aged 55 years.

In Minſter Church-yard in the Iſle of Shepey.

Here Interr'd George Anderſon doth Lye
By fallen on an Anchor he did Dye
In Shereneſs Yard on good Friday
ye 6th of April I Do ſay
All you that Read my Allegy. be alwaies
Ready to Dye——Aged 42 Years.

On the Ballaſt Hills, Newcaſtle, Northumberland.

Here lies James of tender affection
Here lies Iſabell of ſweet complexion
Here lies Katheren a pleaſant Child
Here lies Mary of all moſt Mild
Here lies Alexander a babe moſt Sweet
Here lyes Jannet as the Lord ſaw meet

On the other Side of the ſame Stone.

The Burying place of Alex. Leith Margaret his Spouſe & their Children.

When I enjoy'd The Mortal Life
This Stone I ordered from Scotland Fife
To Ornament the Burial Place
Of me & and all my Human Race.

In the ſame Burial Ground.

Here lies the Body of Eleanor Donniſon who
died in 1769 aged 83.
She was Saxon of this
place upwards of 50 Years.

But

Orate pro āinbus johīs Cokerel et Katarine uxoris eius qui istam
fontem in honore dei fecerunt fieri

But now she'. Gone, her Glafs is out
And left the Living to find out
their Burial Places if that
they muft them Learn
Poor Elean is not here to tell
She is lieing in the Grave.

✢✢✢✢✢✢✢✢✢✢✢✢✢✢✢✢✢✢✢✢✢✢✢✢✢✢✢✢✢✢✢✢✢✢✢✢✢

MISCELLANEOUS PLATE.

The FONT *in the Chapel of Orford, Suffolk.*

THIS beautiful Font ftands in the Chapel at Orford; it is of ftone, but according to the prefent barbarous cuftom fmeared over with paint, by which the delicate touches of the chifel are either hid, or extremely blunted.

Its figure is an octagon, having on each face, within a kind of fquare frame or border, an hieroglyphical figure, reprefenting one of the four Evangelifts, or one alluding to the paffion of our bleffed Saviour. Of the firft kind is an Angel in a chair, holding a fcroll, fignifying St. Mathew——— a winged Lion for St. Mark; the Ox of St. Luke, and Eagle for St. John, all likewife holding fcrolls.

The four other figures are, 1ft, The Virgin fitting on a throne, holding the dead body of Chrift in her lap. The head of Chrift has by fome accident been broken off.

2. The figure of an Angel, holding an efcutcheon in his hands, charged with a reprefentation of the Trinity.

3. The figure of a King feated on a throne, holding between his knees a large crucifix.

4. An Angel holding an efcutcheon, charged with the crofs, fpear, crown of thorns, nails, fcourges, and trumpet.

As feveral of thefe are not fhewn in the View of the Font, they are all placed round the margin of the Plate.

Beneath thefe, at every angle, are the projecting heads of Angels, who, fpreading and intermixing their wings, form an agreeable ornament to the bottom of the Font.

This is fupported by a foot, diminifhing towards the bottom, which is likewife octagonal; round it are four figures of fitting animals, fomewhat refembling Rams, and placed alternately with thofe of four Wild Men, bearing clubs, all on fmall pedeftals.

The whole ftands on an octagonal bafe of three fteps; the edge of the fecond ftep is ornamented with flowers. Round its upper furface, near the verge, is cut the following infcription in old Englifh characters.

Orate pro Animabus Johannis Cokerel et Katerine uxoris ejus qui iftam fontem in honore Dei fecerunt fieri.

In ENGLISH,

Pray for the Souls of John Cokerel and Katherine his wife, who for the honour of God caufed this Font to be made.

No date is added to inform us when it was conftructed, though from the ftile of its workmanfhip it feems very ancient. Its cover, which is a dome or cupalo, crowned with a ball, makes an elegant termination, and confpires with its other parts in giving a picturefque and elegant form to the whole.

To the EDITOR of the ANTIQUARIAN REPERTORY.

SIR,

AMONG the many jocular cuftoms mentioned by Blount in his treatife on thofe fubjects, he has omitted one obferved on making new Freemen at Alnwick in the county of Northumberland, which affords to the full as much matter for mirth as any he has there recorded, and is befides at this time

THE ANTIQUARIAN REPERTORY.

time in full force, having within a very few years been complied with. The history and form of it is as follows:

In the reign of King John, that monarch attempting to ride crofs Alnwick Moor, then called the foreft of Aidon, he fell with his horfe into a bog or morafs, where he ftuck fo faft that he was with great difficulty pulled out by fome of his attendants.

The King, incenfed againft the inhabitants of that town, for not keeping their roads over their moor in better repair, or at leaft for not placing fome poft or mark pointing out the particular fpots which were impaffable, inferted in their charter, both by way of memento and punifhment, that for the future all new created Freemen fhould on St. Marks day pafs on foot through that morafs, called the Freemens well.

In obedience to this claufe of their charter, when any new Freemen are to be made, a fmall rill of water which paffes through the morafs is kept dammed up for a day or two, previous to that on which this ceremonial is to be exhibited, by which means the bog becomes fo thoroughly liquified, that a middle fized man is chin deep in mud and water in paffing over it, befides which unlucky wags frequently dig holes and trenches; in thefe filled up and rendered invifible by the fluid mud several Freemen have fallen down, and been in great danger of fuffocation. In fhort, in proportion as the new made Freemen are more or lefs popular, the paffage is rendered more or lefs difficult; at the beft, however, it is fcarcely preferable to the punifhment of the horfe-pond inflicted by the mob on a detected pick-pocket.

The day being come, the candidates, for they are literally fo, being dreffed all in white, preceded by a cavalcade, confifting of the Caftle Bailiff, the four Chamberlains, the Freemen of the town, and a band of mufic, repair to the fcene of action. And on the word, or a fignal being given, they pafs through the bog, each being at liberty to ufe the method and pace, which to him fhall feem beft, fome running, fome going flow, and fome attempting to jump over fufpected places, but all in their turns, tumbling and wallowing like porpoifes at fea, or hogs in the mire, to the great amufement of the populace, who ufually affemble in vaft numbers on this occafion. This fcene being over, the parties return to the town and endeavour to prevent by good chear the ill effects of their mornings exercife.

A Difcovery

A Discovery by Sea from London to Salisbury.

From the Works of John Taylor, *the* Water Poet.

Continued from Page 168.

MY bonny Barke to Sea was bound againe;
On Thurday morne, we lanch'd into the Maine,
By Folstone, and by Sangates antient Castle,
Against the rugged waues, we tugge and wrastle
By Hyde, by Rumney, and by Rumney Marsh,
The Tyde against vs, and the winde blew harshe,
'Twixt Eolus and Neptune was such strife,
That I ne'er felt worse weather in my life :
Tost and retost, retost and tost againe;
With rumbling, tumbling, on the rowling Maine,
The boystrous breaking Billowes curled locks
Impetuously did beate against the Rockes,
The winde much like a Horse whose wind is broke,
Blew thicke and short, that we were like to choake:
As it outragiously the billowes shaues,
The Gusts (like dust) blown from the bryny waues,
And thus the winds and seas robustious gods
Fell by the eares starke mad at furious ods.
Our slender ship, turmoyld 'twixt shores and Seas,
Aloft or low, as stormes and flaws did please:
Sometimes vpon a foaming Mountaines top,
Whose height did seeme the heau'ns to vnderprop,
When straight to such profundity she fell,
As if she diu'd into the deepest Hell.
The Clowds like ripe Apostumes burst and showr'd,
Their mattery watery substance headlong powr'd;
Yet though all things were mutable and fickle
They all agreed to souse vs in a Pickle,

Of

Of Waters freſh and ſalt, from Seas and Skye,
Which with our ſweat ioin'd in triplicity,
That looking each on other, there we ſaw,
We neither were halfe ſtew'd, nor yet halfe raw,
But neither hot or cold, good fleſh or fiſhes
For Caniballs, we had beene ex'lent diſhes.
Bright Phœbus hid his golden head with feare,
Not daring to behold the dangers there,
Whilſt in that ſtraight or Exigent we ſtand,
We ſee and wiſh to land, yet durſt not land,
Like rowling hills the billowes beate and roare
Againſt the melancholly Beachie ſhore,
That if we landed, neither ſtrength or wit
Could ſave our Boate from beinge ſunke or ſplit.
To keepe the Sea, ſterne puffing Eols breath
Did threaten ſtill to blow vs all to death
The waues amaine (vnbid) oft boorded us,
Whilſt we almoſt three hours beleaguerd thus,
On euery ſide with danger and diſtreſſe,
Reſolv'd to run on ſhore at Dengie Neſſe.
Theſe ſtand ſome thirteene Cottages together,
To ſhelter Fiſhermen from winde and weather,
And there ſome people were as I ſuppos'd,
Although the dores and windowes all were clos'd:
I neere the land, into the Sea ſoone leapt
To ſee what people thoſe ſame houſes kept,
I knock'd and cal'd, at each, from houſe to houſe,
But found no forme of mankinde, Man or * Mouſe
This newes all ſad, and comfortleſſe and cold,
Vnto my company I ſtraightwayes told,
Aſſuring them the beſt way I did thinke,
Was to hale vp the Boate, although ſhe ſinke.
Reſolued thus, we all together pleaſe
To put her head to ſhore, her ſterne to Seas,
They leaping ouerboord amidſt the Billowes,
We pluck'd her up (vnſunke) like ſtout tall fellows.

* No dwelling within neere three miles of thoſe Cottages.

Thus being wet, from top to toe we ſtrip'd,
(Except our ſhirts) and vp and downe we ſkip'd,
Till winde and Sunne our wants did well ſupply,
And made our outſides, and our inſides dry.
Two miles frō thence, a ragged * town there ſtood,
To which I went to buy ſome drinke and food:
Where kindely ouer-reckon'd, well miſus'd
Was, and with much courteſie abus'd.
Mine Oaſteſſe did account it for no trouble,
For ſingle fare to make the payment double:
Yet did her mind and mine agree together,
That (I once gone) would neuer more come thither:
The Cabbins where our Boate lay ſafe and well
Belong'd to men which in this towne did dwell:
And one of them (I thanke him) lent vs then
The Key to ope his hoſpitable Den,
A brazen Kettle, and a pewter diſh,
To ſerve our needs, and dreſſe our fleſh and fiſh:
Then from the Butchers we bought Lamb and ſheep,
Beere from the Alehouſe, and a Broome to ſweepe
Our Cottage, that for want of vſe was muſty,
And moſt extremely ruſty—fuſty—duſty.
There, two days ſpace, we Roaſt, and boile, and broile,
And toyle, and moyle, and keepe a noble coyle
For onely we kept open houſe alone,
And he that wanted Beefe, might have a *Stone*.
Our Grandam Earth (with beds) did al befriend vs,
And bountifully all our lengths did lend us,
That laughing, or elſe lying † downe did make
Our Backes and ſides ſore, and our ribs to ake.
On Saturday the windes did ſeeme to ceaſe
And brawling Seas began to hold their peace,
When we (like Tenants) beggerly and poore,
Decreed to leaue the Key beneath the doore,

             But

---

* The townes name is Lydd, two miles from Rumney in Kent.

† Our beds were Cables and Ropes, every feather at the leaſt 10 fathom long.

But that our Land-lord did that shift preuent,
Who came in pudding time, and tooke his Rent,
And as the Sunne, was from the Ocean peeping,
We lanch'd to Sea againe, and left house-keeping.
When presently we saw the drifling skies
'Gan powt and lowre, and Winde and Seas 'gan rife,
Who each on other plaid their parts so wilde,
As if they meant not to be reconcilde,
The whilst we leape vpon those liquid hills,
Where Porpofes did show their fins and Gills,.
Whilst we like various Fortunes Tennis ball,.
At every stroake, were in the Hazzard all.
And thus by Rye, and * Winchelsey we past
By Fairlegh, and those Rockie cliffs at last.
Some two miles short of Hastings, we perceiu'd
The Lee shore dangerous, and the Billowes heau'd:
Which made us land (to scape the Seas diftresse)
Within a harbour, almost harbourlesse,
(We give God thanks) amongst the Rocks we hit,
Yet were we neither wash'd or sunke, or split.
Within a Cottage nigh, there dwells a Weauer
Who entertain'd vs as the like was neuer,
No meate, no drinke, no lodging (but the floore)
No stoole to fit, no Locke vnto the doore,
No Straw to make vs litter in the night
Nor any Candlesticke to hold the light,
To which the Owner bid vs welcome still,
Good entertainement, though the cheare was ill.
The morrow when the Sun with flushed face
In hie diurnall courfe began to trace,
The wind exceeding stiffe and strong and tough,
The Seas outragious, and extremely rough,
Our Boate laid safe vpon the Beachy sand,
Whilst we to Hastings went or walk'd by land.

Much

* I walk'd to Winchelsey, where I thanke my Couzin Mr. Collins, the Maior there, hee made me kindely welcome.

Much (to that Towne) my thankfulneſſe is bound,
Such vndeſerued kindneſſe there I found.
Three nights we lay there, and three daies we ſpent,
Moſt freely welcom'd, with much merriment;
Kinde Mr. * Maior his loue aboue the reſt :
Me and my crue, he did both feed and feaſt,
He ſent vs Gold, and came himſelfe to vs ;
My thankes are theſe, becauſe his loue was thus.
Mine Hoſt and Hoſteſſe Clayton thus I thanke,
And all good fellowes there, I found ſo franke,
That what they had, or what could there be got,
They neither thought too heavy or too hot.
The windes and Seas continued ſtill their courſe,
Inueterate ſeem'd their rage, vntam'd their force,
Yet were we loth and linger and delay :
But once againe to venture and away.
Thus deſperately reſolu'd, 'twixt hope and doubt,
Halfe ſunke with launching, madly we went out,
At twelue a clocke at noone, and by Sun-ſet
To Miching, or New Haven we did get.
There almoſt ſunke (to ſaue our Boat at laſt)
Our ſelues into the ſhallow Seas we caſt :
And pluck'd her into ſafety to remaine
Till Friday that we put to Sea againe.
Then 'mongſt our old Companions (ſtorms and flaws)
At euery ſtroake neere deaths devouring iawes :
The weary day we paſt through many feares,
And land at laſt quite ſunke o'r head and eares.
All dropping dry, like fiue poore Rats halfe drown'd ;
From ſuccour farre, we halde the Boat on gronnd,
Caſt out our water, whilſt we brauely drop'd,
And vp and downe to dry ourſelves we hop'd.
Thus we our weary Pilgrimage did weare,
Expecting for the weather calme and cleare :

But

* The Maiors name was Mr. Richard Boyſe, a Gentleman, whoſe laudable life, and honeſt gouerment is much beloued and approued.

But ſtormes, flawes, windes, ſeas, tooke no minutes reſt
Continuall fiercely blowing, Weſt South-Weſt,
A Town called Goreing, ſtood neere two miles wide,
To which we went, and had our wants ſuppiide:
There we relieu'd ourſelues (with good compaſſiō)
With meat and lodging of the homely faſhion.
To bed we went in hope of reſt and eaſe,
But all beleaguerd with an hoſt of Fleas:
Who in their fury nip'd and ſkip'd ſo hotly,
That all our ſkins were almoſt turn'd to motly.
The bloudy fight endur'd at leaſt ſixe houres,
When we (oppreſt with their encreaſing pow'rs)
Were glad to yeeld the honour of the day
Vnto our foes, and riſe and runne away;
The night before, a Conſtable there came,
Who aſk'd my trade, my dwelling, and my name:
My buſineſſe, and a troop of queſtions more,
And wherefore we did land vpon that ſhore?
To whom I fram'd my anſwers true and fit,
(According to his plenteous want of wit)
But were my words all true, or if I li'd,
With neither I could get him ſatisfi'd.
He aſk'd if we were Pyrats? We ſaid no,
(As if we had, we would haue told him ſo,)
He ſaid that Lords ſometimes would enterpriſe
T'eſcape and leaue the Kingdome, in diſguiſe:
But I aſſur'd him on my honeſt word,
That I was no diſguiſed Knight or Lord.
He told me then that I muſt goe ſixe miles
T'a Iuſtice there, Sir John, or elſe Sir Giles;
I told him I was loth to goe ſo farre,
And he told me he would my iourny barre.
Thus what with Fleas, and with the ſeuerall prates
Of th'officer, and his Aſſ-ſociats,
We aroſe to goe, but Fortune bade us ſtay:
The Conſtable had ſtolne our oares away,

And borne them thence a quarter of a mile,
Quite through a Lane, beyond a gate and ſtile,
And hid them there, to hinder my depart,
For which I wiſh'd him hang'd with all my heart.
A Plowman (for us, found our Oares againe
Within a field, well fill'd with Barly Graine.
Then madly, gladly out to Sea we thruſt,
'Gainſt windes and ſtormes, and many a churliſh Guſt:
By Kingſton Chappell and by Ruſhington,
By little Hampton, and by Middleton,
To Bognors fearefull Rockes, which hidden lie
Two miles into the Sea, ſome wet, ſome dry:
There we ſuppos'd our danger moſt of all,
If we on thoſe remorceleſſe Rocks ſhould fall:
But by th' Almighties mercy and his might,
We Row'd to Selſey, where we ſtaid all night.
There our neceſſity could have no Law,
For want of beds, we made good vſe of Straw,
Till Sol, that old continuall Traueller
From Thetis lap, 'gan mount his flaming Car.
The weather kept it's courſe, and blow'd and rag'd,
Without appearance it would e'r be ſwag'd,
Whilſt we did paſſe thoſe hills, & dales, & Downs,
That had deuour'd great ſhips, and ſwallow'd towns;
Thus after ſix or fiue houres toyle at leaſt
We paſt along by Wittering, Weſt and Eaſt,
Vpon the Lee ſhore ſtill, the winde full South,
We came neere Chicheſter's faire Hauens mouth,
And being then halfe ſunk, and all through wet
More fear'd then hurt, we did the Hauen get;
Thus in that harbour we our courſe did frame
To Portſmouth, where on Munday morne we came;
Then to the Royall Fleet we row'd aboord,
Where much good welcome they did vs affoord.
To the Lord Generall firſt my thankes ſhall be,
His bounty did appeare in gold to me,

And

And euery one aboord the Prince I found
Inſtead of want, to make their loues abound,
Captaine Pendudduck there amongſt the reſt,
His loue and bounty was to vs expreſt,
Whiche to require, my thankfulneſſe I'l ſhow,
And that I'l euer pay, and euer owe.
On Tueſday morning we with maine and might,
From Portſmouth croſt unto the Iſle of Wight:
By Cowes ſtout Caſtle, we to Yarmouth haſted,
And ſtill the windes and ſeas fierce fury laſted.
On Wedn'ſday we to Hurſts ſtrong Caſtle croſt,
Moſt dangerouſly ſows'd, turmoyl'd and toſt;
Good harbour there we found, and nothing deere,
I thanke kinde * M. Figge the porter there,
He ſhew'd vs there a Caſtle of Defence
Moſt vſeful, of round circumference :
Of ſuch command, that none could paſſe thoſe Seas
Vnſunke, or ſpoyl'd, except the Caſtle pleaſe.
On Thurſday, we our Boat row'd, pull'd and hal'd
Vnto a place, which is Key Hauen call'd.
The winde ſtill blowing, and the ſea ſo high,
As if the lofty waues would kiſſe the ſkye,
That many times I wiſh'd with all my hart,
Myſelf, my Boat, and Crue, all in a Cart;
Or any where to keepe vs ſafe and dry,
The weather raged ſo outragiouſly.
For ſure I thinke the memory of man
(Since windes and ſeas to blow or flow began)
Cannot remember ſo ſtormy weather
In ſuch continuance, held ſo long together,
For ten long weekes e'r that, tis manifeſt,
The wind had blown at South or Weſt Southweſt,
And rais'd the Seas: to ſhew each others power,
That all this ſpace (calme weather) not one hower,

That

* Matthew Figge, a right good fellow.

That whether we did goe by Sunne or Moone,
At any time, at midnight, or at noone:
If we did Iaunce, or if to land we fet,
We ftill were fure to be halfe funke, and wet.
Thus toyling of our weary time away,
That Thurfday was our laft long look'd for day;
For hauing paft, with perill and much paine,
And plow'd, and furrow'd, o'r the dangerous maine,
O'r depths, and flats, and many a ragged rocke,
We came to Chrift-Church Hau'n at fiue a Clocke.
Thus God in mercy, his iuft iudgement fparing,
(Gainft our prefumption, ouer-bold, and daring)
Who made vs fee his wonders in the deepe,
And that his power alone aloft did keepe
Our weather-beaten Boate aboue the waues,
Each moment gaping to be all our Graues.
We finking fcap'd: then not to us, to Him
Be all the glory, for he caus'd vs fwim.
And for his mercy, was fo much extended
On me (whofe tempting had fo farre offended)
Let me be made the fcorne and fcoffe of men,
If euer I attempt the like agen.
My loue, my duty, and my thankfullneffe,
To Sir George Haftings I muft here expreffe:
His deedes to me, I muft requite in words,
No other paymen', poore mens ftate affords.
With fruitleffe words, I pay him for his coft,
With thanks to Mr. Templeman mine hoft.
So leauing Chrift-Church, and the Hauen there,
With fuch good friends as made vs welcome cheer:
Some ferious matter now I muft compile,
And thus from verfe to profe I change my ftile.

THE

ANTIQUARIAN REPERTORY.

THOMAS DE WOODSTOCK.

THOMAS DE WOODSTOCK, fo called from the place of his nativity, (the youngeſt ſon of King Edward III.) Duke of Glouceſter. He was (as Mr. Camden deſcribes him) an ambitious man, and of an unquiet ſpirit; he behaving himſelf arrogantly towards his nephew, fell under his diſpleaſure, and being ſurprized in his way to London, was hurried away to Calais, where he was ſmothered between two feather-beds, A. D. 1397. A little before his death, he made a confeſſion under his hand, (as appears from the parliament-rolls) that by virtue of a patent extorted from the King, he had exerciſed regal authority, appeared armed in the royal preſence, contumeliouſly reviled the King, renounced his allegiance, and entertained a deſign to depoſe him, for which he was attainted of high-treaſon after his death ; and his honour being forfeited, was beſtowed by King Richard II. on Thomas Lord De Spenſer, who was created Earl of Glouceſter by that King.

This curious Portrait is in the Collection of the Right Honourable George Onſlow. Conſidered as a piece of Art it is no mean performance, and muſt have been the work of one of the beſt Maſters of the time wherein it was painted. To the Collectors of Engliſh Heads it will be a valuable acquiſition, no Head of this Duke having before been engraved.

Epitaph

Epitaph in St. Nicholas *Church at* Newcastle-upon-Tyne.

HERE lyeth buried underneath this Stone
Of John Bennet both body and Bone
Late of thefe parts, Mafter of the Ordinance
Which deceafed by God's providence
The 8th Day of this Month of July
In perfect Faith, love & Charity;
A thoufand 5 hundred 60 & Eight
Whofe Soul Heaven be trufted went ftreight
Thro God's Great Mercy, Bloodfhed & Death
Which only he trufted to during his breath
So truft we his Wife & children that caufed this,
And Captain Carel a Friend of his.

In the Parifh Regifter *of* Fordwich *in* Kent.

Directed thus from the P. Councell Decr 12th 1566 K & Q^s apparel of Fordwich

For our loving Friend the Mayor and Jurats of Fordwich in Kent.

One Cloake guarded with Velvett
A Jacket velvett embroyderd wth Silver lace
2 Velvett Caps Laced
A p^r of Breeches embroyderd Silver lace.
A Kirtell embroyderd Silver Lace
A Kirtell of Taffata embroy'd Silver Lace
A Kirtell of Sattin Embroy^d D^{o.}
A P^r of Crimfon Sattan Sleeves
A Vardingall, a velvet Jerkin a piece of Satten Embroyd.

Sold 1574. This Apparel with others Sold A^o---Eliz.
N. B. On what Account thefe Clothes were fent is not known.

To.

THE ANTIQUARIAN REPERTORY.

To the EDITOR of the ANTIQUARIAN REPERTORY.

SIR,

IF inferting the following Anecdote is confiftent with your Plan, it is much at your Service; the Authenticity of it may be depended on.

I am, Sir, yours,

Z. N.

ON the 20th of February, 1772, fome labourers employed in breaking up a part of the old Abbey Church of St. Edmond's-Bury, Suffolk, difcovered a leaden coffin which contained an embalmed body, as perfect and entire as at the time of its death; the features and lineaments of the face were perfect, having been covered over with a kind of mafk of embalming materials, which came off entire; the very colour of the eyes were diftinguifhable, the hairs of the head a brown intermixed with fome few grey ones, the nails faft upon the fingers and feet as when living. The body meafured about fix feet, and feemed genteelly formed. The labourers, for the fake of the lead, which they fold to a neighbouring plumber for about fifteen fhillings, ftript the body of its coffin, and threw it out among the rubbifh. A furgeon in the town, hearing of the wonderful prefervation in which this corpfe was found, was induced to make fome obfervations on it, in order to difcover the method formerly ufed in embalming; for which purpofe he made feveral incifions into different parts of the body and limbs, all which he found amazingly perfect, confidering the length of time it had been interred. The brain in particular was very little worfted, and contained in it proper membranes, not being extracted, as was the cuftom among the Egyptian embalmers. After thefe experiments, the remains were put into a ftrong oak coffin and buried eight feet deep, clofe to the north-eaft pillar which formerly affifted to fupport the Abbey belfrey. The furgeon, it is faid, kept one of the arms, which he preferved in fpirits; he has alfo the mafk, before faid to have covered the face, in which the form of the features are fairly imprinted. From the place where this body was found, and the expence and care evidently employed for its prefervation, it was judged to be the remains of Thomas Beaufort, third fon to John of Gaunt, Duke of Lancafter,

Lancaster, by his third Dutchess, Lady Catherine Swineford, relict of Sir Otho de Swineford of Lincolnshire. He took the name of Beauford from the place of his birth, a castle in France so named, belonging to the Duke his father. He was half-brother to King Henry the Fourth, and was, Anno 1410, created Duke of Exeter and Knight of the Garter. In 1410, appointed Lord Chancellor, and in 1412, High Admiral of England, and Captain of Calais.

At the battle of Agincourt, fought the 25th of October, 1415, he commanded the rear guard of the army of his nephew Henry the Fifth; and on the death of that King was jointly with his brother Henry, the Cardinal and Bishop of Winchester, appointed by the parliament to the government, care and education of the royal infant Henry the Sixth. He married Margaret, daughter of Sir Thomas Nevil, by whom he had issue only one son, who died young. He was a great benefactor to this Church, and died at East Greenwich, Anno 1427, whence he was removed hither in obedience to his last will, and buried near his Dutchess, close to the wall at the entrance into the Chapel of our Lady.

It was reported that the body of the above mentioned Lady was also found about the same time, and if deposited in lead, it was in all likelihood treated with as little, or rather less ceremony than that of her Lord, since it does not appear to have been re-interred.

Several other persons of royal and noble blood are buried in this Church, whose remains are threatened with a like disturbance, which though it may not in the least affect the dead, yet as it gives great offence to many of the living, it is much to be wished that any future invasions on these small and silent mansions, may be prevented by the proprietor of the ruins. Indeed a reverence for the sepulchres of their forefathers, and a dread of violating them, seems almost innate, being universally prevalent among the generality of mankind, both civilized and barbarous.

A View

THE ANTIQUARIAN REPERTORY.

A View of ST. JAMES's from the Village of CHARING.

THIS Plate is engraved from an ancient view, fuppofed to have been drawn by Hollar. It appears to have been taken fomewhere about what is now the Eaft fide of St. James's-ftreet.

This Palace ftands on the fite of an Hofpital founded by fome well-difpofed citizens of London, as Tanner fays, " beyond the memory of man, and, (as fome think) long before the conqueft." It was dedicated to St. James, and endowed for the reception and maintenance of fourteen women afflicted with leprofy, and afterwards, by new benefactions, eight brethren were added, who were to perform divine fervice. This Hofpital is mentioned as early as 1100, in a MS. in the Cotton Library.

It was rebuilt in the reign of Henry III. when it was under the government of a Mafter, though the Abbot of Weftminfter claimed a jurifdiction over it, till Henry VI. granted the perpetual cuftody of it to Eaton College, where it continued till the twenty-third of Henry VIII. It was by them furrendered to that King, being then valued at 100l. per ann. and exchanged for Chattifham, &c. in Suffolk. On the fuppreffion, penfions for life were granted to the fifters.

Henry the Eighth having thus obtained the poffeffion of this Hofpital, pulled it down and built in its place the prefent Palace of St. James's: he alfo drained and planted the Park, which was then a wet, marfhy field. This Palace has ever fince the year 1697, when that at Whitehall was confumed by fire, been the refidence of moft of our Kings in the winter feafon, and has from time to time undergone feveral alterations and amendments; the Park in particular was confiderably enlarged by Charles the Second, who added to it feveral fields, planted the limes, and laid out the mall.

IF the annexed Deed of Foundation and Statutes of the Free Grammar School in Morpeth come within your Plan, they are much at your Service; they have not before been printed; I send you with them a short Description of the Building, and am,

Sir, yours, &c.

I. B.

THE Chantery founded at Morpeth was situated on the north-east of the bridge, as you enter the town, very near the side of the river Wansbeck, in a beautiful vale of wood and water, as most of the religious houses in the north are. It was partly pulled down at the dissolution of the monasteries, and remained in that situation till in the sixth year of King Edward the Sixth, when a Grammar School was founded here, and endowed with the whole estates, as appears by the grant annexed—The middle area to the west is entire, except enlarging the windows, and breaking convenient doors, for the original entrance to the west, is built up with a window in the belfry. The north area is almost demolished, and many houses built out of the materials on the ground; in a yard behind these houses, the ground plan may be traced with the greatest ease, which has been cruciform. A very handsome modern built chapel, for the use of the town, was built some years ago on the south, and the Grammar School is kept in the west part, which is entire. I am well informed that some of the estates and revenues mentioned in the grant of Edward VI. have been alienated from the good Purposes of the Founder, are fallen at last into private property, and are so held to this day. It were to be wished that the bailiffs and burgesses would prosecute those invaders on the face of this deed, to recover what is due to the charity. This place, from its healthful situation, the conveniencies of life in great plenty and cheapness, the smallness of the town, added to the abilities of the masters, will, I hope, revive this once flourishing seminary of education; though I could wish, the more readily to effect it, that the masters would exert themselves in some things, and render themselves more publickly known.

An Abstract of a Grant of Lands from Edward VI. *to establish a Grammar School to the Bailiffs and Burgesses in* Morpeth.

EDWARD the Sixth, by the Grace of God of Great-Britain, France, and Ireland, King, Defender of the Faith, and over the Church of England and Ireland Supreme Head. TO all whom these our present Letters shall come, greeting, Know ye that we, as well upon the humble Petition of William Lord Dacre, Greystock and Gilsland, as of the Bailiffs and Burgesses of the Town of Morpeth in our County of Northumberland, and many other of our subjects of the whole Country there adjoining, for founding and erecting a Grammar School there for the instruction and education of youth, do of our special favour, and of our certain knowledge, mere motion and will, grant and ordain, that from henceforth there shall be one Grammar School in the said Town of Morpeth, which shall be called the Free Grammar School of King Edward the Sixth, to be continued for ever. AND we do by these Presents declare, that the said School shall have one Master and Assistant. KNOW ye, that of our special favour we have granted of our free will and pleasure to the Bailiffs and Burgesses of the said Town of Morpeth in the County of Northumberland, all those two late Chanterys in Morpeth in the said County, and all that late Chantery of St. Egidius founded in the Chapel of Witton in the Parish of Hartburne in the said County, with all their Rights, &c. &c. AND all and singular our messuages, lands, tenements, cottages, gardens, meadows, pastures, feedings, rents, reversions, services and hereditaments whatsoever, situate and being in Morpeth and Netherwotton and elsewhere, in the said County, to the said late Chanterys belonging, which had been formerly granted or appointed for the support of any of the Presbyters or Ministers formerly ministring in the said late Chanterys, or any of them. AND also all and singular our messuages, lands, &c. &c. situate and being in Morpeth aforesaid, and in Ponteland, Milburne, Dorris-Hall, High-Callerton, Berwick-Hill, Low-Callerton, and Denington, or elsewhere, in our said County, which have been granted for the support of any Presbyters or Ministers formerly ministring in Morpeth, for the support of the School of Morpeth, or for the support of the Presbyter or Minister in Ponteland in the said County, and the

rever-

reverfions of all and fingular the faid premiffes, in as ample manner to hold as any of the Minifters of the late Chanterys, or any Mafter of the School in Morpeth, or any Perfon whatever, formerly had occupied or enjoyed the fame, as all and fingular the faid premiffes have or ought to have come to our hands, by reafon of any act paffed in our parliament held at Weftminfter in the firft year of our reign, amongft other things made and provided concerning the diffolution and determination of diverfe Chanterys, Colleges, Free Chapels, Gilds and Fraternities, or ought to remain in our hands, which meffuages, lands, &c. &c. are only computed at the clear yearly value of 20l. 10s. 8d. TO HOLD the faid meffuages, lands, &c. &c. to the faid Bailiffs and Burgeffes of Morpeth for ever, to hold of us, our heirs and fucceffors, as of our manor of Eftegrenewicke in our County of Kent, by fealty only of free foccage. YIELDING and paying to us, our heirs and fucceffors, yearly and every year, the fum of 10s. 8d. of lawful money of Great-Britain, to be paid at the feaft of St. Michael the Archangel, for all rents and fervices and demands whatever. AND we alfo give to the faid Bailiffs and Burgeffes, the profits growing out of the fame, from the feaft of the annunciation of the bleffed Virgin Mary laft paft to the date hereof, without fine or gift to us or our heirs and fucceffors for the fame. AND further we grant to our faid Bailiffs and Burgeffes and the major part thereof, power with the then Bifhop of Durham to appoint Mafters when neceffary, to make ftatutes and laws in writing for the government of the fame, the falary, the direction and management of the rents, &c. for the fupport of the faid School for ever. AND we further empower our faid Bailiffs and Burgeffes to take and receive to them and their fucceffors, or of any other Perfon, manors, meffuages, lands, tenements, rectorys, tythes and other hereditaments whatfoever within the kingdom of Great Britain, or elfewhere within our dominions, fo as they do not exceed the yearly value of 20l. as well to fupport the faid School as for the fupport of the Bridge, or other neceffary Buildings in Morpeth, befides the faid meffuages, lands, &c. &c. to the faid Bailiffs and Burgeffes and their fucceffors aforefaid, granted the ftatute of mortmain concerning lands and hereditaments, or any other ftatute, act, or ordinance had or provided to the contrary. AND it is our will and pleafure that the faid Bailiffs and Burgeffes have our letters patent, duly made out and fealed under our great feal of England without any fee or fine, great

or

THE ANTIQUARIAN REPERTORY.

or small, to be made, paid or given for the same, in our *Hanaper* office * or elsewhere.

In witness hereof we have caused these our letters to be made patent at Westminster, the 12th day of March, in the sixth year of our reign.

Inrolled in the office of Richard Hochonson, Auditor of our Lord the King, in the said County of Northumberland, 26th day of March, in the sixth year of our reign. } Signed

NEL BEAUMONT.

E. SHAWFELD.

Statutes and Orders concerning the Free Grammar School of King Edward *the Sixth, founded at* Morpeth, *made and agreed upon by the Bailiffs and Burgesses of* Morpeth, *and confirmed by the Right Reverend Father in God* William *Lord Bishop of* Durham, *the 7th Day of* January, *in the twelfth Year of the Reign of our Sovereign Lord* George, *Anno Dom.* 1725.

1. ALL former statutes and orders being hereby made null, it is ordered that the grant from King Edward the Sixth of certain lands and rents therein mentioned, to be given to the Bailiffs and Burgesses of Morpeth, for the use of a Free Grammar School there, and all grants and deeds executed by any other person or persons for the benefit of the said School, and all counterparts of leases heretofore granted of any of the School lands, and all other deeds, papers and writings, rentalls, terriers, books of account and remembrances, and all other writings whatsoever in any wise relating to the said School, shall be carefully searched for and taken from all papers and writings which relate to the Corporation of Morpeth, and be kept separate and by themselves in the library made, or to be made, for the use and service of the said School, and locked up in a chest or box to be made for that purpose, which chest or box shall be kept under two locks and keys, one key to be kept by the Head Bailiff for the time being, and the other by the Head Master of the School.

2. If the grant from the Crown, or other writing, deed or evidence, be taken out of the common chest and not returned presently, a memorial thereof shall be entered in a book to be made and kept in the said common

* *Hanaper* office is an office in Chancery, Anno 2 Edw. 4. c. 1. The clerk was called the Warden of the Hamper, whose duty was to receive all monies due to the King for the seals of charters, patents, commissions and writs.——Now the Exchequer.

cheſt, which ſhall be called the Book of Remembrances of all things relating to the School, which memorial ſhall be croſt when ſuch grant, deed, writing, or other evidence ſhall be reſtored.

3. A true and perfect rental or ſchedule ſhall be made within the ſpace of ſix months, of all the houſes, lands and tenements, rents and revenues, which were heretofore given and are now belonging to the ſaid School, and in the making of the ſame particular care ſhall be taken to diſcover and come at the knowledge (if poſſible) of any lands or rents which are not now received, or at this time not perfectly known; which rentall, when ſo made, ſhall be put into and kept in the ſaid common cheſt.

4. That a true and perfect account of all leaſes heretofore lett of the ſaid School lands, together with their ſeveral dates and times of expiration, and the rents reſerved thereupon, ſhall be inſerted in the ſaid Book of Remembrances.

5. That a catalogue ſhall be alſo taken of all the books heretofore given to or for the uſe of the ſaid School, and that the ſame and all other books which ſhall hereafter be given to or for the uſe of the ſaid School, ſhall be carefully kept in the ſaid library for the uſe and ſervice of the maſter, uſher, and ſcholars of the ſaid School.

6. That the Bailiffs of the Corporation for the time being, ſhall act and be eſteemed as Governors of the ſaid School, and ſhall from time to time, as often as there is occaſion, repair the School-houſe and keep the ſame in good order, by and with the rents and profits of the School lands, laying out only ſo much as ſhall be abſolutely neceſſary upon that occaſion.

7. That a true ſurvey ſhall be taken of all the lands belonging to the School within the ſpace of ſix months, and that not only the ſaid lands, but all the houſes and tenements belonging to the School, ſhall be deſcribed, and the rentalls and boundaries of them ſhall be particularly ſet down in the ſaid Book of Remembrances, that the ſaid lands and houſes may be the better known for all times to come.

8. That none of the lands and houſes belonging to the School ſhall be lett to any perſon any otherwiſe than by leaſe in writing, and no leaſe ſhall be lett for any longer term than twenty-one years.

9. That on Eaſter Tueſday in every year the two Bailiffs ſhall view, or cauſe workmen to view, all the houſes, gardens and hedges belonging to the School lands, and to ſee that they be kept in good repair and condition.

10. In the choice of the Master singular care and circumspection shall be used, that he be of a healthful constitution and of exemplary life and conversation; pious, sober, grave, diligent and industrious, and of authority to encourage virtue and discourage vice; he shall be a Master of Arts and excellently skilled in the Latin and Greek tongues, and all niceties of both; a man dexterous in teaching, of temper and moderation, rather by fair means persuading to learning and goodness than forcing by severity, and of discretion wisely to distinguish between defects in nature and wilful negligence; such a Master shall be treated with all due respect and encouragement.

11. The Usher or Under-master shall be qualified, as near as may be, like the Master, and none shall be elected Usher or Under-master who has not taken the degree of Batchelor of Arts.

12. When either the Master or Usher shall be chosen and admitted, all Statutes and Orders concerning this office and charge shall be read, and they shall subscribe them with promise to observe them.

13. That the Master and Usher shall instruct in good manners as well as literature, and teach poor mens children with as much care and diligence as the rich; they shall teach all freemen and brothers children gratis, yet may receive what is voluntarily offered.

14. That the sons of all tenants and farmers who have not a freehold estate above the value of twenty pounds per ann. shall be taught for twenty shillings per ann. and the Master and Usher shall ask no more.

15. That the Usher shall teach by the direction and appointment of the Master.

16. That besides the usual performances of the School, the Master shall yearly against Christmas, Easter and Whitsuntide, appoint the two upper forms particular exercises to be recited publickly, and upon recital of those exercises before Easter, he shall give a book to each of the three best performers as an honorary reward for their merit.

17. The Master and Usher shall not both at one time be absent from School, unless for an hour or two at most upon extraordinary occasions, nor shall either of them be out of town in the whole year above twenty days (unless in times of vacation) to be accounted jointly and severally, except upon some great occasion, to be allowed of by the Bailiffs for the time being, or by the Bishop of Durham for the time being.

18. That neither Master nor Usher shall have any benefice with cure, or any curacy, nor any other employment which may hinder their constant and

diligent

diligent attendance at School, and in cafe either the Mafter or Ufher fhall at any time hereafter accept or be poffeffed of any fuch benefice, curacy or employment, and within three months after an admonition given by the Bailiffs, with the advice and approbation of the Bifhop of Durham for the time being, fhall not refign the faid benefice, curacy or employment, he the faid Mafter or Ufher fhall be removed from the School by the Bailiffs.

19. That neither Mafter nor Ufher fhall be a frequent haunter of taverns or alehoufes; he fhall not lodge in a public-houfe.

20. That neither Mafter nor Ufher fhall give up or defert the School without fix months warning firft given to the Bailiffs and Burgeffes, unlefs they can provide themfelves fooner to their content.

21. That if any difference or contention fhall happen between the Mafter and Ufher, the Bifhop of Durham for the time being fhall determine the fame; and in cafe either party refufe to fubmit to his determination, he fhall be removed from the School by the Bailiffs, the confent of the Bifhop of Durham being firft had and obtained.

22. Both Mafter and Ufher in cafe of evil converfation, neglect of the fchool, or breach of thefe ftatutes or orders, may, after two admonitions from the Bailiffs, be removed; yet not without three months warning, and without the Bifhop of Durham firft judging the caufe of fuch removal to be juft.

23. The Ufher fhall take care that the School and all things in it, and belonging to it, fhall be kept clean and in order.

24. The Ufher fhall take care that the School-doors be opened every morning and afternoon to let the Scholars in, and fhut always when the School is done.

25. On every School-day, between the 10th of October and the 10th of February, the Mafter and Ufher fhall be at School at feven of the clock in the morning, and after the 10th of February till the 10th of October, they fhall be there every morning at fix; after dinner they fhall be at School at one and ftay there till five; all the Scholars are to obferve the fame hours; provided always, that on every Thurfday the School fhall be difcharged at three o'clock.

26. No Scholar fhall appear at School with unwafhed hands or face, with dirty or tattered cloaths or fhoes, or any thing elfe that is flovenly or indecent.

27. All

27. All Scholars shall be sufficiently furnished with penknives, pens, ink, paper, and convenient books, all which they shall carefully preserve.

28. No Scholar, when in School, shall remove out of his place without just occasion, or make any disturbance in the School.

29. No Scholar shall quarrel, fight, steal, swear, lie, speak ribaldry, or use cards, dice, or any other unlawful gaming.

30. Every morning, half an hour after the time appointed for the Master and Usher appearing at School, shall be read with a distinct and audible voice, all the morning prayers in Latin, and in the afternoon before dismission of the School, all the evening prayers in English, which morning and evening prayers shall be the same which are used in the Free Grammar School at St. Edmundsbury in Suffolk; and at these prayers shall every Scholar present himself meekly and decently upon his knees.

31. On every Sunday the Scholars shall be present at Church from the beginning to the end of divine service, behaving themselves all the time soberly, attentively and devoutly, the Master always walking at the head of them and the Usher in the rear.

32. Every Saturday, or when else the Master shall think convenient, an account shall be taken by the Master and Usher of all offences committed the week before against any of the Statutes or Orders, or otherwise against piety or good manners, and punishment shall be inflicted accordingly, regard being always had that more favour be shewn to such as offend but seldom and through infirmity, than to frequent and obstinate offenders.

33. If any Scholar shall break the School windows, or do any injury to the School-house or any thing belonging to it, the parents or friends of that Scholar shall make full satisfaction; and in case of refusal, the offending Scholar shall be banished the School for ever by the Bailiffs.

34. In case any Scholar shall be incorrigibly vicious, or after a whole year's experience be found incapable of learning, or shall be much absent from School unless upon sickness, the Master, with the consent of the Bailiffs for the time being, shall dismiss him from the School.

35. On every Saturday all the Scholars shall be instructed in the principles of the Christian Religion, the Master and Usher taking special care that every Scholar shall be able to repeat perfectly, without book, the Catechism set down in the Church of England's Liturgy.

36. Besides the English Catechism nothing shall be taught in School but Latin and Greek, except the rudiments of Hebrew, which the Master may teach such as shall desire it.

37. Every form shall learn such books as the Master shall judge to suit best their several capacities.

38. Exercises shall constantly be enjoined to every form according to their abilities, as oppositions, translations, dialogues, epistles, themes, verses, imitations and declamations.

39. The Scholars of those forms who are capable of speaking Latin, shall constantly do so in School, and the Master and Usher shall often admonish their Scholars to speak Latin when they are out of School.

40. The Master and Usher shall take great care that all their Scholars read and pronounce articulately with due sound and accent, that they well understand their Lectures, and know what phrases are in them, what tropes and figures, and what else remarkable, and repeat deliberately and perfectly, without book, what is requisite.

41. On Fridays account shall be taken of all Orders in the foregoing week, or so much of them as the Master shall require.

42. Times of vacation shall be these and no other, from Osapientia till Monday after Epiphany, Monday and Tuesday next before Ash-Wednesday, from Saturday sevennight before Easter till the Monday after Easter-week, and from the Saturday before Whitsuntide till the Monday sevennight after, all Holidays, all Days of public Humiliation and Thanksgiving.

43. No play shall be granted but for Thursday afternoon, or upon an extraordinary occasion for Tuesday afternoon, the Master to judge of such occasion.

44. That all these Orders shall be fairly engrossed on parchment and put into a frame, and hung up in some public place in the School, that the Master, Usher and Scholars may the better know what they are to do, and what will be required of them to discharge their several duties.

45. That another copy of these Orders fairly engrossed on parchment, shall be kept by the Head Bailiff of Morpeth for the time being, and at the end of his year shall be delivered over by him to the next succeeding Head Bailiff, that they may in their respective years frequently look into the same, and enquire how they are observed and kept by the several persons concerned therein.

I do

I do hereby confent and approve of the abovefaid Statutes and Orders for the Free Grammar School at Morpeth, containing in number forty-five, and do as much as in me lyes (as vifitor of the faid School) ratify and confirm the fame. Witnefs my hand and Epifcopal feal this 12th day of February, Anno Dom. 1725.
W. LS. Durefme.

L. Common Seal of the Corporation of Morpeth.

✣✣✣✣✣✣✣✣✣✣✣✣✣✣✣✣✣✣✣✣✣✣✣✣✣✣✣✣✣✣✣✣✣

PONT Y PRIDD BRIDGE.

PONT Y PRIDD, or the New Bridge over the River Taafe in Glamorganfhire, lies fix miles from Cardiff, in a moft romantic country; the river in fummer is extremely low, fcarce covering its pebbly bed, but after heavy rains fwells to a deep, irrefiftible torrent.

This Bridge, for its extraordinary lightnefs and the width of its fpan, ftands unrivalled not only by any Bridge in England, but even in Europe, and perhaps the whole world, exceeding the arch of the Rialto at Venice by 50 feet, and that of the center of Black-Friars by 40 feet.

It is in figure the fegment of a circle; its chord meafures 140 feet, and the height of the key-ftone, reckoned from the fpring of the arch, is 34 feet.

This Bridge is a proof that extraordinary genius will rife fuperior to every impediment or difadvantage. Both the Mafon who defigned and executed it, and the Workman who formed the center, were common country artificers, unpatronized by the Great, and neither graduated in any Univerfity, nor fellows of any Academy; and fo far were they from having vifited Italy, in order to avail themfelves of the knowledge of the Ancients, or to view the works of the Moderns, that they probably were hardly ever out of their native country; were perhaps ftrangers to the names of Vitruvius and Palladio, and never heard of the Rialto. However, in compenfation for thefe deficiencies, they poffeffed good fenfe, which, as Mr. Pope obferves, " although no fcience is fairly worth the feven."

The name of the Mafon is William Edward; he contracted with the county for a certain fum of money to build them a Bridge which fhould ftand at leaft fix years; and accordingly built one of three arches, but a flood
hap-

happening, which is no uncommon event in this mountainous country, it was carried away by the impetuofity of the river.

He next conceived the defign of conftructing his Bridge of one fingle arch, and accordingly completed it; but here he was again foiled; for the preffure of the abutment not being in equilibrio with that of the crown of the arch, fqueezed it out at the top. Not difheartened at this, and feeing wherein he had failed, he fet about contriving how that fault might be avoided, and hit on the prefent method, by making three cylindrical apertures through each fide, thereby not only confiderably leffening the weight of lateral preffure, but adding greatly to the picturefque form and elegance of the Bridge; which bids fair to tranfmit his fame to future generations. The name of the Artift who formed the center, is Thomas Williams, by trade a Millwright.

The appearance of this Bridge is much hurt by the rude workmanfhip of its parapet; but when it is confidered how great a lofs the contractor fuftained by the failure of his two other Bridges, it is not to be wondered at, that he fhould finifh every part in as cheap a manner as poffible. Beneath this arch a number of ftallectites hang like ificles, perhaps formed by the mortar which the vaft preffure has caufed to exfude through the interftices of the ftones. As the ramp or afcent of this Bridge is very fteep, pieces of wood are laid acrofs the way to give a firm foot-hold to the horfes which pafs over it. The Drawing from which this Plate is engraved, was made by Major Hayman Rooke, Anno 1774.

✣✣✣✣✣✣✣✣✣✣✣✣✣✣✣✣✣✣✣✣✣✣✣✣✣✣✣✣✣✣✣✣✣✣✣✣

To the EDITOR of the ANTIQUARIAN REPERTORY.

SIR,

LOOKING lately over Pafquier's *Recherches de la France*, a Book replete with curious articles relating to ancient manners, cuftoms, and inventions, many of them common to both that and this country, I found the following ingenious conjecture concerning the origin of the numeral letters V, X, C, L, M, D; that is, refpecting the reafon why they were

firft

firſt put to ſignify the ſums of five, ten, an hundred, fifty, a thouſand, and five hundred; and as I do not recollect ever to have met with it in any Engliſh author, think it will not be unworthy of a place in your Repertory, and have therefore here ſent you the ſubſtance of that diſſertation.

The firſt obvious method of reckoning, Mr. Paſquier ſuppoſes to have been upon the fingers, each finger ſtanding for one, and repreſentable by an upright ſtroke, ſo that the number four was repreſented by IIII; but there being no more fingers on one hand, wherewith to continue the account, the number five was conſidered as formed by the firſt finger and thumb, which, when the hand is diſplayed, has ſomething of the V like figure.

The repreſentation of five being thus fixed on, its double or ten was produced by joining together of two V's at their points, which formed a figure ſo like an X, that that letter is made to ſtand for it, being compounded of two V's.

The letter C, antiently written Ⅽ, being the initial letter of the Latin word *centum*, was a very obvious and natural abbreviation of that number; and being divided in two horizontally, each half was a kind of L; that letter was therefore adopted to ſignify fifty. For the like reaſon, the letter M, the initial of the Latin word *mille*, ſignifying a thouſand, is made to ſtand for that ſum; it was anciently wrote thus, ⓜ which being divided down the middle, ſplit into two letters, each reſembling a D, and D accordingly is the numeral letter for five hundred, or half of one thouſand.

Whether theſe conjectures are grounded on truth I will not take upon me to determine; they are, however, it muſt be allowed, plauſible and ingenious.

I am, Sir, your moſt obedient ſervant,

P. B.

To the EDITOR of the ANTIQUARIAN REPERTORY.

SIR,

THE following Account of Carfax Conduit in Oxford, is taken from a Manuscript formerly belonging to Mr. Hanwell, Deputy Treasurer of Christ Church College in that University, which he had transcribed from some of the public Libraries. As it contains an accurate Description of a very curious piece of Architecture, you may perhaps think it worth printing; if so, it is much at your service.

I am, Sir, yours, &c.

EDWARD ISTED.

Some Account of the Conduit at Carfax, *which, in French, is* Quatre Voiz, *or, in English,* Four Ways; *with an Explanation of the Symbols and Figures thereto belonging.*

THE Conduit is a curious piece of fine Architecture, built in the year 1610, as appears by the date facing the East, by Mr. Otho Nicholson, M. A. The building thereof, with the charge of bringing the water by pipes from the Conduit-house near Hinksey, cost no less than 2500l. The Founder was afterwards made Treasurer to King James the First. He was much skilled in the Oriental tongues, and had travelled abroad into several countries. He was a Gentleman well beloved, and whose death was much lamented.

In Christ Church Library, as it is at present, but formerly was a Chapel, near to the stone pulpit is a small monument, containing an inscription well worthy the inspection of a curious eye, the year of our Lord, at that time, being so promiscuously placed by capital letters, as to make up the date of the year in gold letters; over which is a coat of arms, bearing the same in likeness as is carved on every side of the Conduit, viz. E. W. N. and S. of the Ornaments that adorn that Building: first, The whole is exactly square, built with fine polished stone, and was formerly more beautiful than now it is, the four sides being made with hard stones cut all over like the waves of the sea, indented one in each other; but since the University had it repaired

repaired where it was damaged or decayed by time, notwithstanding the great weight of stone work above the stone walls, it was so well contrived with props and pullies whilst doing, as to support the whole top while the sides of the old work were pulled down, and fitted up again, as it now stands, being of free stone, also with the arms of the University, City and Founder, under the cornice: thus on the east side stands the University, City, and Founder's arms, the last of which is azure, two bars ermine, and in chief, three suns shining in their full glory, alluding to his name, viz. Nicholson. On the west side is the City, University, and Founder's coats of arms. On the north side is the Founder's, University, and City arms, and the same on the south; on each corner above the cornice are placed on the three sides of each cube, as many sun dials, making in all twelve; that is, three at the north, three at the south, a like number at the east and west points; between each corner dial facing the north, east, south and west, is finely carved a kind of open work, consisting of the capital letter O, a small figure of a mermaid holding a comb and looking glass; then the capital letter N [*], and a small figure of the sun, and these again successively repeated.

On the four side walls hereof, proceeding from the corners of it, stand as many curious arches, which concentre in the top, or upper part, supporting a stately fabric of an octangular figure. Under and between those arches is contained a large cistern, over which stands carved by a good hand, Queen Maud, sister to the Emperor, riding on an ox [†] over a ford, alluding to the name Oxford or Oxon; the water which comes from the fountain head or conduit house near Hinksey above-mentioned, is conveyed into the body of the carved ox, and thereby the city is supplied with good and wholesome water issuing from his pizzle, which continually pisses into the cistern underneath, from whence proceeds a leaden pipe, out of which runs wine on extraordinary days of rejoicing. Above the foot of each grand arch which supports the other work, is one of the supporters to the royal arms of England, according to the times they were used, in manner following. To the north-west point is an Antelope, borne as a supporter to the English arms in the reign of King Henry the Eighth. To the south-west point is a dragon, used in the reign of Queen

---

[*] The letters ON ON compose a Rebus, being the initial letters of his name, and was an antient way of expressing devices, when there is some analogy between the arms and the name of the person using it.

[†] At present, the figure of the Queen on the Ox is surrounded with brass network.

Elizabeth.

Elizabeth. To the south-east point is a lion, as now used on the dexter side of the arms of England, and to the north-east point is an Unicorn, used on the sinister side as at present. Each of these supporters is sejant, or sitting, holding in their fore feet a banner, containing the several quarterings of the royal arms of England, Scotland, France, and Ireland. Between the above supporters are carved various ornaments, as boys, obelisks, flowers, and fruitage, interchangeably transposed on all the four sides of the Conduit. Above the middle of each arch that supports this curious and stately fabric, stands figures neatly carved, representing the four Cardinal Virtues: 1. To the north-west stands Justice, richly habited, holding in her right hand a sword, in her left a pair of scales, and her eyes covered, to shew the impartial administration of justice. 2. To the south-east stands Temperance, with a rich robe, pouring of wine out of a large vessel into a smaller measure, a fit emblem of it. 3. To the north-east stands Fortitude, holding in her right arm a broken pillar or column, in her left the capital belonging thereto of the Corinthian order in architecture. 4. To the south-west stands Prudence, or Wisdom, holding in her left hand a serpent in a circular form, the tail being in the mouth, denoting Eternity as having no end.

Where the aforesaid four arches meet, at top stands a curious pile of stone work of an octangular form, or eight sides, having as many niches, in each of which stands a fine statue under a canopy, which is fluted within, each figure having a crown of gold on his head, a sceptre in his hand, and a shield on his arm, containing his device or coat of arms. These figures, which stand in the above-mentioned niches, are the Seven Worthies; and our worthy King James the First made up the number eight, as follows: 1. To the east stands King David crowned, holding in his right hand a sceptre, in his left a shield, on which is depicted his device, viz. Blue, a harp gold, stringed with silver, within a bordure diaper'd with red and black. 2. Alexander the Great, crowned with gold, holding a shield of the same, whereon is a lion rampant regardant, or, armed and langhed azure, i. e. tongued and claw'd blue. 3. Godfrey of Bulloin crowned with thorns, in imitation of our Saviour, he being the chief of the Christian Worthies that were then engaged in a war against the Grand Turk, to enlarge the borders of Christianity. From thence it was called the Holy War. He bore on his shield a cross potent between four crosslets, or. 4. Andaticus, or Stapila Roydes Lapides or Gepids, whose shield is or. 5. Corbex volant, Charlemain or Charles the Great, whose shield is parly per pale, or and azure, three fleur de lis, or.

6. King

6. King James the First, on whose shield is depicted the royal arms of England and France quartered with Scotland and Ireland. 7. Hector of Troy, whose shield is or, a lion gules sejant in a chair, purpure, holding a battle ax, argent. 8. Julius Cæsar, the first of the twelve Roman Emperors, whose shield is or, an eagle displayed with two heads sable. Above these Eight Worthies, stand out at some distance several curious figures, representing the liberal sciences; one of which is Orpheus with his harp, representing the science of music, embellished with several sorts of musical instruments, as trumpets, lutes, bases, violins, music books, some open and some shut; figures of boys singing. On the top of all, over the niches, and above the four grand arches which support the rest, stand two figures of human shape back to back, representing Janus, being an old man, looking westward, holding in his left hand a shield, whereon is carved and painted a bat with its wings displayed: the other is a young woman with a scepter in her hand, and both standing under a canopy, above which is an iron rod, on the top of it is a vane shewing the several points of the wind, and over that is a cross representing the four cardinal points of the heavens; also between the niches wherein stand the Eight Kings, that is, the Eight Worthies, are contained ornaments, consisting of a woman upwards and scales of fish downwards, and tapering towards their feet, under which are interchangeably placed the royal badges of the four kingdoms, viz. The Rose for England, the Thistle for Scotland, the Fleur de Lis for France, and the Harp for Ireland. Janus was an ancient King of Italy, usually painted with two faces, representing Time past and to come; also War and Peace. Much more might have been said in commendation of so curious and well-contrived a structure, which for usefulness, beauty, and neatness, is not to be exceeded in the three kingdoms.

Thus far concerning the Conduit is copied verbatim from an original Manuscript, only at the conclusion of that MS are added thus: " But I leave a more elegant account to be done by a better hand; only I say this, he that won't commend me, let him come and mend me;" and so his Manuscript concludes with a FINIS.

To the Editor of the Antiquarian Repertory.

SIR,

THE following elegant Epitaph on Evan Rice, Huntsman to Sir Thomas Mansel, is said to have been written by Bishop Atterbury. As I do not recollect to have seen it in print, I think it well worthy a place in your Work, and am, Sir, yours, &c.

A. B.

VOS qui colitis Hubertum
   Inter Divos jam repertum
Cornu, quod concedens fatis
Reliquit vobis, insonatis
Lætus solvite canores
In singultus et dolores
Nam quis non tristi sonet ore
Conclamato Venatore
Aut ubi dolor justus, nisi
Ad tumulum Evani Risi
Hic per abrupta & per plana
Nec pede tardo, nec spe vana
Canibus et Telis egit
Omne quod in Sylvis deget
Hic evolavit mane puro
Cervis Ocyor ac Euro
Venaticis intentus Rebus
Tum cum medius Ardet Phœbus
Indefessus adhuc quando
Idem Occidit venando
At vos venatum, illo duce
Non surgetis alia Luce
Nam Mors, mortalium Venator
Qui ferinæ nungnam Satur
Cursum prævertit humanum
Proh dolor rapuit Evanum

THE ANTIQUARIAN REPERTORY.

Nec meridies nec Aurora
Vobis reddent ejus ora
Reftat illi nobis flenda
Nox perpetuo dormienda
Finivit multa laude motum
In ejus fita large notum
Reliquit Equos, cornu, canes
Tandem quiefcant ejus manes
   Evan Rifi
Thomas Manfel fervo fidelis Dominus
  Benevolens pofuit.

THE following Extract is copied from a Survey, called, *The Booke of Bothool Baronrye*, in Northumberland, moft beautifully written, and in high prefervation; the property of his Grace the Duke of Portland, to whom that Barony now belongs. It was taken the 20th day of June, 1576, by Cuthbert Carnabie, Robert Maddifon, and John Lawfon, Tenants of that Manor, by virtue of a commiffion granted by Cuthbert Lord Ogle, and directed to the aforenamed Cuthbert Carnabie, Robert Maddifon, Jacob Ogle, Efquires; Anthony Ratcliff and John Lawfon, Gents. the whole five, or any four, three, or two of them. Dated at Bothole, the fixth day of May in the faid year.

TO this Manor of Bothoole belongeth ane Caftell in circumference ccclxxxx foote wharto belongeth ane Caftell greate Chaulmer, parler, vij Bedchuulmers one Galare, Butterie pantrie Lardenor Kitchinge backhoufe brewhoufe, a Stable, an Court called the Yethoufe wharin thare is a Prifon a Porters loge and diverfe faire chaulmeringe an common ftable and a Towre called Blanke Towre, a Gardine ane Nurice, Chapel and an Towre called Ogles Towre and Paftrie with many other prittie Beauldingis here not fpecified ffaire gardinges and Orchettes wharin growes all kind of Hearbes and Flowres and fine Appiles Plumbes of all kynde Peers Damfellis Nuttes, Wardens, Cherries to the blacke & reede Wallnutes & alfo Licores verie fyne worthe by the yeare xx^l.

                  This

This Survey is well worthy the notice of the Curious, even on account of the ancient Caftle therein defcribed, but more particularly fo for the information it gives us, refpecting the forts of fruit then ufually found in our Englifh orchards, which, from the fpecimen here exhibited, feem to have been far better furnifhed than is ufually imagined, efpecially when the Northern fituation of Bothoole is taken into confideration.

To the Editor of the Antiquarian Repertory.

SIR,

YOUR publication of the Draught and Defcription of the Curfew, led me to fearch the Writings of the French Antiquaries for fome information on that head, but to my great furprize I have not been able to meet with the leaft account of any fuch Utenfil, or even any thing refpecting the cuftom which gave occafion and ufe to it, except in Pafquier's *Recherches de la France*, and there fo little light is thrown on the fubject, that I am apt to believe it was no French cuftom, but a meafure fuggefted to the Conqueror by his prudence, and the fear of a revolt among his newly conquered and diffatisfied fubjects.

Monfieur Pafquier fays, the ringing of the Curfew bell was a cuftom long eftablifhed in particular towns in France, and originated, as he fuppofes, in times of tumult and fedition. But the earlieft inftance he gives, is no farther back than the year 1331, when the city of Laon, which had forfeited its privileges, was reinftated therein by Philip de Valois, who directed that for the future a Curfew bell fhould be ringed in a certain town in that city, at the clofe of the day. He then, from Polidore Virgil, cites the regulation of William the Conqueror, (refpecting that fignal) and fays, that he does not fee that he brought it from France, nor does he believe that the French took it from him. If he had affigned any reafons for this pofitive incredulity, it would have given his readers a better opinion of his candour. He adds, that under the reigns of Charles the Sixth and Seventh it came much in ufe; though from what can be gathered from his vague, and even contradictory manner of treating this queftion, it feems doubtful whether it was ever univerfally practifed in France.

THE

ANTIQUARIAN REPERTORY.

The BRIDGE of BRIDGENORTH, SHROPSHIRE.

NEITHER the Builder of this Bridge, nor the Time when it was built, occur in any of the accounts publifhed of this town. The view here given, fhews it was a handfome ftructure, adorned and defended by a Gatehoufe, to ftop the paffage in cafe of any riot or fudden infurrection; though fuch ftoppage could avail but little, the river juft near it being fordable. Great part of this Bridge was demolifhed by a flood in the fummer of the year 1774. It either has, or is to be (as it is faid) repaired or rebuilt with caft iron.

For the ANTIQUARIAN REPERTORY.

IN the Parifh of Berlen near Snodland, in the County of Kent, are the veftiges of a very old Manfion, known by the name of Groves. Being on the fpot before the workmen began to pull down the front, I had the curiofity

curiofity to examine its interior remains, when, amongft other things well worth obfervation, appeared in the large oak beam that fupported the chimney-piece, a curious piece of carved work, of which the following is an exact copy:

Its fingularity induced me to fet about an inveftigation, and to my fatisfaction was not long without fuccefs. The large bowl in the middle is the figure of the old Waffell-bowl, fo much the delight of our hardy Anceftors, who, on the vigil of the new year, never failed (fays my author) to affemble round the glowing hearth with their chearful neighbours, and then in the fpicy Waffel-bowl (which teftifies the goodnefs of their hearts) drowned every former animofity, an example worthy modern imitation. Waffell was the word, Waffell every gueft returned as he took the circling goblet from his friend, whilft fong and civil mirth brought in the infant year. This annual cuftom, fays Geoffrey of Monmouth, had its rife from Ronix, or Rowen, or, as fome will have it, Rowena, daughter of the Saxon Hengift; fhe, at the command of her father, who had invited the Britifh King Vortigern to a banquet, came in the prefence with a bowl of wine, and welcomed him in thefe words 𝕷𝖔𝖚𝖊𝖗𝖔𝖐𝖎𝖓𝖌 𝖂𝖆𝖋𝖋𝖍𝖊𝖎𝖑, he, in return, by the help of an interpreter, anfwered, 𝕯𝖗𝖎𝖓𝖈 𝖍𝖊𝖎𝖑𝖊, and, if we may credit Robert of Glofter,

𝕶𝖚𝖋𝖋𝖊

𝕶𝖚𝖘𝖘𝖊 𝖍𝖎𝖗𝖊 𝖆𝖓𝖉 𝖘𝖎𝖙𝖙𝖊 𝖍𝖎𝖗𝖊 𝖆𝖇𝖔𝖚𝖓𝖊 𝖆𝖓𝖉 𝖌𝖑𝖆𝖉 𝖉𝖗𝖔𝖓𝖐𝖊 𝖍𝖎𝖗𝖊 𝖍𝖊𝖎𝖑
𝕬𝖓𝖉 𝖙𝖍𝖆𝖙 𝖜𝖆𝖘 𝖙𝖍𝖔 𝖎𝖓 𝖙𝖍𝖎𝖘 𝖑𝖆𝖓𝖉 𝖙𝖍𝖊 𝖛𝖊𝖗𝖘𝖙 𝖜𝖆𝖘-𝖍𝖆𝖎𝖑
𝕬𝖘 𝖎𝖓 𝖑𝖆𝖓𝖌𝖚𝖆𝖌𝖊 𝖔𝖋 𝕾𝖆𝖝𝖔𝖞𝖓𝖊 𝖙𝖍𝖆𝖙 𝖜𝖊 𝖒𝖎𝖌𝖍𝖙 𝖊𝖛𝖊𝖗𝖊 𝖎𝖜𝖎𝖙𝖊
𝕬𝖓𝖉 𝖘𝖔 𝖜𝖊𝖑𝖑 𝖍𝖊 𝖕𝖆𝖎𝖙𝖍 𝖙𝖍𝖊 𝖋𝖔𝖑𝖈 𝖆𝖇𝖔𝖚𝖙, 𝖙𝖍𝖆𝖙 𝖍𝖊 𝖎𝖘 𝖓𝖔𝖙 𝖞𝖚𝖙 𝖇𝖔𝖗𝖌𝖚𝖙𝖊.

Or, (if I may presume)

Health, my lord king, the sweet Rowena said,
Health, cry'd the chieftain, to the Saxon maid;
Then gayly·'rose, and 'midst the concourse wide,
Kifs'd her hale lips and plac'd her by his side;
At the soft scene such gentle thoughts abound,
That health and kisses 'mongst the guests went round;
From this the social custom took its rise,
We still retain, and must for ever prize.

Thomas De Le Moor, in his life of Edward the Second, says partly the same as Robert of Glofter, only adds, that 𝕸𝖆𝖘𝖘-𝖍𝖆𝖎𝖑𝖊 and 𝕯𝖗𝖎𝖓𝖈-𝖍𝖆𝖎𝖑 were the usual phrases of quaffing amongst the earliest civilized inhabitants of this island.

The two Birds upon the Bowl did for some time put me to a stand, till meeting with a communicative person at Hobarrow, he assured me they were two Hawks, as I soon plainly perceived by their bills and beaks, and were a Rebus of the Builder's Name. There was a string from the neck of one Bird to the other, which, 'tis reasonable to conjecture, was to note that they must be joined together to shew their signification; admitting this, they were to be red Hawks. Upon enquiry, I found a Mr. Henry Hawks, the owner of a Farm adjoining to Groves; he assured me, his father kept Grove Farm about forty years since, and that it was built by one of their name, and had been in his family upwards of four hundred years, as appeared by an old Lease in his possession.

The Apple Branches on each side of the Bowl, I think, means no more than that they drank good Cyder at their Wassails. The Saxon words at the extremities of the Beam are already explained, and the Mask carved Brackets beneath, correspond with such sort of work before the fourteenth century.

T. N.

WESTON

WESTON HOUSE, WARWICKSHIRE.

THIS is the Manfion Houfe of the ancient Manor of Wefton, an account of which Manor, as far back as the reign of Edward the Firft, is preferved in Dugdale's Hiftory of Warwickfhire.

It was built in the reign of Henry the Eighth by William Sheldon, Efq; who obtained licence from that King in the thirty-feventh year of his reign, to impark three hundred acres of land, meadow, pafture, and wood, to be called by the name of Wefton Park for ever, as alfo a Charter of Free Warren to himfelf and heirs.

Queen Elizabeth vifited Wefton: an apartment in that Houfe ftill retains the name of the Queen's Chamber, as does another that of the Maids of Honour's Room; her Coat of Arms ftill remains over the front door.

The working of Tapeftry was, it is faid, firft introduced into England by the above-named William Sheldon, who, at his own expence, brought Workmen from Flanders, and employed them in weaving Maps of the different Counties of England, feveral of which ftill hang in the large room here.

This Houfe is fituated on a fine Knole, from which the lawn gradually defcends, and is bounded by clumps and a grove of very large trees; the extenfive profpects, the inequality of the ground, and the luxuriancy of the trees, make the whole extremely picturefque and beautiful.

This Drawing was taken in the Year 1773.

THE

THE following Sketch, &c. entitled, "A Defcription of England and Scotland," was written by one Stephen Perlin, an Ecclefiaftic, and publifhed at Paris, Anno 1558. It was dedicated to the Dutchefs of Berri. This Book was extremely fcarce, but has lately been re-publifhed with another Tract, likewife very rare, defcribing the Entry of the Queen-Mother of France into Great-Britain, Anno 1639; with many valuable and ingenious Notes. As the French in which it is written is almoft obfolete, and in many Places obfcure, the Editor hopes the following Tranflation will not be unacceptable to his Readers.

THE Author feems to have imbibed every national Prejudice, which ought to have been excluded from the Mind of a Traveller: yet it is not to be doubted, but what he fays refpecting this nation, was then the general Opinion of moft of his Countrymen, perhaps of moft Foreigners; and, probably, his Portraits of Englifh Manners, though overcharged, may not be totally deftitute of Likenefs. As a literary Compofition, little can be faid for it.

ENGLAND for beauty is the fecond city in Chriftendom, rich, opulent, and, if compared with other fmall kingdoms, great. It may meafure four hundred miles; that is to fay, two hundred leagues in length; certainly it is a great length from England to Scotland; but its breadth is fmall, and in my opinion does not exceed thirty leagues, in fo much that it is a long, narrow gut of land. This kingdom is fituated in the ocean, main, or great fea, which encompaffes the whole earth; for, according to Cofmographers and poets, there are four forts of feas; that is to fay, the Ocean, Mediterranean, Adriatique, and Frozen Seas. This land is alfo at the extremity of the world, and feparated from the reft of the earth, as is teftified by that moft excellent and fcientific poet, Virgil, in his firft Bucolick, where he introduces Melibœus converfing with Tityrus. Tityrus [a] complaining of having loft his lands and country of Mantua, fays, "The greater part of

[a] Our author here quoted by memory. The paffage he alludes to is thus rendered by Trap. It is fpoken by Melibœus, and not by Tityrus.

    But we to diftant climes, muft banifh'd go,
    Some to parch'd *Africk*'s fands; to Scythia, fome;
    To *Crete* and turbulent Oäxe's ftream,
    And *Britain*, quite from all the world disjoin'd.

us shall inhabit the cold Scythia, the rest the arrid Africa, and afterwards we shall come to the rapid river of Oaxus; and from thence scattered abroad, wander towards the English, separated from the rest of the world. England has, from the earliest ages, been called the Greater Bretaingne; in it are three principal dutchys, namely, the dutchy of Wales, the dutchy of Norct, and the dutchy of Cornuaille; it is true, there are other little dutchys, such as the dutchy of Northumberland, &c. In this little kingdom are many woods, oxen, cows, and calves; many herds of swine, which are generally small, and either black, or at least spotted with black. There are some considerable tracts of arable land, as when you have passed London to go to Cabruches [b], Bristo, Neuchastel; and near the road leading towards Scotland, you meet with some tolerable good land.

Here is plenty of silver money, and the gold coin is large; there is also a great abundance of hides, linens, woollen cloth, metals, good tin, lead, and many fisheries, which bring in considerable revenues.

Their capital city is called in French Londres, in English London; it is a very beautiful and excellent city, and, after Paris, one of the most beautiful, largest and richest places in the whole world; one must not mention with it Lisbon, the capital and metropolitan city of Portugal; nor Antwerp; nor Pampelune, a city of Navarre; nor Burgos in Spain; nor Naples; nor divers others, neither for extent nor riches: for, first, this city is rich in grocery, in cloth, linens, fisheries, and has one of the most beautiful bridges in the world. In it are several streets, as the street of *Blanchapton* [c], *Paternostre* [d] street, and the street of *Sodouart* [e]. There are beautiful suburbs, which are even greater than the city itself; as the suburbs of *Oisemestre* [f], the suburbs of *Oincestre* [g], and those of *Sodouart*. Their principal church is dedicated to St. Paul, which they call in their language, Paules; and when they would say, which is the way to St. Paul's church? they say, *ou es ou est goud ad Paules*.

In London you will see the apprentices in their gowns, standing against their shops and the walls of their houses bare-headed, in so much that passing through the streets you may count fifty or sixty thus stuck up like idols, holding their caps in their hands.

In this city are many beautiful mansions and palaces, which are the dwellings of the milors, or chief nobility; whilst I was in England there were

[b] Cambridge. [c] Perhaps Whitechapel. [d] Pater-noster. [e] Southwark. [f] Westminster. [g] Winchester.

milor

THE ANTIQUARIAN REPERTORY. 223

milor Notumbellant [h], milor Marquis [i], milor Ouardon [k], Cobham, Grec [l], Arondelle, and milor Suphor [m]; and then the bifhop of Winchefter, and the milor Courtenay, were prifoners in the Tower. Monfieur Badaulphin was ambaffador for the king, and governed the little king Edward; for that lord had many great banquets, and honourable entreated the moft noble king Henry of Valloys, and at that time there was a noble feftival [on account of the wedding] of the daughter of milord Notumbellant to the fon of [n] the duke of Suphor; who would have thought that fortune would have turned her robe, and exercifed her fury upon thefe two great lords?

The king of this country caufes himfelf to be titled King of France, at which I was provoked almoft to death. His ftile is thus proclaimed in Englifh, *Edouart of grace lorde ged the quin and Angleterre, and France and Irelande*; which is to say in French, Edward by the Grace of God King of France, England and Ireland.

But a time will come that the prognoftick fhall be accomplifhed, and that Henry fhall no longer bear a crefcent for his device, for the half-moon fhall be completed, and the motto, *donec totam impleat orbem*, fhall no more be ufed. The ftars promife him all Italy fhortly, as the kingdom of Naples, Sicily, and the dutchy of Milan, for all Italy is probably deftined to change hands, and this is a great fecret; and then a little king of England fhall no longer arrogate to himfelf this honour, and this land fhall become one of the defolated kingdoms, and that not without caufe.

One may fay of the Englifh, they are neither valiant in war, nor faithful in peace. Cæfar, in his Commentaries, fays, That England is an ifland in the fea, ferving as a retreat for thieves and robbers; for it being inhabited, many banifhed perfons and vagabonds fixed their refidence there; in fo much that the emperor Julius Cæfar fays, their language is compofed from all the different nations, and is an affemblage or jumble of all tongues; which, in truth, I find to be true, for their language partakes as well of the German as of divers others; on which account, the poets of paft times have defpifed their pretences to antiquity, and have always eftimated them as a ftrange and barbarous people, not deducing their origin from the Aborigines, but from ftrangers, barbarians, and runaways; as when any country has been deftroyed

[h] Northumberland [i] Thomas Parr, Marquis of Northampton. [k] Warden of the Cinque Ports. [l] Probably, Grey. [m] Duke of Suffolk. [n] Suffolk had no fon, he here confounds the parties. It fhould be the duke of Northumberland's fon and the duke of Suffolk's daughter.

by

by war, the inhabitants have come by sea and settled in Great-Britain. The people of this country have a mortal hatred for the French as their ancient enemies, and in common call us *France chenesve* [o], *France dogue* [p], which is to say, French rascals and French dogs; they also call us *or son* [q], i. e. vile sons of whores.

In this kingdom there are few fortified towns, for, according to my judgment, and the observations I have made in travelling, there are not above twenty-five towns enclosed with walls and ditches; true it is, there are several good and rich hamlets, in which are many fine mansions. You have Rye, D'ovre [r], Gravezin [s], and other handsome towns. Rie, which is opposite to Normandy, and has a castle. Douure [t] has a castle situated on a high mountain, which commands the sea on all sides. Opposite, in Picardie and parts belonging to the king of France, is Calais, which is his property; it is a very strong city, well fortified on every side, the sea flowing into its ditches; without is a castle, half a league or thereabouts in the way from Boulogne, with many marshes and strong grounds. The said county of Calais is very small, for from Calais to Huiffan, which belongs to the king, it is but two leagues, and from Huiffan to Ambreteuil two more. The English make much use of tapistry and painted cloths, which are well executed, and in which are a profusion of fine crowned roses, also fleur de lis and lyons [u], there being few houses in which you will not find these tapistrys. The common people are proud and seditious, of an evil conscience, and unfaithful to their promises, is apparent by experience. These villains hate all sorts of strangers, and although they are placed in a good soil, and a good country, as I have before alledged, they are wicked and extremely fickle, for at one moment they will adore a prince, and the next moment they would kill or crucify him. They may boast that they have conquered the French; but in answer I say, they were driven out like mad dogs. Secondly, the kingdom of France was then small, it has since been increased seven-fold, I may truly say twenty times, as well in force as riches; in so much as to render that kingdom equal in value to all the rest of Christendom. It displeases me that these villains, in their own country, spit in our faces, although when they are in France, we treat them like little divinities, in which the French demonstrate themselves to be of a noble and generous spirit. If one may

[o] French knave. [p] French dog. [q] Whoreson. [r] Dover. [s] Gravesend. [t] Dover.
[u] The King's Arms.

speak

speak of the genealogy of the French, we shall find they are descended from the Trojans, the most valiant people in the world, and most addicted to chivalry, for from them came the Romans, who vanquished the whole world. In this kingdom of England are two Universities, that is to say, Cäbruches and Auxonne, called in Latin Auxonia; Cambruche, in Latin, is called Cambrusium. The people of this country scarcely ever travel, or but little, and are not much given to letters, but only to vanity and ambition, and to all sorts of merchandize, The Italians frequent this country much on account of the Bank. Mr. Badaulphin was here at the same time as I, and afterwards came Monsieur de Nouailles with his wife, who had much trouble from the English.

The Service of their Church is performed in English, their Sermons in several Languages; that is, in the Flemish Church their Sermons are in Flemish; at the Church of St. Anthony, which was the French Church, the preaching was in French; the preacher was called Master Francis, a fair man; and another preacher was named Master Richard, a man with a black beard. The English several times attempted to set fire to the Church of St. Anthony. Good Lord, what a Sedition was I witness to! It happened that King Edward was sick at the Castle of Grenois [a]; his illness lasted three months, at the expiration of which he died. Then might you every where behold the people trembling, groaning, and beating their breasts; then were all the milors much troubled, not knowing what steps to take. Hereupon, milor Notombellant called together all the chief Nobility, called lors, and set forth in several speeches, that Henry the Eighth, King of England, had several wives, of which one was the Mother of Madam Mary, who then pretended to the Crown, and who is at present Queen, whose Mother having been found guilty of Adultery, was condemned by the Privy Council of England, and all her posterity bastardized, and deprived of all claims to royalty; and that thereupon the King had, by his last will, directed that his Young Son [b] should be King, without having any regard to Madame Marie and Madame Elizabeth, his daughters, which will was signed by the hand of the said Henry the Eighth, and approved and confirmed by an arret; of which will the Duke of Notombellant availed himself, and remonstrated to the Council that his daughter ought to be Queen, and that she was by her

[a] Greenwich.
[b] Petit fils, says the Original, which is in reality Grandson.

Mother's side nearly allied to the Crown; for different from all other Kingdoms, the Females here succeed to the throne. Many milors sided with him, and principally the Duke of Suphor, the milor Arondelle, and the milor Marquis; and the said Notombellant caused his daughter, named Madam Jane, to be proclaimed Queen of the Country, who, as I have before said, was married to milor Suphor. At her proclamation, the people neither made any great feasts [c], nor expressed any great satisfaction, neither was one bonfire made. The milor Notombellant set out to apprehend Madam Mary, in order to bring her prisoner to the Castle of the Tower, and took with him the duke of Suphor, the milor Arondelle, and the milor Marquis, accompanied with fourteen or fifteen hundred horse.

But here Fortune proved adverse to him and his enterprize, for being abandoned by his people, the poor Prince, he, and the duke of Suphor, and the milor Arondelle, were ignominiously and basely taken prisoners, without having struck one stroke, or shewed themselves men of courage. This behaviour was undoubtedly very pusillanimous. They were conducted to the Castle of the Tower, under an escort of about eight hundred men. The poor Prince was ill advised, he ought, notwithstanding any opposition that might have been made against him, to have sent milor Arondelle to take possession of the Castle of d'Ovre, the good man Suphor to occupy the Tower, the milor Marquis to the Castle at Rie, and his son-in-law to some other port, which he might have easily effected, for I am certain that the whole Kingdom trembled at his nod; and he, on the other hand, ought to have given battle to the Queen, and have drawn to his party this seditious and noisy people, by the promises of money, which he might without difficulty have done, for the deceased King left treasure in the Tower. But God, who alone distributes victories, would not permit it; and cities are in vain guarded by great captains and armed men, if God does not protect them: wherefore, in the government of a Kingdom, God ought to be implored on all occasions, he being our most faithful Guardian, which the royal prophet David has well taught us. The afore-mentioned prisoners were taken to the Tower; the mob called the milor Notumbellant vile traitor, and he furiously eyed them with looks of resentment; two days afterwards he was taken by water in a little bark to Ousemestre [d], a royal palace, principally to indict and try him; his tryal was not long, for it did not last more than fifteen days at.

[c] My grad Joye, to agree with the rest of the sentence ought to be, ny grand Joye.
[d] Westminster.

most;

moſt; and he, the duke of Suphor, and the milor Arondelle, were condemned by an arret of Council to be beheaded in an open place, before the Caſtle of the Tower; and they had all three the pain of ſeeing one under the hands of an hangman, before whom a whole kingdom had trembled, which, reader, was a lamentable ſpectacle. This hangman was lame of a leg, for I was preſent at the execution, and he wore a white apron like a butcher. This great Lord made great lamentations and complaints at his death, and ſaid this prayer in Engliſh, throwing himſelf on his knees, looking up to heaven, and exclaiming tenderly: *Lorde God mi fatre prie fort ens poore ſiners nend vand in the koore of our teath*; which is to ſay in French, Lord God my father, pray for us men and poor ſinners and principally in the hour of our death. After the execution, you might ſee little children gathering up the blood which had fallen through the ſlits in the ſcaffold on which he had been beheaded. In this country the head is put upon a pole [e], and all their goods were confiſcated to the Queen, who cauſed the images to be replaced, and brought back the ſervice to the Latin language, and made ſeveral proclamations, edicts and prohibitions throughout all England againſt eating of fleſh on Fridays and Saturdays, on pain of being hanged and ſtrangled. And then you might have ſeen thoſe which had been Biſhops, who had been diſplaced by the young King Edward, and his late father Henry, coming in great joy and magnificence about the town, mounted on mules and little pompous horſes, dreſſed in great gowns of black camblet, over which were beautiful ſurplices, their heads covered with ſattin hoods like thoſe worn by the Monks, being joyous on account of the Queen's victory.

In the mean time the Queen made her public entry into London in great ſtate and magnificence, the citizens [f] children walking before her magnificently dreſſed, afterwards followed gentlemen habited in velvets of all ſorts, ſome black, others in white, yellow, violet and carnation; others wore ſattins or taffety, and ſome damaſks of all colours, having plenty of gold buttons; afterwards followed the mayor of the city, with ſeveral handſome companies, and the chiefs or maſters of the ſeveral trades; after them the

[e] Billiant de bow, may likewiſe be tranſlated a block. In France criminals are beheaded kneeling, ſo that the laying of the head on the block, as is the cuſtom here, might, probably, appear to a Frenchman ſtrange and worth remarking.

[f] Les enfans de la ville, perhaps meant charity children, though their being magnificently dreſſed ſeems to contradict this ſuppoſition.

milors

milors richly habited, and the most considerable knights; next come the ladies, married and single, in the midst of whom was Madame Mary, Queen of England, mounted on a small white ambling nag, the housings of which were fringed with gold thread; about her were six lacqueys, habited in vests of cloth of gold. The Queen herself was dressed in violet-coloured velvet, and was then about forty years of age, and rather fresh coloured. Before her were six lords bareheaded, each carrying in his hand a golden mace, and some others bearing the arms [g] and crown. Behind her followed the archers, as well of the first as the second guard.

Those of the first guard were clothed in scarlet, bound with black velvet, and on their escutcheons they had a golden rose, which is called in English *Rose peni*, and under this rose was a golden crown with high leaves, in form of an imperial crown. The second guard were clothed in scarlet, bound with black velvet, and on their escutcheons was interwoven a true lover's knot, and an E in the middle, and on the other side an R, done in order to make a distinction between the two guards. She was followed by her sister, named Madame Elizabeth, in truth a beautiful princess, who was also well accompanied by ladies, both married and single. Then might you hear the firing of divers pieces of artillery, bombards and cannons, and many rejoicings made in the City of London; and afterwards the Queen being in triumph and royal magnificence in her palace and castle of Oycemestre [h], took it into her head to go to hear mass at *Paules*, that is to say, at the church of St. Paul, and she was attended by six hundred Guards, besides the Ceré [i], that is to say, the servants of lors and nobles. In English, the word *lors* means lords, the *milors* are princes of the council, and those nearly allied to the crown; these we in French barbarously call *milours*, but in English they are stiled *milors*, as those well know who have visited this country, and speak good English. These servants carried halberts [k]. It happened that an Englishman, during mass, threw a dagger at the priest, making a great tumult, mass not having been celebrated in this country for six or seven years. This man was immediately seized, indicted and tried, and on the spot instantly condemned to death. There was also in my time another disturbance in a little church in the Borough of Southwark, respecting a priest

---

[g] Swords of state. [h] Westminster.
[i] Ceré, perhaps Ciré, a name given in Flanders to those who bear wax tapers at public processions. [k] It is possible these servants might carry both halberts and tapers.

who narrowly escaped being killed whilst saying mass; the Queen made use of such horrible punishments, and by the effusion of human blood so established her authority, that every body was astonished and terrified at remaining in the kingdom. After this proclamation was made, that all strangers should depart the realm, and then all the English preachers left England, some going to the kingdom of Denmark, and others to the kingdom of Suest, otherwise called the kingdom of Sweden, and others elsewhere. And then the canons of St. Paul's might be seen saying their vespers and mattins as in France. In this kingdom are many beautiful ships, so handsome are hardly to be seen elsewhere in the whole world; and in this country are many fine islands, and much fine pasture, so that being on the water it affords great pleasure to see the fine islands, in which are plenty of game, for these are all surrounded with woods and thick hedges, and it is not at all uncommon to see at one time an hundred rabbits running about in one meadow. In this country the men, as well nobility as traders and husbandmen, never lard their meat, but only anoint it with butter. The King of this Country levies great taxes on his subjects, as charges, descents, acquittances, appenage, and other great royal taxes; and on those leaving the kingdom, what is called *feuliage* [a], for when strangers are leaving the kingdom of England they are searched, and footmen may only carry out ten crowns, and horsemen twenty crowns, for if they have much wealth they must convert it into merchandize, as the gold and silver must remain in the country; this I have in my time seen practised. An ambassador who has his passport is not subject to this regulation, neither he nor his retinue are searched. Whilst I remained in England there were garrisons all over the country. The people of this country make good cheer, and dearly love junketting; and you will see many rich taverns, and the tavern-keepers have commonly large purses, in which are three or four smaller ones full of money, whence you may gather that this country is very rich, and that people in trade gain more in one week, than those in Germany or Spain do in a month; for here you may commonly see artizans, such as hatters and joiners, play at tennis for a crown, which is not often seen elsewhere, particularly on a working-day, and continually feasting in a tavern upon rabbits, hares, and all kinds of meat. The naturalized French residing in this country, are Normans of the district of Caux. They are a cursed and wicked sort of Frenchmen, worse than all the English.

[a] Perhaps *fouillage*, a fee for searching, from the verb *fouiller*.

Both fish and butter are cheap, for I once bought nine place for a denier, but you muſt underſtand that the denier is worth nine tournois French money, or thereabouts, and is called a *peni*. In this country there are many ſorts of money, the firſt piece is called a *fardin*, another a *hahapeni*, which is to ſay, the half of a penny, another is called a *peni*, another a *gros* [b], another *ſixpens*, another a *chelin*, and five ſhillings a *courone*. The Engliſh are very fond of French crowns, which they call in their language *Franche couronne*, and value it at nineteen and twenty gros. The men are large, handſome and ruddy, with flaxen hair, being in a northern latitude. Their women, of any eſtimation, are the greateſt beauties in the world, and as fair as alabaſter, without offence to thoſe of Italy, Flanders and Germany, be it ſpoken: they are alſo chearful and courteous, and of a good addreſs.

The Engliſh in general are chearful and great lovers of muſic, for there is no church, however ſmall, but has muſical ſervice performed in it. They are likewiſe great drunkards; for if an Engliſhman would treat you, he will ſay in his language, *vis dring a quarta rim gaſquim oim heſpaignol, oim malvoyſi*, that is, will you drink a quart of Gaſcoigne wine, another of Spaniſh, and another of Malmſy. In drinking or eating they will ſay to you above an hundred times, *drind iou*, which is, I am going to drink to you; and you ſhould anſwer them in their language, *iplaigiu*, which means, I pledge you If you would thank them in their language you muſt ſay, *god tanque artelay*, which is to ſay, I thank you with all my heart. When they are drunk, they will ſwear blood and death that you ſhall drink all that is in your cup, and will ſay thus to you, *bigod ſol drind iou agoud oin*. Now remember (if you pleaſe) that in this land they commonly make uſe of ſilver veſſels when they drink wine, and they will ſay to you at table, *goud chere*, which is, good cheer. The ſervants wait on their maſter bare-headed, and leave their caps on the buffet. It is to be noted, that in this excellent kingdom there is, as I have ſaid, no kind of order; the people are reprobates, and thorough enemies to good manners and letters, for they don't know whether they belong to God or the Devil, which St. Paul has reprehended in many people, ſaying, be not tranſported with divers ſorts of winds, but be conſtant and ſteady to your belief.

In this country all the ſhops of every trade are open, like thoſe of the Barbers in France, and have many glaſs windows, as well below as above in the chambers, for in the chambers there are many glazed caſements, and that in all the tradeſmens houſes in almoſt every town, and theſe houſes are like the Barbers ſhops in France, as well above as below, and glazed at their

[b] A Groat.

open-

openings. In the windows, as well in cities as villages, are plenty of flowers, and at the taverns plenty of hay c upon their wooden floors, and many cushions of tapestry, on which travellers seat themselves. There are many bishopricks in this kingdom, as I think sixteen, and some archbishopricks, of which one is esteemed the principal, which is Cantorbie, called in English *Cantorberi*, where there is a very fine church, of which St. Thomas is patron. England is remarkable for all sorts of fruits, as apricots, peaches, and quantities of nuts; and in this country there are no wolves; their flag is the red common cross; the Bourgignons have a red cross of St. Andrew. There was in my time a milor, a man white with age, wise and discreet, called milor Ouardon, at whose house (though unworthy) I was several times feasted. He was very rich in pasture land, and kept upon his own estates five thousand sheep, this I have heard both himself and servants and dependents often declare. The country is covered and very shady, for the lands are all enclosed with hedges, oaks, and many other sorts of trees, so that in travelling you seem to be in one continued wood; but you will find many little flights of steps, which are called *amphores*; over these foot passengers go by little paths into the grounds, here horsemen cannot come, but are obliged to keep the high road among trees and bushes. Here are no shepherds to keep the sheep, they are commonly left morning and evening in the woods and the common fields. As to the manner of living of the English, they are rather unpolite, for they belch at table without reserve or shame, even in the presence of persons of the greatest dignity. They consume great quantities of beer, double and single d, and do not drink it out of glasses, but from earthen pots with silver handles and covers, and this even in houses of persons of middling fortune; for as to the poor, the covers of their pots are only pewter, and in some places, such as villages, their pots for beer are made only of wood.

They eat much whiter bread than that commonly made in France, altho' it was in my time as cheap as it is sold there: with their beer they have a custom of eating very soft saffron cakes, in which there are likewise raisins, which gives a relish to the beer, of which there was formerly at Rye some as good as I ever drank. The houses of the people of this country are as well furnished as any in the world. Likewise, in this country you will scarcely find any nobleman, some of whose relations have not been beheaded. For my part (with reverence to my reader) I had rather be a hog driver and keep my head, for this disorder falls furiously on the heads of great lords. For

c He means, perhaps, rushes, with which the floors of most houses were then strewed.
d Strong and small.

a while

a while you may see these great lords in vast pomp and magnificence, and the next instant you behold them under the hands of the Executioner. Wherefore I will quote you a proverb, which says, That heretofore were many persons who might have lived securely and without constraint, if they had remained in their humble stations, but being raised to an elevated rank, they thereby fell into many dangers and troubles, which you may see verified in this kingdom as frequently as in any other in the world, In France, we have no accounts of a prince having fallen into such misfortunes, for every one, as well prince, as noble and ignoble, lives peaceably, and zealously and affectionately obeys his king, and exerts himself to succour his prince even to the last drop of his blood, and assists him with money according to his abilities, and by this means the enemies are confounded and repressed, and the kingdom, by this means, rendered invincible, and the king rendered the greatest sovereign in the world, and the best obeyed, and his kingdom the best ruled and governed, insomuch that it might be esteemed the monarchy of the whole world, and the principality of the whole earth, which, without flattery, is the truth, as any one may see at a view; and its justice is well administered, not tyrannically, as in England, which is the pest and ruin of a country, for a kingdom should be governed, not by shedding human blood in such abundance as to make it run into the rivulets, thereby disturbing the good people.

Alas, Lord God, how happy is he who lives under a good king and a good lord, one who studies virtue above all things, and governs his people by council, authority and prudence, whose sole endeavour is to keep his people in peace, and to cause every one to be secure in his dwelling, and secure as well on the sea as in the fields, and who does every thing for the public good; by these means he is loved, honoured and revered, feared and dreaded, every where and by every body, and not feared for his power only. The office of such a king, or lord, is to exalt the good, and constrain and exterminate the wicked. In England the legal punishments are very cruel, for a man is put to death for a trifling offence; for a crime which in France would be only punished with a whipping, a man would here be sentenced to death. It is true, they have here but two sorts of executions, hanging and beheading, and by this means a man is as severely punished for a trifling as a more heinous offence, which ought not to be, and is better regulated in France, for there are several sorts of torments according to the crime. In this island they do not practise breaking on the wheel, nor any other kind of punishments than those I have mentioned. They execute the poorer criminals

nals out of the town on wooden gibbets, if they are not milors, barbaroufly in French called *milours*, who were put to death at London to ftrike terror into the people. They have a cuftom of holding their great days [a] every three months, and it is likewife to be noted, that the fervants carry pointed bucklers, even thofe of bifhops and prelates, and the men commonly exercife themfelves with the bow. The hufbandmen, when they till the ground, leave their bucklers and fwords, or fometimes their bows in the corner of the field, fo that in this land every body bears arms; and for the fea-ports of this country it rains there frequently, on account of ftorms at fea. It is good living here, as I found it in my time. Let this fuffice for England.

Of the Kingdom of Scotland.

Having before fpoken of England, my fovereign Princefs, with all poffible truth and exactnefs, it at prefent remains to touch lightly on the kingdom of Scotland. Scotland is a kingdom beyond England, and is very cold and feptentrional, that is to fay, approaching the north, and ftill colder than England, for the farther one goes beyond the feas, tending towards the kingdom of d'Anemark and Sueft, otherwife barbaroufly called Sueden, the colder it is; for in thofe kingdoms the cold would even fplit a ftone. Scotland is one of the parts of the Greater Britain, which Britain is divided in two parts, that is, into England and Scotland; in fo much that thefe two kingdoms were formerly but one, but have been divided by war, which was done by two brothers. England, which is the greater part, fell to one; the leffer and worfe part of Greater Britain, which is Scotland, fell to the other; to eftimate the difference between thefe two, let us fuppofe that England is Paris, and Scotland the fuburbs of Saint Marceau; as that city is preferable to the fuburbs, fo in like manner is England preferable to Scotland, to which it bears no comparifon. They are feparated from each other only by a fmall river. It is to be underftood, that the Kings of England and Scotland are defcended from the fame houfe, but (as the cuftom is) for the great to endeavour to devour the fmall: fo the rapacious Kings of England, not content with their own limits, have endeavoured to invade and conquer the country of their neighbours and allies, infomuch that they have exerted themfelves to ravage, burn, and ruin the Kings of Scotland and this kingdom. The Scots fpeak like the Englifh, or at leaft there is not a greater difference than between the fpeech of the Normans and that of the Picards. The country is but poor in gold and filver, but plentiful in provifions, which are as cheap

[a] Quarter Seffions.

as in any part of the world; and truly the milors of that country and the *gentillemans*, that is to say, the gentry, labourers, and tradefmen, who have any money, may live very comfortably. The arable lands of that country are but indifferent, and the greateft part of the country is a defert. As to the fize of the kingdom, you muft underftand it is of a great compafs; but with refpect to habitable lands, it may be ftiled fmall, that is to fay, that there is much bad and wild uncultivated land; but that the country is fmall with refpect to the fize of its cities and villages. The Scots have always been allied to the crown of France, and have always been faithful to the noble fleur de lis, infomuch that they have been hitherto preferved from their ancient enemy, who is worfe than a dragon, ferpent, crocodile, or afp; and without the affiftance of the Kings of France, their country would have been loft, and fallen into the hands of the Englifh: the Kings of France never abandoned their friends in diftrefs, for once the Englifh took many of their places, and burned much of their country, but they had fuccour and affiftance from the French, who with great diligence drove the Englifh out of Scotland like mutineers and villains, where the faid Scots fhewed themfelves as bold and courageous as lions, at which time there was a great defeat of the enemy. On this point it is to be obferved, that if thirty thoufand French fhould enter England through Scotland, they might foon conquer and overrun the whole country, this is certain, but the Englifh always keep up an alliance with the emperor, otherwife both they and their country would foon be reduced to duft. Since that time, the noble and valiant King of France has caufed feveral fortreffes to be built in Scotland, and repaired others, for the fafeguard and defence of that country, which has coft an immenfe fum of money, but the faid kingdom of Scotland ferves him as a buckler againft his enemies, and a means for conquering England; and it is to be underftood, that within thefe fifty years it is nearly doubled, and is worth fix times its former value; and fince Madame the Dowager of Scotland has been married to the King of Scotland, fhe has caufed feveral eftates to be tilled and cultivated, which before were of no great eftimation, and has rendered the uncultivated part of the country much better than it was before, in fo much that throughout the kingdom the fands are rendered tolerable, as I leave the world to imagine. The ftile of the Queen is thus proclaimed in Scotch, *Marie Stouart of grace lorde god the quinne Scottellement*, that is to fay in French, Mary Stouart, by the grace of God Queen of Scotland. They are, of perfon, bold and gallant enough, but are not fo well armed as the French, for they have very little well made, clean and polifhed armour, but

French,

use jackets of mail in exercising daily with the French, and have the custom of using little ambling nags and small horses; their lances are small and narrow, and they have scarce any large horses, and few are brought to them except from France. Their houses are badly built and proportioned, at least those of the common people. They have plenty of cows and calves, on which account their flesh is cheap, and in my time bread was tolerably cheap. In this place there are no vines, and wine is very dear, but the Scots drink beer, *godalles* and *alles*, with a quantity of milk. In this kingdom there are twelve bishopricks, with an archbishoprick called St. Andrews, where there is a castle. Their capital city is called in Scotch, Ennebroc, in French, Lislebourg, which is about the size of Pontoise and not bigger, having been formerly burned by the English. Here are some other sea-ports, as Dumbars [c], Domberterand [d], and other little cities and towns. Their Regent is named Madame de Longeville, a lady of honour, born of an ancient house, that is to say, of the house of Gaudefroy de Baillon, King of Hierusalem and Cicile and Duke of Lorrain, one of the most valiant families in the world, without depreciating any other. This country, although it is in a bad neighbourhood, being near a haughty, treacherous and proud enemy, has neverthelefs sustained itself in a manly sort by the means and assistance of the most noble King of France, who has many times let the English know what were the consequences of the anger of so great a monarch and emperor. But thanks to God, the affairs of this country have been regulated, and every thing goes on well, and for their benefit and that of their kingdom. How happy oughtest thou to esteem thyself, O kingdom of Scotland, to be favoured, fed, and maintained, like an infant, on the breast of the most puissant and magnanimous King of France, the greatest lord in the whole world, and future monarch of that round machine, for without him thou wouldst have been laid in ashes, thy country wasted and ruined by the English, utterly accursed by God. Thou knowest well if I lye, he helpeth thee with gold, silver, and garrisons, and affords thee succour of every sort, and loves thee like his own. In this country there is much broom, and the people do not warm themselves with wood, but with coals. A merchant in this country is well esteemed who has an annual rent of four hundred livres, and is among the richest men of the country, which is very far from having twelve or fifteen thousand livres per annum, as is often the case in France, Flanders, Germany, Spain, Portugal, and England. The richest man in Scotland, at the time I was there, was the archbishop of St. Andrews.

[c] Dunbar.   [d] Dumbarton.

The bishopricks of this country, as I understand, are but small, one ought however to praise their fidelity and firm attachment to the French, by the assistance of which all England may be undermined and burned. One thing I find reprehensible among the Scotch, which is that it is difficult to obtain a lodging from them. If you say to an ordinary sort of man in Scotch, *Guede gueduit goud maistre praie qui mi longini,* which is to say in our language, Good night, my master, I pray you to give me a lodging; they will answer you haughtily in their tongue, *eft eft no bet,* which is to say, there is no bed; and will not vouchsafe to lodge you, unless they expect a considerable recompence. However, some are more compassionate and humane, there being here, as in other countries, both good and bad. There is but one dutchy in this country, which is called the dutchy of Hampton [e]; there are many small counties. They carry bucklers like the English, and use the bow, and in other respects live like them, except that they are not so great dealers and tradesmen, and have not, as every one knows, such weighty purses; in other points they do not differ from the English, either in dress, conditions and stature. The then Admiral of France was called Milor Boduet [f], and the King's Lieutenant, Mosieur Dozay, who was the Governor of the French, and a man faithful even to death; and the Dowager of Scotland has the government of the Scots; they administer justice very uprightly, according to their customs, and receive money from France.

In this country (as I have seen it practised) a man who is possessed of an hundred golden, or sun crowns, will lend them to a merchant, for which the merchant will maintain him a whole year in his house, and at his own table, and at the end of the year will return him his money. All the cities and places of this kingdom are small, except St. Andrews, which is pretty large. The Scotch who apply themselves to letters, become good philosophers and authors. I knew formerly at Paris two doctors of divinity, who were the most learned that were to be met with, and principally in philosophy; they had all the books of Aristotle at their fingers ends; one was called Master Simon Sanefon [g], living at the college of Sorbonne, and the other Monsieur Cranston [h], who had been rector; they are both now bishops in Scotland, and in great reputation and honour, and augment and amplify the kingdom by their honour and virtue. The arms of Scotland is a lion, sprinkled with

[e] Hamilton. [f] Earl of Bothwell.

[g] Simon Simson, doctor of the Sorbonne, flourished Anno 1585; he is mentioned by Dempster and Sir George Mackenzie.

[h] David Cranston, Professor of the Belles Lettres in the University of Paris, in Montacute College, A. D. 1519. He was first a Batchelor, and afterwards a Doctor of Divinity.

fleurs

fleurs de lis. The kings of this country chuse to be without guards, and their subjects are bound to go to the wars at their own charge and expence, whenever they are commanded. On the death of the King Stouart, the crown came to his noble daughter, who is at present married to Monsieur the Dauphin; and although there are many Kings and Queens richer than the Queen of Scotland; she is nevertheless well allied and related, being not only related to Princes but also to Kings and Queens, particularly to the Queen of England and the King of d'Annemarc, insomuch that in default of heirs, she may lineally, and of right, succeed to the crowns of both kingdoms; and I do not know whether I might not venture to say, that the kingdom of England belongs to her at present, without speaking at random, as knowing a secret from those who have much frequented England. It is to be noted, that the House of Scotland is a most noble House and Lineage; and it ought likewise to be known, that the crown has for three or four hundred years remained in the family of the Queen of Scotland, bearing her name, by which it may be understood, that it is one of the most ancient royal houses in the world: and for as much as the kingdom of Scotland ought to be extremely happy in its alliance with France, so should we Frenchmen be glad to have the alliance, affinity, and friendship of the said Scots, for from Scotland we may repulse the English, and from thence enter easily into their country, which gives no great odds against them, and thus enables us to curb and check them. Monsieur de Termes was formerly in Scotland, where he performed many great acts of prowess and valour, and with an army of some few French and Germans, restored peace and tranquility to that whole kingdom, and drove the English out of Scotland, where they had taken seven or eight places from the Scots, and but for this relief would have made themselves masters of all the kingdom; and this gallant Seigneur de Termes, for council and judgment another Hannibal and Cato, retook *Tinton*[i], *Quincornes*[k], and *Lisle aux Chevaux*[l], and other towns and fortresses, and gave battle to the English, and in a succession of time quitted the whole kingdom. It is to be remarked, that in this kingdom of Scotland there are many towns, as Dombarres[m], Dombertrant[n], Thinton, Quincornes, Lisle aux Chevaux, Lislebourg, otherwise called Ennebroc, Sainct André, and many other little towns and castles.

It is to be noted, that nothing is scarce here but money; wine is brought them from Bourdeaux and Rochelle; and it must be understood, that the Scots do not pay for the wine they buy from the people of Bourdeaux, but in lieu thereof give them other merchandize. In their country they have barley, plenty of peas and beans, and in my time the poor people put their

[i] Perhaps Tantalon Castle.   [k] Kinghorn.   [l] Lisle aux Chevaux, or the Horses Island; perhaps Inch Keith.   [m] Dunbar.   [n] Dumbarton.

dough between two irons to make it into bread, and then made it what is esteemed good food in that country. In this place there are many churches highly ornamented, and plenty of monasteries, in which there are plenty of religious; and it is to be noted, that the ecclesiastics are richer than the housekeepers or nobles; wherefore, my most esteemed princess, I shall put an end to this little tract of Scotland, which I have delineated as accurately as I could; and no one ought to be offended that I have said that money is scarce in this kingdom, nor need any one to be scandalized thereat, as it behoves an historian to follow truth, and not to lye in any thing, but to describe things as they are, without change or alteration: in like manner as if a man in describing France should say it was a bad country, would deserve to be put in a sack and thrown into the water, as was very properly done by Julius Cæsar, who himself described the wars, and when he could not take a town or castle, declared the resistance which he had met with, and that exactly without addition. This little country is useful and necessary to us, as much so as the richest; and it is to be noted in concluding, that in this region the gentlemen take codfish and salmon in their moats; also it is to be noted, that there are some savages* in some of the counties of Scotland, and that from day to day the country strengthens and amends, and is in a daily state of improvement. Now to conclude, (Madame and most esteemed Princess) I shall pray the Saviour and Redeemer, Jesus Christ, to augment your noble Majesty, and prosperity in this lower region, and in the other to bestow on you the crown of justice, always submitting myself to your very puissant Majesty, and promising at all times of my life to be your poor servant and subject, even to the last drop of my blood; praying you most heartily to hold me recommended to the King our Sire, who, of his benign grace and royal and imperial liberality, when I was presented to him at the Tornelles by Monsieur the Constable, promised, on notice being given him of a vacancy, to bestow on me some genteel benefice, on which promise I have always relied, and which has given me the greater courage to continue my studies. My sovereign Princess, as long as I live I shall study to render service to the king and his kingdom, and that for the amplification and augmentation of his crown, praying the Lord to give him prosperity, and an increase of all good things. In the same manner as my family have served him (as being his well beloved) faithfully and loyally even to death, so I also, with the permission of God, hope to do as much according to my small abilities; and for you, Madam, I most sincerely promise you for the rest of my life, to pray to God for your singular and very exalted Majesty. And this will suffice, at present, concerning the kingdom of Scotland, in expec-

* Quelque sauvage; this is a doubtful expression, and many mean a desart, though more probably alludes to the Highlanders, frequently by ignorant foreigners considered as savages.

tation, by the grace of God, of another cofmography, and ſhort defcription of all the world and the divifions thereof, with the changes of kingdoms, which will be of great uſe for the perfect underſtanding and knowledge of geometry; for cofmography is coufin-german to geometry, and one cannot be known without the other; for how ſhould a geometrician or engineer be able to fortify a place, if he does not know the fituation and defcription of the fpot, the bounds and limits of the waters and feas, and he by means of knowing the cofmography, will the more eafily make the platforms, bulwarks, trenches, batteries, approaches, gabions, ditches with cuvettes, ſtrong walls and ramparts, terraces, caſtles, and other fortreſſes, mines and countermines, cofmography being abfolutely neceſſary for the art military.

✣✣✣✣✣✣✣✣✣✣✣✣✣✣✣✣✣✣✣✣✣✣✣✣✣✣✣✣✣✣✣✣✣✣✣

LONG MEG and her DAUGHTERS.

THIS venerable Druidical Monument, which is by the country people called Long Meg and her Daughters, ſtands near Little Salkeld in the county of Cumberland.

It confiſts of fixty-ſeven maſſy Stones, of different forts and fizes, ranged in a Circle of near 120 paces diameter; fome of theſe Stones are granite, fome blue and grey limeſtone, and others flint; many of them are ten feet high, and fifteen or fixteen in circumference; theſe are called Long Meg's Daughters.

On the fouthern fide of this Circle, and about feventeen or eighteen paces out of the line, ſtands the Stone called Long Meg, which is of that kind of red ſtone found about Penrith. It is ſo placed, that each of its angles faces one of the cardinal points of the compaſs; it meaſures upwards of eighteen feet in height and fifteen in girth, its figure being nearly that of a ſquare prifm. It weighs about fixteen tons and a half.

In the part of the Circle the moſt contiguous, four large Stones are placed in a ſquare form, as if they had been intended to ſupport an Altar; and towards the eaſt, weſt, and north, two large Stones ſtand a greater diſtance from each other than any of the reſt, ſeemingly to form the entrances into the Circle. It is remarkable, that no ſtone quarry is to be found hereabouts. The appearance of this Circle is much hurt by a ſtone wall built crofs it, that cuts off a confiderable ſegment which ſtands in the road. The encloſed part, in 1774, when this view was drawn, was fowed with corn, and it being then nearly ripe, many of the Stones which had fallen down, were thereby hidden.

The fame ridiculous Story is told of theſe Stones, as of thoſe at Stonehenge, i. e. that it is impoſſible to count them, and that many perſons who have made the trial, could never find them amount twice to the fame number. It is added, that this was a holy place, and that Long Meg and her Daughters were a company of Witches transformed into Stones, on the prayers of fome Saint, for venturing to prophane it; but when, and by whom, the Story does not fay. Thus has Tradition obfcurely, and clogged with fable, handed down the deſtination of this ſpot, accompanied with fome

of

of that veneration in which it was once undoubtedly held, though not sufficiently to protect its remains from the depredations of avarice, the enclosure and cultivation of the ground bidding fair to destroy them.

These Stones are mentioned by Camden, who was either misinformed or misreckoned their number; unless, which seems improbable, some have been taken away. " At Little Saikeld (says he) there is a Circle of Stones, " seventy-seven in number, each ten feet high; and before these, at the " entrance, is a single one by itself, fifteen feet high. This the common " people call Long Meg, and the rest, her daughters; and within the Cir- " cle are two heaps of Stones, under which they say there are dead bodies " buried; and, indeed, it is probable enough that this has been a monu- " ment erected in memory of some victory."

The History of the British and Druidical Antiquities, having been thoroughly investigated since Camden's time, these Circles are now universally agreed to have been Temples and Places of Judgment, and not Sepulchral Monuments. Indeed his Editor has, in some measure, rectified his mistake by the following Addition. " But as to the Heaps in the middle, " they are no part of the Monument, but have been gathered off the plowed " lands adjoining, and (as in many other parts of the county) thrown up " here in a waste corner of the field; and as to the occasion of it, both this, " and the Rolrick Stones in Oxfordshire, are supposed by many to have been " Monuments erected at the solemn Investiture of some Danish Kings, and " of the same kind as the Kongstolen in Denmark, and Moresteen in Sweden; " concerning which, several large Discourses have been written."

The tall Stone under the two Crows, is that called Long Meg.

DRUIDICAL CIRCLE, near KESWICK, CUMBERLAND.

THIS Druidical Monument is not mentioned by Camden, neither has it yet acquired any name, and indeed seems little known. Mr. Pennant says, it was discovered by Dr. Brownrigge, who resides somewhere near it.

It stands on the flat summit of a hill, close under that mountain called Saddleback, about two miles from Keswick, and near the road from that town to Penrith. It is composed of stones, mostly granite, of divers shapes and sizes, evidently collected from the surface of the earth, being rude and untouched by any instrument.

They are ranged nearly in a circular figure, some standing and others lying; the diameter from east to west is thirty paces or yards, and that from north to south measures thirty-two. The stones at the north end are the largest, being near eight feet in height and fifteen in circumference.

At the eastern end a small inclosure is formed by ten stones, in conjunction with those of that side of the circle, three sides of it are right lined, the fourth being a small portion of the circle, is necessarily rounding. On the whole, not attending to this rounded side, but considering it as straight, the shape would be what is called an oblong square. This is supposed to have been the Adytum, or Sanctum Sanctorum, into which it was not lawful for any but the Druids to enter. It is on the inside seven paces in length from east to west, and three in breadth; here probably the Altar was placed. On the west side, opposite this Adytum, a single stone lies about three paces out of the Circle. The whole Monument consists of fifty stones, forty of which form the Circle, and ten are employed in the Adytum.

THE

ANTIQUARIAN REPERTORY.

PORTRAIT of JOHN EVANS.

EVANS, whose portrait is here exhibited, was one of those professors of Astrology and Magic, vulgarly stiled Fortune-tellers, or Cunning-men, who gulled the credulous and ignorant, by pretending to resolve questions, recover stolen goods, and predict future events, from certain positions of the planets; a study much in vogue, as late as the time in which he lived, and in the pursuit of which many well-meaning persons so besotted their understandings, as to become dupes to their own visionary absurdities.

Very little is known of this Evans except what is related by William Lilly, his pupil, who tells several very extraordinary stories concerning him, which are here transcribed; but on the whole, from the character given of him, he appears to have been more knave than fool. His countenance, which was scarcely human, seems to have been admirably calculated to strike an awe into his superstitious consulters. "It happened on one Sunday,
" 1632 (says Lilly) as myself and a justice of peace's clerk were before ser-
" vice, discoursing of many things, he chanced to say, that such a person
" was a great scholar, nay so learned, that he could make an Almanack,
" which to me then was strange. One speech begot another, till, at last he
" said, he could bring me acquainted with one Evans in Gunpowder-alley,
" who

"who had formerly lived in Staffordshire, that was an excellent wife man,
"and studied the Black Art. The same week after we went to see Mr.
"Evans; when we came to his house, he having been drunk the night
"before, was upon his bed, if it be lawful to call that a bed whereon he
"then lay; he roused up himself, and after some compliments, he was con-
"tent to instruct me in Astrology; I attended his best opportunities for
"seven or eight weeks, in which time I could set a figure perfectly: books
"he had not any, except Haly de Judiciis Astrorum, and Orriganus's
"Ephemerides; so that as often as I entered his house, I thought I was in
"the wilderness. Now something of the man. He was by birth a Welsh-
"man, a master of arts, and in sacred orders; he had formerly had a cure
"of souls in Staffordshire, but now was come to try his fortune at London,
"being in a manner enforced to fly for some offences very scandalous, com-
"mitted by him in those parts where he had lately lived; for he gave judg-
"ment upon things lost, the only shame of Astrology: he was the most
"saturnine person my eyes ever beheld, either before I practised or since;
"of a middle stature, broad forehead, beetle-browed, thick shoulders, flat
"nosed, full lips, down looked, black curling stiff hair, splay-footed; to
"give him his right, he had the most piercing judgment naturally upon a
"figure of theft, and many other questions, that I ever met withal; yet for
"money he would willingly give contrary judgments, was much addicted
"to debauchery, and then very abusive and quarrelsome, seldom without a
"black eye, or one mischief or other. This is the same Evans who made
"so many antimonial cups, upon the sale whereof he principally subsisted;
"he understood Latin very well, the Greek tongue not at all: he had some
"arts above, and beyond Astrology, for he was well versed in the nature
"of spirits, and had many times used the circular way of invocating, as in
"the time of our familiarity he told me. Two of his actions I will relate,
"as to me delivered. There was in Staffordshire a young gentlewoman,
"that had for her preferment married an aged rich person, who being de-
"sirous to purchase some lands for his wife's maintenance; but this young
"gentlewoman, his wife, was desired to buy the land in the name of a gen-
"tleman, her very dear friend, but for her use; after the aged man was
"dead, the widow could by no means procure the deed of purchase from
"her friend; whereupon she applies herself to Evans, who, for a sum of
"money, promises to have her deed safely delivered into her own hands;
"the sum was forty pounds. Evans applies himself to the invocation of

"the

" the angel Salmon, of the nature of Mars, reads his Litany in the Com-
" mon Prayer Book every day, at select hours wears his surplice, lives
" orderly all that time; at the fortnight's end Salmon appeared, and having
" received his commands what to do, in a small time returns with the very
" deed desired, lays it down gently upon the table, where a white cloth
" was spread, and then being dismissed, vanished. The deed was, by the
" gentleman who formerly kept it, placed among many other of his evi-
" dences, in a large wooden chest, and in a chamber at one end of the
" house; but upon Salmon's removing and bringing away the deed, all that
" bay of building was quite blown down, and all his own proper evidences
" torn all to pieces. The second story followeth. Some time before I be-
" came acquainted with him, he then living in the Minories, was desired
" by the Lord Bothwell and Sir Kenelm Digby, to show them a spirit. He
" promised so to do: the time came, and they were all in the body of the
" circle, when lo, upon a sudden, after some time of invocation, Evans
" was taken from out of the room, and carried into the field near Battersea
" Causeway, close to the Thames. Next morning a countryman going by
" to his labour, and spying a man in black clothes, came unto him, and
" awaked him, and asked him how he came there; Evans, by this, under-
" stood his condition, enquired where he was, how far from London, and
" in what parish he was, which when he understood, he told the labourers
" he had been late at Battersea the night before, and by chance was left
" there by his friends. Sir Kenelm Digby and the Lord Bothwell went
" home without any harm, and came next day to hear what was become of
" him; just as they in the afternoon came into the house, a messenger came
" from Evans to his wife to come to him at Battersea. I enquired upon
" what account the spirit carried him away; who said, he had not, at the
" time of invocation, made any suffumigation, at which the spirits were
" vexed. It happened, that after I discerned what Astrology was, I went
" weekly into Little-Britain, and bought many books of Astrology, not
" acquainting Evans therewith. Mr. A. Bedwell, minister, of Tottenham-
" High-Cross, near London, who had been many years chaplain to Sir Henry
" Wotton, whilst he was ambassador at Venice, and assisted Pietro Soave
" Polano, in composing and writing the Council of Trent, was lately dead,
" and his library being sold in Little-Britain, I bought amongst them my
" choicest books of Astrology. The occasion of our falling out was thus:
" a woman demanded the resolution of a question, which when he had done,

" she

" she went her way; I standing by all the while, and observing the figure, asked him why he gave the judgment he did, since the signification shewed quite the contrary, and gave him many reasons; which when he had pondered, he called me boy, and must he be contradicted by such a novice? But when his heat was over, he said, had he not judged to please the woman, she would have given him nothing, and he had a wife and family to provide for; upon this we never came together after."

The Drawing from which this Plate is engraved, was communicated to the Editor by the late worthy and ingenious Mr. Grainger, from the Collection of the Right Honourable Lord Cardiff. It is of the same size as the Print, and evidently drawn with much care and attention.

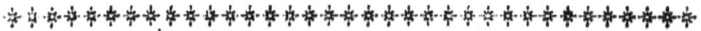

NETLEY ABBEY, HAMPSHIRE.

THE pleasing melancholy inspired by contemplating the mouldering towers and ivy mantled walls of ancient buildings, is universally felt and acknowledged, by observers, of every sort and disposition; but these scenes receive a double solemnity, when the remains are of the religious kind, such as Churches and Monasteries.

In considering a decayed Palace, or ruined Castle, we recollect, that it was the seat of some great Lord, or warlike Baron, and recur to the history of the gallant actions which have been atchieved on that spot, or are led to reflect on the uncertainty of all human grandeur, both, perhaps, from the fate of its lordly owner, and its own tottering state; but these are subjects which are like to affect the generality of beholders but very slightly; persons in the middling walk of life, happily for them, being almost excluded from those violent convulsions and sudden reverses, to which men of a more elevated rank are frequently subjected, and which is a sufficient retribution for all their so much envied superiority.

Religious ruins not only strike pious persons with that reverential awe, which the thoughts of their original destination must always command, but as places of sepulture excite ideas equally applicable to all ranks and opinions, from the monarch to the beggar, whether believers or sceptics, it being impossible to walk over a spot of ground, every yard of which covers the remains

of

of a human being, once like ourselves, without the intrusion of the awful memento, that we must soon, very soon, occupy a like narrow tenement of clay; a consideration which will, for a moment, overcloud the most chearful temper, and abstract from trifling pursuits, at least for a while, those of the most dissipated turn, and oblige them to bestow some thoughts on that inevitable moment, when they are to depart hence. Over and above these, there is something in the stile of building more particularly gloomy than that either of Castles or Mansions, occasioned by the peculiarity of the Gothic windows, the number of the arches and recesses, and the long perspective of the aisles.

Netley Abbey, in Hampshire, an inside view of which is here given, stands eminently distinguished among the monastic ruins of this country, for its peculiar fitness to excite those solemn ideas just mentioned. For this it is indebted not only to the elegance of its construction, its size and extent, but also to the profusion of ivy with which it is overgrown, and which half closes its figured windows, serving by its sober colour to set off the more lively green of a variety of trees and shrubs, which have spontaneously grown up within its walls, and out of the huge fragments fallen from its fretted roof, so as to form a sort of grove in the body of the church, which, by limiting the coup d'oeil of the spectator, husbands out the beauties of the scene, and, in appearance, trebles its real magnitude.

Among these ruins, several of the different offices of the monastery are distinguishable, particularly the abbot's kitchen, in which opens a vault, said, by the person who shews the place, to communicate with the adjacent Castle. The Historians of the spot, likewise, commonly point out the place where a sacrilegious mason met that fate with which he had been threatened by dreams and visions; that is, was crushed to death by the fall of part of a window he was attempting to take down, having first demolished the roof.

The History of this House is comprized in a few words: respecting the founder, authors are not agreed; some attribute that honour to King Henry the Third, and others to Peter de Rupibus, Bishop of Winchester; but all allow it was founded about the year 1239. It was a Cistertian House, and the Monks were brought from the Monastery of Beaulieu, in the same county. It was dedicated to the Virgin Mary and St. Edward, and at the dissolution had an abbot and twelve monks. The site and buildings were granted, 28th of Henry VIII. to Sir William Paulet; and since that time have passed through various hands; and, as report says, were once inhabited by an Earl of Huntingdon. For the sake of its materials, it has been repeatedly dilapidated

pidated and plundered by different perfons, till within thefe few years; Mr. Dummer, the prefent proprietor, has caufed it to be fhut up, and a key to be left with a neighbouring cottager, who picks up a maintenance by fhewing it to the parties that come by water, from Southampton, to drink tea among thefe ruins; an expedition the Editor of this work recommends to all perfons of tafte.

The river runs within an hundred yards of the Abbey, which ftands on an eminence furrounded by woods. Clofe to the water's edge is an old fort, feemingly built about the reign of Henry VIII. probably at the fame time as thofe of Hurft, Calfhot, and Cowes. Near the Abbey are the mounds of feveral large fifh ponds, once, doubtlefs, well ftored with frefh water fifh, for the ufe of the Monaftery.

꧁꧂꧁꧂꧁꧂꧁꧂꧁꧂꧁꧂꧁꧂꧁꧂꧁꧂꧁꧂꧁꧂꧁꧂

The TOMB of HENRY the Fifth Earl of WESTMORELAND, and his WIVES.

THIS Tomb is ftill extant in the ftate here reprefented, in the choir of the parifh church of Staindrop in Yorkfhire. It is of oak, and fuppofed to have been made in his life-time, from a paffage in his will, dated Auguft 18, 1563, wherein he directs that his body fhall be buried in the choir of the parifh church of Staindrop, under the tomb laft made, near to Jane his wife. This Earl had three wives; firft, Anne, daughter of Thomas Manners, Earl of Rutland; fecond, Jane, daughter of Sir Richard Cholmondeley, Knight; third, Margaret, but whofe daughter fhe was is not known; this third wife is not mentioned in Edmondfon's peerage, where there is a miftake refpecting the name of the fecond.

The dimenfions of this Tomb are:

Length of the inner part —	6 feet	6 inches.
Breadth ditto	6	6½
Length of the outward part	7	9
Breadth ditto	7	6
Height of the whole —	3	3½

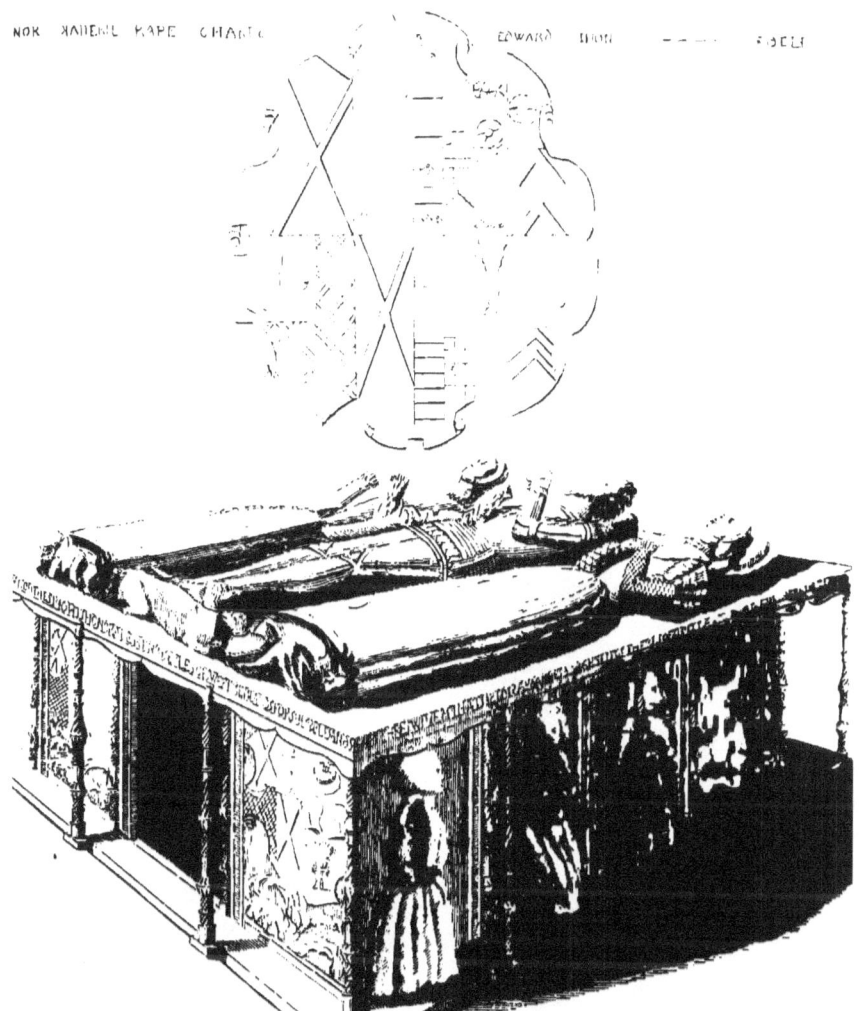

The north and south sides are divided each into four parts or niches, in every one of which is placed a figure of one of his children, with his or her name above, except over the seventh, where it is obliterated; they stand in the following order, beginning at the west end of the south side, ELENOR——KATHERNE——RAFE——CHARLS——EdWARd—IHON—a name lost—AdELF. Note, the last or eighth figure is lost.

The east and west ends had each three carved shields, charged with different quarterings, as are shewn in the engraving; that here shewn apart over the Tomb was placed on the southernmost pannels of both the east and west ends. The middle pannel is out, and lost on the east end.

At the bottom of the pannel, under the arms at the west end, are these inscriptions in ancient capitals, with stops between each word.

On the Northernmost.

All yow that come
To the Churche to praye   a
Pater Noster and a Crede for

On the Southernmost.

To have mercy
Of us and all owr progenye

East End.

On the Southernmost { made bi the Ha
                     ndis of John Tarbotons.

On the Northernmost there is no inscription.
Round the margin of the Tomb in like letters.

On the West End.

This Tomb made in the yere of owr Lord God and in second yere of Elizabeth

South Side.

By the Grace of God Quene of England and Franc and Ireland defendor of the faith   by the

Eaft End.

commandments of the Right Honorable Heni Erle of Weftmorland for himfelf and

North Side.

his thre wives that is to fay Anne daughter to the Erl of Rutland and Jane Margaret daughters.

The reft of the infcription is loft.

On the top or table of the Monument lies the Earl between two of his wives; he is in armour, they in the drefs of the times, all of them with joined hands, as in the act of prayer. The hands of the women are broken off and loft.

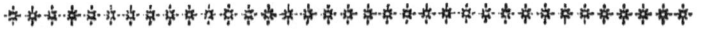

Hiftory of the Entry of Mary de Medicis, *the Queen Mother of* France *into* England, *Anno* 1638, *tranflated from the* French *of the* Sieur de la Serre, *Hiftoriographer of* France, *publifhed Anno* 1639.

THEIR Majefties of Great-Britain having been informed by Mr. de Monfigot, refident for the Queen in England, of the Refolution fhe had taken to vifit them, the news was fo agreeable that they already awaited that happinefs with impatience.

Their expectation was not long protracted, for a fhort time after the Sieur de la Montaigne, a gentleman of the Queen's body guard, was difpatched to give notice to Monfieur Monfigot, of her Majefty's embarkation in Holland, which he communicated to the King, her fon-in-law, and the Queen, her daughter, who received it with great fatisfaction.

Inftant orders were given by the King, with his own mouth, to the Earl of Northumberland, as one of the firft Earls and Lord High Admiral of England, Councellor both of State and of the Privy Council, defcended from the Dukes of Braband, and from the Stem of Charlemagne, of which he glorioufly fupports the honour, to receive the Queen at the firft port at which fhe fhould arrive, with all the honours due to her rank; an employment which this Lord readily accepted, in order to acquit himfelf thereof, although he was juft recovered from a fit of ficknefs, and his health was not thoroughly eftablifhed.

He

He was accompanied by the Vifcounts Convvay[a] and Grandifon, both very confiderable perfonages, by the Baron Goring, mafter of the horfe to the Queen, and one of the moft accomplifhed noblemen of the court, as alfo the Chevalier Vane, grand comptroller of the King's houfehold, and member both of the ftate and privy councils; heretofore ambaffador to the late King of Sweden and the States of the United Provinces of the Low Countries; employed as paymafter for the expences of his Majefty and of all his court, and at prefent treafurer of the King's houfehold.

Monfieur de Monfigot, as one of the moft zealous in his duty, did not fail to be of the body, accompanied by five or fix of the Queens gentlemen who had refided fome time in England.

Monfieur the Chevalier Finet, mafter of the ceremonies, a gentleman of great eftimation for his probity, with his marefchal of office, having received orders to provide a number of coaches drawn by fix horfes, without reckoning thofe of the King, the Queen, the Prince and Princefs, and thofe of many other Lords, for the conveyance of her Majefty and her train from the port of Dover, where fhe was expected, to Rochefter, where the King and Queen, followed by the whole court, had planned their meeting. Thefe orders and regulations were executed, but ufelefsly, occafioned by the continuation of a contrary wind; fo that the Lord High Admiral returned to London, being obliged thereto by a relapfe of his diforder; and the King fent Monfieur, the Duke of Lenox, his near relation, one of the gentlemen of his bed-chamber, whofe merit is as well known as his name. He was accompanied by his brother, who bears that quality worthily; he is called Monfieur, the Earl Ludovic; by Meffeurs the Vifcounts Conway and Grandifon, the two elder fons of the Earl of Morton; Milord Goring; the Chevalier Vane, grand comptroller; Mr. Finet, mafter of the ceremonies, and many other lords, knights, and gentlemen of his Majefty's privy chamber. All being arrived at Canterbury, they remained there a confiderable time, waiting for a change of the wind; but confidering, that according to the feafon of the year, they might wait a long time, they returned to London, where they, and news of the Queen's landing at the port of Harwich, arrived at the fame time, by means of Mr. de Mafure, lieutenant of the company of the hundred gentlemen of the body guard of the Queen, who rode exprefs to acquaint their Majefties therewith. The Duke of Lenox had frefh orders from his Majefty to fet out immediately with his whole company to meet

[a] Probably, Conway.

her, and at the entrance into his kingdom to offer her, from him, the authority of his sceptre and his crown.

Mr. le Monsigot, accompanied in particular by those of the Queen's gentlemen who had remained in England, made one in order to pay his duty to her. But whilst the whole are on the way, notwithstanding the haste they make both day and night, they shall afford me leisure to inform you of every thing that passed at the landing of her Majesty at this port of Harwich.

The Queen could not land till Thursday in the morning, on the 29th of October, on account of the storm, although her vessel was within sight and even cannon shot from the preceding Tuesday, but that did not prevent the governor of the castle from going to pay his first devoirs to her Majesty, and to inform her at the same time, on the part of the King his master, of the express order issued to him to receive, lodge, and treat her, and all her court with more respect and attention, than if the King himself was present in person, for which the Queen returned him thanks. I am obliged to tell you, *en passant*, that no one imagined her Majesty would make for this port, on account of its perilous situation, and the evident dangers attending the entrance.

On Friday, in the morning, the Queen landed with an incredible joy, having been seven whole days in a continual storm; but certainly the compassion her Majesty had for her ladies and maids of honour, gave rise to the greatest part of this satisfaction; and not to speak falsely, the graces and attractions of these ladies were a little in disorder on their leaving the ship, for in so great and continual a storm, they were more attentive to the alleviating their uneasinesses, than the preserving their beauty; every thing about them seemed so sorrowful and so deplorable, that the most beautiful among them touched the hearts of the beholders more with pity than love; although after so many apprehensions of shipwreck, the joy to see themselves safe in port possessed them so absolutely, that one might observe at the same time, the appearance of present joy and the marks of a past sorrow.

The Queen alone having always appeared as it were insensible to the fatigues of the sea, by an unparalelled force of mind and body, excited the admiration of every one with her accustomed air and majesty.

All the port was filled on both sides with the soldiers of the guard and the citizens, both equally armed, as were all the streets through which the Queen was to pass. For my part, I so fully employed my mind in the consideration of the honours and respects shewn to the Queen by a crowd of people of all ages and

and fexes, by a thoufand different actions, to which the zeal with which they were done gave both a value and a grace, that I could fcarcely diftinguifh the noife of the cannons from the different acclamations of joy, altho' the founds were extremely diffimilar.

The Queen was lodged in the Mayor's houfe, as being one of the handfomeft; and from the next day after the news of her arrival, feveral neighbouring lords and gentlemen came to offer their fervices to her, and they had the honour to make their reverences to her, by the affiftance of Monfieur le Vifcount de Fabrony, who bore frefh teftimony of their good will.

The fame day towards the evening, the Duke of Lenox arrived at Harwich with all his train, and as foon as he had enquired of Monfieur the Vifcount de Fabrony, concerning the Queen's health, not thinking he fhould have the honour at that hour to pay his reverence to her Majefty; he informed him in particular of his orders: but as the Queen was immediately acquainted with his arrival, Mr. le V. de Fabrony telling him, at the fame time, how impatient her Majefty was to fee him, led him to an audience, and prefented him to the Queen, who received him gracioufly, and with all the demonftrations of a fenfible pleafure.

Mon^r. the Duke of Lenox told her Majefty, that the King, his fon-in-law, and the Queen, her daughter, rejoiced equally at her happy arrival and her good health, and that he was commanded to affure her, on their part, that fhe fhould be as abfolute as themfelves over the lands fubjected to them.

This firft compliment was received with great tokens both of joy and gratitude, and were expreffed by her Majefty both in her countenance and her acknowledgements.

Then all the lords and gentlemen who had accompanied the Duke of Lenox, each according to his rank, quality and merit, made their obeifances to the Queen, at which her Majefty expreffed the fatisfaction fhe received; neither did they fail, at a proper time and place, to acquit themfelves handfomely of their devoirs to the ladies of the court.

Monf^r. de Monfigot paid his perfonal refpects to the Queen, in order to give her a final account of the exact attention he had obferved in executing her commands, when he received from her own mouth praifes which recompenfed him with prodigality. I fhall change the difcourfe.

The fun was no fooner fet, than there appeared fuddenly the lights of artificial fire-works, not lefs agreeable than his rays; and the much more fo, as they served to give light to a thousand different amusements, to which the violins, bagpipes and drums, added animation, sweetness and grace.

Her Majesty remained a whole week in this first town, to refresh herself after her disagreeable voyage, where, by the good orders given by Monsieur, the grand comptroller, and by his continual attention, she was as splendidly treated by her whole court, as if she had been in London; besides, the Sieur de Labat, valet de chambre to the Queen, and appointed by his Majesty to the office of his quarter-master, had very little difficulty, though much care, to mark out here the lodgings for the court, because every one vied with his neighbour in offering his house, as if they had considered it as a mark of honour to see their door chalked, since it was for the service of so great a Princess.

The Duke of Lenox, and the Lords who had accompanied him, paid their court every day with great assiduity, being constrained constantly at her Majesty's hour of dining to clear the room of a world of people, who, instigated by the curiosity of seeing, before they died, one of the greatest Queens of the earth, caused always a croud in the hall in which the table was laid.

In the mean time the roads from London to Harwich were so beaten by the frequent passing of gentlemen, who their Majesties of Great-Britain sent to the Queen, in order to be informed every day of the state of her health, that strangers needed no guide to that place.

Her Majesty set out on Saturday, 6th of November, in the coach appointed by the King, accompanied by Madam the Marchioness de Sourdiac and Madame de Fabrony. The Queen caused the Duke of Lenox to be sent for, to whom she gave a place in her coach.

A great number of other coaches were filled with equerries, maids of honour, women of the bed-chamber, and gentlemen domestics of the Queen, and other considerable persons of her suite.

The Lords who came to meet her Majesty and accompany the Duke of Lenox, having each of them their coach, altogether in order, made a magnificent appearance.

The people of the town, alarmed at so sudden a departure, had ranged themselves in divers companies along the streets and ways, so that even at day-break the Queen was necessitated to give them this last satisfaction, of seeing once more that great Princess, in whose favour every one put up vows to heaven; and although their language was unknown to me, their action

was

was accompanied with so much ardour, and so much humility, that therein it served me for a linguist and interpreter.

The Queen arrived betimes at Colchester, where they had marked the first lodging; and as she was expected with impatience by the inhabitants, a number of them were come forth to do themselves the honour of first congratulating her Majesty on her happy arrival, by a thousand acclamations of joy and contentment.

And to say the truth, that notwithstanding the preparation already made for her entry into that town, the marks of joy which that day appeared on every countenance, so occupied my mind with admiration, that I had only eyes for them.

The Queen was no sooner at the gates of the town, than the citizens and youths of the town, both under arms, made her the first harangue on the part of the people, to the noise of an infinite number of discharges from musquets, which in their language spoke nothing but rejoicings, whilst the mayor of the town, accompanied with the magistrates, advanced slowly by degrees to the door of her Majesty's coach, where, after having anew assured her on the King's part of the commands he had received to render her all sort of obedience, he made her a present of a large cup of silver gilt, according to a custom observed at the entries of Kings.

This present was very agreeable to the Queen, who estimated its value by the zeal with which it was offered to her: her Majesty likewise, by thanks, amply rewarded him for it; as also for the care he had taken to oblige her on this occasion, amply I say, since the least word from so great a Princess, bestows an honour on all those to whom she addresses herself. Her Majesty was conducted as far as the Castle by the townsmen, all armed, a party of whom were appointed for her guard. Monsieur the Viscount de Fabrony had an apartment there also.

This house belongs to Mr. Lucas, a Cavalier of distinction, and to whom this particular notice is due for the care he had in the absence of Monsieur, the grand comptroller, to send all sorts of necessary provision to Harwich, for the use of the Queen and her whole court.

The Sieur Labat, who constantly exercised the office of quarter-master, had the same privilege at the entrance into this town, of marking the doors of all sorts of houses, which were the most commodious for him to appoint for lodgings; and certainly the power which was herein granted him, made it evident that this Princess was great in all things, since even only on the first news of her Majesty's arrival, those who had not yet had the honour of seeing her, made themselves as it were lodgers in one part of their own houses, in order to lodge more commodiously some of her suite in the other.

This grand day of the entry of her Majesty, was a solemn holiday in that town, and although the shops remained open, they were only filled with people occupied at divers pastimes, in order to celebrate it honourably.

The ensuing night was illuminated by a thousand fires, whose brightness seemed to outshine that of the stars, and produced such joyous and happy effects, that those of the most melancholy disposition changed at once their humour, in order to join in the general rejoicing.

The Queen was, as usual, treated magnificently, with all her court; for besides her table, to which nothing could be added, those of her ladies, maids of honour, and women of her bed-chamber, which were all separate, there was likewise that of M. le Visc. de Fabrony, of M. Brinonet, steward to the Queen, who had served to the present time since his entry into the Low Countries; those of the gentlemen of the body guards, those of the officers, without reckoning a fresh one covered twice each day in the town for all the gentlemen domestics, and other considerable persons of her Majesty's suite, who lodged out of the Castle; all served with three courses, with such an abundance of meat, that one was constrained to acknowledge, on seeing so great a distribution, that it could only be made by a great King, and that Monsieur the Chevalier Vane alone, who was then comptroller, could possibly have executed the orders which had been given him. I made this remark as a fresh testimony of his attention, that the greatest part of the officers, and other persons destined for the service of all these tables, spoke French for the convenience of every one.

The Queen passed her Sunday in this place, in order to perform her devotions in the morning, and to divert herself after dinner with walking in the fine gardens here; and though the approaches of winter had already withered all the flowers, art, like an able gardener, compensating for the poverty of the parterres, had embellished the walks with an ever-growing turf, the softness and verdure of which made it so agreeable an object, that one could never be tired with walking on it.

The Queen of Great-Britain, notwithstanding the obstacle of her being very big with child, having resolved, in company with the King, to meet the Queen, her mother, on the way; M. de Monsigot had orders to find her Majesty, and to entreat her from the Queen, her mother, not to undertake

this

this journey in the fituation wherein fhe was, and to tell her, moreover, if the requeft thus made had not fufficient weight, that fhe commanded it in quality of mother, which obliged her to alter her refolution, to fhew publicly by her obedience, that the crown and the fceptre which fhe bore, were much lefs abfolute than the commands of the Queen, her mother. I return to my fubject.

Her Majefty left this beautiful manfion the 8th of November, to fleep near the town of Chensford[a], in a caftle belonging to Monfieur de Mildmay, a Chevalier of diftinction, as well for his perfonal merit as for the antiquity of his family.

The Queen arrived here at four o'clock in the evening, but certainly I cannot relate the new and agreeable magnificence with which her entry into this place was accompanied. Reprefent to yourfelf, that all the neighbouring peafants, men and women, being affembled in different companies on the road by which her Majefty was to pafs, without any other order or command, than that which their own zeal had that morning impofed on them; fome led by a violin, the others by a bagpipe, all together received the Queen, dancing to the founds of thefe inftruments, enlivened by a thoufand acclamations of joy. And not to lye, this action appeared to me fo pompous in its fimplicity, and fo magnificent in its innocence, that I fhall for ever remember it.

Her Majefty was lodged in this fine caftle, where M. the Vifcount de Fabroni had his cuftomary apartment; the gentlemen, domeftics, and other perfons of the fuite, were lodged in the town, diftant about a cannon fhot, but all very commodioufly, by the care of the Sieur Labat; being alfo privately entertained by their landlords, according to the good cuftom of the country, or rather according to the fentiments of public joy, with which they were animated at the arrival of fo great a Queen, mother of their own.

The fame order for the entertainment of her Majefty, and her whole court, was obferved with the fame deliveries, and all the fame tables were ferved, with an equal fplendor to that of the firft day, to the particular praife of Monfieur the grand comptroller, who acquitted himfelf therein worthily of his charge.

In the mean time the King, informed of the Queen's approach, fet out from London on Monday after dinner, in order to fleep in his caftle of Havering, diftant five leagues, followed by the Earl of Pembroke and of Mont-

[a] Chelmsford.

gomery, his grand chamberlain, a nobleman of great worth, as well for his birth and his fervices, as for thofe good qualities which raife him above the vulgar; by the Earl of Holland, one of the gentlemen of his bed-chamber, a nobleman of great importance, whether confidered for the great embaffies he has been employed in, or for that public eftimation which he has acquired in all places; by the Earl of Morton, captain of the guards, who is in great reputation, and by many other lords and knights, as alfo by an infinite number of gentlemen of his privy chamber.

On the morrow, the Queen being ready to depart, and in the very action of leaving her chamber to get into the coach, notice was given to her Majefty, that the King, her fon-in-law, was arrived, and juft then entering the caftle; whereupon fhe came down from her chamber with all poffible expedition, to the door of the hall which opened into the court, where the King meeting her Majefty, who was coming to him, having bowed to her, kiffed her, and faid:

" That after having caufed an offer to be made to her, on her entry into
" the kingdom, of all the power he was poffeffed of: he now came to make
" her an offer of his perfon, to honour and ferve her, according to thofe incli-
" nations he had ever enteatained."

The Queen, who was already fenfibly touched with the fweet object of his prefence, was not lefs affected with the fincerity of his difcourfe, and had doubtlefs remained filent from joy, if her generofity had not loofened her tongue, to fay to him, " That the civility of all thefe offers loaded her
" equally with honour and fatisfaction, and that fhe was greatly confoled in
" her misfortune, fince it had given her the occafion of feeing him." Their Majefties then made mutual enquiries after the ftate of each others health, changing their complimentary difcourfes into words, both more ferious and full of affection.

Madame the Marchionefs de Sourdiac, and Madame de Fabrony, the Queen's ladies, being near his Majefty, the King kiffed them with her permiffion, alfo the others who were there.

The King prefented to the Queen, Monfieur the Earl of Pembroc, his grand chamberlain; Monfieur the Earl of Holland, one of the principal gentlemen of his bed-chamber, who had the honour of being long before known to this great Princefs, in an extraordinary embaffy he made into France; and Mr. the Earl of Morton, his captain of the guards; and they all, one after the other, made their reverences to her Majefty.

The

The Queen prefented, likewife, to the King, Monfieur the Vifcount de Fabroni, Monfieur the Prefident le Coigneux, and Monfieur the Colonel d'Ouchant, and all three did themfelves the honour of making their reverences to him.

The lords of his fuite making a proper ufe of the occafion, did not fail to falute the ladies, whilft the King led the Queen by the hand to her coach, wherein he took a place. Monfieur the Duke of Lenox, Madame the Marchionefs of Sourdiac and Madame de Fabroni were feated in the fame coach.

The other coaches were filled with equerries, maids of honour, women of the chamber, and the Queen's gentlemen, according to the fame order which had before been obferved.

Monfieur the Earl of Pembroke, and Monfieur the Earl of Holland, as alfo all the other great lords of the King's train, having each of them their own coach, got into them, after having acquitted themfelves of the devoirs to the ladies, by handing them into theirs.

But certainly it was very pleafant, during thefe actions, to hear the flourifhes of a dozen trumpets of the King's train, who were ranged in a circle, in the firft bafe court of the caftle, where the croud of people was fo great, that it was extremely difficult to get a paffage through them.

Their Majefties arrived in the evening at the caftle of Giddi-hall, belonging to a widow lady, very confiderable as well for her virtue as nobility, which caftle was prepared to ferve for the Queen's laft lodging on the road.

The King flept at his caftle of Havering before mentioned.

The Queen and her whole train were, according to cuftom, magnificently entertained in this fine houfe, in which Monfieur le Vifcount de Fabroni had alfo his lodging. The gentlemen, domeftics, and other confiderable perfons, were lodged in the town of Rumford before the palace; but all found the fame kind of hofts that they had before met with; that is, with refpect to the goodnefs of their entertainment. It is to be remarked, that all the different caftles at which the Queen lodged in her way, was fo fuperbly ornamented, and with fo much fplendor, that one might have taken thefe houfes for fo many louvres, as well for the magnificence of the feafts, as for the richnefs of the furniture, all different, with which the Queen, her daughter, had caufed them to be adorned, not lofing one fingle opportunity of teftifying the honour and joy fhe received by the arrival of the Queen, her mother.

On the morrow, Wednefday the tenth day of November, the King having rejoined the Queen, their Majefties left this fine houfe at noon, in order to arrive in London early; whilft they were on the road, I made ufe of the opportune leifure it gave me, to make you a recital of the magnificences of this beautiful entry into this fuperb city, of which this is a little fketch:

Defcription of the City of London.

London is feated in a plain, the avenues to which are very agreeable, having that famous river the Thames, which ebbs and flows, bounding its extent on the eaft fide, and a thoufand fertile fields, which limit it alike towards the weft. I would reprefent the fpaces it contains, if my pen had the virtue of Jacob's ftaff. I will only tell you, that thofe who have meafured them, maintain that they are of the fame extent as thofe of Paris; and not to lye, the map points out to us few larger or more populous cities than thefe, and as it is a fea-port favourable to all nations, profit draws hither, from all parts of the world, an infinite number of ftrangers, who enrich it dayly by their ordinary commerce.

Palaces are very common, and the other houfes built with brick and of a fimilar ftructure, embellifh the ftreets where they are fituated, although their breadth and long extent make them handfome of themfelves. Among the great number of temples fumptuoufly built, thofe of St. Paul and of Weftminfter, are the moft ancient and the moft magnificent. The firft is repairing, and at prefent enlarging anew, but with fo great an expence, where, by the King's example, every one is fo willing to appear pioufly generous, according to his abilities and zeal, that before the work now began is finifhed, it will exceed two millions of livres.

The other Temple is a place deftined to ferve for a burial place for kings and princes, whence it happens, that there are there to be feen a great number of fepulchral monuments, of which the magnificence, though difmal, equally aftonifhes and ravifhes the mind with admiration.

The fields, the gardens, and the parks, are on one fide the neareft limits of its compafs, and on another the Thames, which contains inexpreffible beauties from its great width, its gentle courfe, and the elegance of the fuperb buildings erected on its banks, altogether render this fpot fo agreeable, that there are many who believe that its ifland is one of thofe fortunate ones, of which the poets have only reprefented the ideas.

Nothing is talked of but feafts and dances, and in all public places, violins, hautbois, and other forts of inftruments are fo common, for the amufement of particular perfons, that at all hours of the day, one may have ones ears charmed with their fweet melody.

The police is, neverthelefs, fo well obferved, that they live here without diforder and without confufion, and there is fo much fafety in the ftreets even

during

during the night, that one may walk as freely as in the day, without any other arms than those of the confidence one has in the goodness of the people.

The royal palace, the greatest and most commodious of any this day to be found in Europe, is situated at the extremity of the suburbs upon the banks of the Thames, from whence one may observe, with some sort of astonishment, this superb city, on the same side that the sun every morning contemplates its magnificences. But after all, when I consider the gentleness and probity of its inhabitants, I cease to admire the beauty of its superb edifices.

It is true, that being governed by a great monarch, whose virtuous inclinations causes them always immediately to obey all the just laws he imposes on them: I am forced to believe, that the sole example of his innocent and all-glorious life, is the strongest chain with which he retains his subjects in their duty.

Besides, as the queen, his spouse, gains as many praises by her merit, as respects by her greatness, it must be acknowledged, that their majesties together, serve at present for a flambeau, not only to their subjects, but also to all the world, to light them to chuse the paths of virtue, and to avoid those of vice. I return to you.

The Lord-Mayor having received the King's orders, before his departure from London, to make the preparatives for this entry, acquitted himself at the time very worthily.

He caused immediately to be erected on one side, in the great street of London, for above a league in length, benches with backs, and enriched with ballusters three feet high, all covered over equally with blue cloth, and commanded all the companies, or fraternities, of the different trades, in all amounting to fifty, to appear in the citizens gowns, with trimmings of marten skin, sitting on the benches the day of the entry, and every company to have its banner with their arms, in order that they might be distinguished one from the other, when all assembled, which was executed.

Six thousand soldiers [a] chosen and belonging to the city separated in divers companies, every one having their proper officers, all being gentlemen, were destined to form a haye or line on the other side of the street, all armed richly, some with muskets and others with piques. And although the shops, the balconies, and the windows, were to be filled anew with a great number of ladies; there were orders to hang tapestry on the houses, nevertheless, according to the discretion of the owners, being well assured that all persons would endeavour to shew their zeal by their magnificence, in so much that

[a] The trained bands.

though

though this great street contained in its length many other streets, the different merchants of the one and the other ornamented it so richly, and every one according to their own invention, that nothing more sumptuous nor more superb could be seen.

This place was dressed up with woven tapestry, that with Flemish or embroidery; one with Chinese, and another with Indian tapestry; the scarcity of which made it inestimable. The street of the Drapers was hung on both sides with scarlet, which was worthy to be remarked; the other streets of the suburbs of the city, and of the same extent, were differently ornamented, and on both sides, the companies of the soldiers of Westminster, and those of the citizens of the quarter, were ranged in a haye to Saint James's, being the name of the palace fixed for the Queen's lodging.

At the entry of the first gate [b] of the city a theatre was erected, of the height of the ballusters, covered with a canopy richly ornamented with tapestry, where my lord-mayor, dressed in his robes of crimson velvet, accompanied by the criminal judge [c], dressed in his ordinary robe; and also the twenty-four aldermen of London, all clothed in their scarlet robes, lined with marten skins, each wearing a gold chain, waited for their Majesties to acquit themselves of the duties of their offices.

And certainly in such a great train, where the spectators were without number, the strict order which was here kept, rendered the magnificence without an example.

The day was very fine, and as it was already made a holiday, on account of the public rejoicing, of which their Majesties of Great-Britain had themselves set the example, all their subjects seemed to vie with one another in celebrating it with as much zeal as satisfaction.

The noise of trumpets constrain me to change my discourse, to make a recital of all that passed at the entry of their Majesties into London, since they are already very near the gates.

At the entrances of the city, all the King's officers dressed in their royal liveries, who waited for their Majesties in a certain assigned place, ranged themselves in order, every one according to his rank, to follow them when they should alight from their travelling coach, and assume, as they did, another of parade, of red or crimson velvet, embroidered with gold, both within and without, and drawn by six horses of great price; in which M. the Duke

[b] Aldgate.   [c] The Recorder.

of

of Lenox and Madame the Marchionefs de Fabroni had the honour of places.

A litter with the fame covering, carried by two mules fuperbly harneffed, followed the coach. The following is the order which was obferved in the ceremony of the entry:

The gentlemen ufhers, well mounted, led the way, two and two, dreffed in their liveries of fcarlet, enriched before and behind with the king's arms embroidered in gold.

Twelve trumpeters clothed in the fame fluff, although the fafhion of their habits were different, followed after; and as their flourifhes drew every body to the balconies and windows, they obliged even thofe of little curiofity to obferve and admire them.

A company of fifty gentlemen of the band of penfioners, who are a fort of *gens d'armes*, each according to the order of their eftablifhment, maintaining three horfes, for which they receive an annual penfion from the King; thefe marched after his lieutenant, but all well mounted, and as well equipped.

The ferjeants of arms, gentlemen who commonly go before the King on days of folemnity, made their appearance in their places, each carrying on his fhoulder a large mace of filver gilt, crowned with a clofe crown of the imperial form and of the fame metal.

The coach of Monf. the Vifcount de Fabroni followed next, and that of the Queen's equerries appeared in fuite.

Two of the King's equerries went immediately before the coach wherein were their Majefties. The other equerries were ranged round about it, and the King's footmen, with thofe of the Queen, followed together on each fide of the doors of the coach.

The Earl of Salifbury, captain of the penfioners, and the Earl of Morton, captain of the guards, both members of the ftate and privy council, marched on horfeback in the fame rank with Monfieur de la Mafure, lieutenant of the hundred gentlemen of the Queen's body guard, all well mounted.

That handfome litter embroidered with gold, with the fame covering as the coach, having been provided by the exprefs commands of the Queen of Great-Britain, for the convenience of the Queen, her mother, followed alfo in its place, carried by two mules.

The coaches of the maids of honour, of the women of the chamber, the gentlemen domeftics and penfioners, as alfo thofe of the officers of his Majefty, came afterwards with an infinite number of others. But certainly all this pompous train appeared of itself so magnificent, in the order in which it marched, that nothing could be added to make it more admirable.

In the mean time the cannon in the Tower of London, being elevated over its proud battlements, as centinels, gave the watch word by their tremendous voices, to all the others which had been prepared on the banks of the Thames, in number two hundred, to announce the entry of their Majesties into the city, which though it trembled with the surprize of this first advertisement, its inhabitants at the same time leaped with joy.

The sounds of these cannon had no sooner ceased, than my Lord-Mayor, accompanied by the Recorder and twenty-four Aldermen of London, advanced to the door of the coach in which their Majesties were, and kneeling, presented to the King his sword of justice, which the King took and returned to him immediately, saying to the Queen, that my Lord-Mayor should wait on her to pay his duty to her; and then the Recorder made the following speech to her Majesty:

Harangue of the Recorder to the Queen.

" Madam,
" Although the news of your Majesty's arrival in this kingdom had struck
" us dumb with joy and satisfaction, we this day make an effort to recover
" our voices, since a public joy, like ours, is better expressed by shouts
" than silence. Nevertheless, when we suffer our minds to dwell on the con-
" sideration of the virtues and greatness of your Majesty, of which the
" brightness is increased by that of the King, your son-in-law, and our
" master, who accompanies you; it is to no purpose that our tongues are
" loosened, they know not what to say to speak worthily: insomuch that it
" is only permitted to us to admire and be silent; but before we observe
" this new silence which your Majesty imposes on us, we most humbly sup-
" plicate you graciously to accept the respects and submissions which we in
" body render you, on the part of all the citizens; we say in body only,
" Madam, since the King, who is the soul, has in this action already pre-
" vented us. We farther join to these most humble prayers, the vows which
" we make for the accomplishment of your wishes, and the conservation of
" your health."

The Queen, who had listened with great attention to this speech, answered him:

" That

" That she was too sensible of the testimonies of good will which the peo-
" ple had shewn at her arrival, ever to lose the memory thereof; and that in
" respect to them she should always remain obliged to them for the part
" they therein took."

At these words the cannon begun again to cause the sweet melody of their noise to be heard, as being no longer frightful, for even the children, already used to the terror which their surprize could cause, only laughed with joy, suffering themselves to be carried away by the general example, rather than by the weakness of their courage.

But in what terms shall I represent, at present, the splendour, the pomp, and the magnificence of this entry, so beautiful, so superb and so royal, since all the objects I contemplated, confounded my mind with admiration. When I considered their Majestys in that sumptuous coach, I imagined to myself that it was the goddess Cybele, who coming to visit her son Neptune, they were both seated in his triumphal chariot, and passing over the demesnes of his empire.

When I cast my eyes upon an infinite number of beautiful ladies superbly habited, and suspended in air in the balconies, I found myself obliged to believe that all the celestial goddesses were descended upon earth, followed by the wood and water nymphs, in order to celebrate the festival of this entry in favor of the mother of the gods.

Farther, if I contemplate that world of people of different nations, who filled both the windows and streets, I was persuaded at the same time, that all the gods were assembled together in London to be spectators of the magnificences of that superb entry.

In effect, to speak more soberly, the splendour of the rich coach in which their Majesties rode ; the beauties of these foreign ladies assembled in crouds in a thousand places; the gravity of the citizens, of whom one half appeared armed, and the other half in these balustres decently dressed; and in fine, that great quantity of people of both sexes and all ages, equally filled with zeal; all these objects together, dividing my mind between admiration and joy, oblige me to confess, that I had never before seen so many wonders together: and as their portrait was light by the beauty of those who lighted it, the least curious and the most insensible, touched with a secret extacy and with an extreme pleasure, avowed apart, what I now publish to all the world.

It was then that I found by a new experience, that the eyes are never tired with viewing any more than the ears with hearing: for in truth, tho' more than a thousand different beautiful objects presented themselves before my eyes all at once at every step I advanced, so far from being tired with contemplating them, I never closed my eye-lids but with regret, altho' the interval that action gave to my pleasure was imperceptible.

Let the most fruitful imaginations represent to themselves the satisfaction to be received even in the admiration of beauty, naturally displayed by the hands of nature, upon an infinite number of faces, which differed one from the other only to shew the diversity of attractions and graces, which love makes use of to snatch hearts and captivate our liberties; for if one arrested for a while my eyes and attention, another a moment after exercising her empire, charmed my soul into complaisance and admiration: if that, I say, at length persuaded me by force of her attractions to esteem her alone, this, seizing my judgment, and keeping it in suspence, determined it at last to prefer her to all together; but that pleasure I had no sooner resolved, than a new object all adorable made me in an instant repent in her favour of the precipitancy of my judgment; so that I can assure you, without falsity, that an hundred and an hundred times again, I bestowed and resumed the apple from a great number of ladies, without being able at last to make a definitive present; so equally was my mind diverted and occupied in the contemplation of their different and uncommon perfection.

If my eyes found their paradise in these pleasures, my ears were yet charmed with new pleasure by the melody of the cries of joy, the harmony of trumpets, and other sorts of instruments, which had the virtue of exciting the most melancholy minds to bear their part in the concert of public joy.

It is time, nevertheless, for me to forward their Majesties, in order to represent to you the new magnificences of the palace of Saint James, which was prepared for the Queen. Behold a new plan of my invention.

It is situated at the extremity of the same suburb as that wherein the castle of Whitehall stands, from which it is distant only the extent of a park that divides them. Near its avenues is a large meadow always green, in which the ladies walk in summer. Its great gate has a long street in front, reaching almost out of sight, seemingly joining to the fields, although on one side it is bounded by houses, and on the other by the royal tennis court.

This Caftle is very ancient, very magnificent, and extremely convenient, it is built with brick, according to the fafhion of the country, having the roof covered with lead in form of a floor, furrounded on all fides with crenelles, which ferve for an ornament to the whole body of the building. Its firft court or entrance is very extenfive, from it is the afcent to the Grand Guard Chamber.

This firft Hall was decorated with tapeftry, the beauty and invention of which were ftill admirable, and fhewed its former value, as a piece of furniture of a houfe truly royal.

The fecond Hall, with a canopy of the fame fize, was ornamented with a new fuit of tapeftry, which forcibly excited the admiration of the moft incurious.

The Privy Chamber, in which was both a chair of ftate and a canopy, was embellifhed with another tapeftry, which the induftry of the Artizan had made ineftimable from the time he had completed it; for, without falfity, the pencil itfelf, though favoured by nature, has nothing more lively nor more animated, and what made it ftill more wonderful, was that the innumerable figures therein feem all different, reprefented fo naturally both in their countenances and poftures, the actions they were to perform, according to the defign of the workman, that though filent they made themfelves underftood, notwithftanding the eyes which were the interpreters, were equally dumb.

The Prefence Chamber had its decorations different in beauty and in price, by another tapeftry all of gold and filk, where the flowers of the fpring were fo well and naturally depicted by the pencil of the needle, that one might eafily perfuade onefelf, that the Artizan who made that tapeftry, had originally been a Gardener, and thereby having his imagination always filled with the different forts of flowers which he had formerly fown, he had very happily planted them anew in his work, fince they feemed here blown with the fame beauty as in the parterres.

The Imperial Bed, all of gold embroidery, which the Queen had put into the hands of the embroiderers in order to ornament this Chamber, not having been finifhed, fhe caufed another to be immediately fet up. It was of black velvet, enriched every where with gold fringe, and lined with faffron-coloured fattin. All the furniture of the Chamber were of the fame ftuff, and equally enriched, not to mention the cryftal chandeliers fufpended in the middle, and the filver fconces for flambeaux fixed to both fides, to the tapeftry.

The Bedchamber was ornamented with a new tapeſtry, all of ſilk, juſt new from the hands of the workman, repreſenting the Twelve Worthies; and certainly this work was ſo rare and precious, that Europe cannot boaſt any thing ſimilar; and the challenge the Artizan gave to all his brother Artificers to imitate his induſtry was ſo reaſonable, that his vanity was praiſed inſtead of condemned.

The Queen's Chapel near her cloſet, not having any ornaments more precious than the relicks which her Majeſty brought with her, I ſhall not amuſe myſelf in ſaying any thing more about it, although it was decorated with a brocaded tapeſtry.

A gallery open at both ſides, through which lay the way to the great Chapel, was alſo in the ſuite from the Queen's chamber, as a place deſtined for a private walk, and where the mind might be deliciouſly diverted by the number of rare pictures with which its walls were covered. And among others the Twelve Cæſars, by the hands of Titian, were much admired. I ſay the twelve, notwithſtanding this famous painter only drew eleven, ſince Monſieur the Chevalier Vandheich has repreſented the twelfth, but ſo divinely, that to me to admire it ſeems too little; for as he has in this work raiſed up Titian from the dead, the miracles of his induſtry makes it ineſtimable.

There is likewiſe to be ſeen a Deluge by Baſſan, but ſo ingeniouſly repreſented, that the terror there repreſented touches the hearts of the beholders with equal violence.

A picture of the Fainting of the Virgin by the Chevalier Vandheich, attracts the admiration of even the moſt incurious. And in truth the Painter has, in this work, repreſented Death ſo beautiful, and Sorrow ſo reaſonable, that this object equally diſpoſes the hearts of the wiſeſt to ſigh, and the mind of the moſt timid to deſpiſe life.

The ſcene of Tintoret has its place in the public eſteem; and truly as he repreſents the Feaſt of Grace, where ſouls are rather fed than bodies, the minds are much more ſatisfied than the eyes in admiration of him; conſidering the wonders of this work in the virtu of the pencil of him who did it.

There are alſo an infinite number which cannot have been bought, according to their value, but by a great monarch. It ſhall ſuffice me, for fear of tiring you, to ſay only, that at one of the ends of this three-ſided Gallery there is a portrait of the King of Great-Britain, in armour and on horſeback, by the hand of Monſieur the Chevalier Vandheich: and not to lie, his pencil in preſerving the majeſty of this great Monarch, has by his induſtry

ſo

so animated him, that if the eyes alone were to be believed, they would boldly affert that he lived in this portrait, so striking is the appearance.

The Great Chapel of the Castle is placed at one of the ends of this Gallery; its situation, its building, and the ornaments with which it is adorned, are equally worthy being remarked.

To express to you the great number of Chambers all covered with tapestry, and superbly garnished with all sorts of furniture, where the court was to be lodged, without reckoning the other apartments, which were reserved, and of which Mr. le V. de Fabroni had one of the principal, would be impossible. You shall only know that the Sieur Labate, who continued to execute the office of Quarter-Master, had liberty to mark with his chalk fifty separate Chambers of entire apartments, and the whole were furnished by the particular commands of the Queen of Great-Britain, who seemed to convert all her ordinary diversions into continual cares and attention to give all sorts of satisfaction to the Queen her Mother. And this great expence on so great a quantity of rich furniture, shewed anew the riches and power of a great Monarch, since in only one of his pleasure-houses there was sufficient room to lodge commodiously the greatest Queen in the world, with her whole court.

There were besides two grand Gardens, one with parterres of different figures, bordered on every side by a hedge of box, carefully cultivated by the hands of a skilful Gardener; and in order to render the walls on both sides which it enclosed appear the more agreeable, all sorts of fine flowers were there sowed; and as there are many which are only the daughters of summer, some of autumn, and others of winter; if only a part blow in the spring, every one of the other seasons in their turn produce their tribute towards the public benefit, so that at all times the eyes find their diversion by the beauty of the different colours with which they are enamelled.

The other Garden which was adjoining, and of the same extent, had divers walks, some sanded and others of grass, but both bordered on each side by an infinity of fruit-trees, which rendered walking so agreeable, that one could never be tired.

This Garden is bounded on one side by a long covered Gallery grated in the front, where one may admire the rarest wonders of Italy, in a great number of stone and bronze statues; and as the King to whom they belong, never finds any of these works too dear, although by being unequalled they

are

are ineftimable, they are brought to London from all parts of the world as to a fair, where there is always a fuccefsful fale.

Thefe two gardens are bounded by a great park, with many walks, all covered by the fhade of an infinite number of oaks, whofe antiquity is extremely agreeable, as they are thereby rendered the more impervious to the rays of the fun. This park is filled with wild animals, but as it is the ordinary walk of the ladies of the court, their gentlenefs has fo tamed them, that they all yield to the force of their attractions, rather than to the purfuit of the hounds.—— It is time to change the difcourfe.

The Queen of Great-Britain was waiting in the chamber of the Queen her mother, with all the greateft and moft beautiful ladies of the court; but in truth, that princefs, notwithftanding her advanced pregnancy, bore away the prize from them all, both for grace and majefty, in which her equal is not to be found: I do not fpeak of the greatnefs of her virtue, nor of the excellence of her wit, fince both are the objects of public admiration.

The frefh report of the great guns advertifed me of the approach of their Majefties, befides, the flourifhes of the trumpets, and the crouds of people who affembled in the lower court of the Caftle of St. James's, powerfully perfuaded me they were not far off; and what ftill the more confirmed me in this opinion, was the particular information which the Queen of Great-Britain received exprefs from a gentleman, which obliged her to defcend from the chamber wherein fhe was to the bottom of the great ftairs, accompanied by the Prince of Wales, the Duke of York, her two fons, and the two Princeffes, her daughters, followed by all her ladies.

Imagine to yourfelf the impatience of her Majefty, under the expectation of the honours and fatisfaction of feeing the Queen her mother. In truth, the coach in which fhe was, with the King her fon-in-law, had no fooner entered the bafe-court of St. James's, than the Queen, her daughter, arofe from her chair, and going feveral fteps all alone to meet her, got even to the coach-door, which fhe would willingly have opened, but had not fufficient ftrength; when, in effect, being prevented, fhe threw herfelf on her knees at the feet of the Queen her mother. The inftant fhe alighted from the coach, and her Majefty had no fooner raifed her by the fole effort of her firft embraces, in order to kifs her, than this virtuous Princefs, filled with joy and contentment, threw herfelf once more at her feet for the fecond time, as if fhe had there already eftablifhed her throne, which once more obliged

the

the Queen her mother to make ufe of the fame violence which fhe had before exercifed to oblige her to rife, which fhe did by the force of careffes.

You muft not here expect oratory. Extreme joy, like great forrow, renders all people dumb, and fince love and nature both acted in this meeting, they caufed their fovereignty to be known, in tying up the tongues, clofing the hearts, and holding open the eyes alone, to give paffage to a thoufand tears of joy, after having taken away the bounds from the fource which produces them.

Truly, I never before faw fo much joy and fo many tears together; for as all thofe who were witneffes of this action, found themfelves touched with an extreme joy, which they could exprefs only by the eyes; thefe they moiftened with tears drawn from their hearts, to witnefs its excefs by this eloquent language.

In the mean time thefe two great Queens, equally fpeechlefs through joy, were fo ftrongly occupied, the one by her tender embraces inceffantly renewed, the other with her moft humble fubmiffions, of which fhe feemed never to tire, that I was a thoufand times ravifhed with admiration of an object, where nature and love, joy and humility, were in difpute for the preeminence.

But at length the Queen of Great-Britain, who was always endeavouring to render new devoirs to the Queen her mother, prefenting to her the Prince of Wales, the Duke of York, the Princefs, and her Sifter, they all together, from the example of their mother, threw themfelves at her feet to receive her benediction, which was accompanied by new careffes which her Majefty beftowed on them, of which I confefs my inability to exprefs either the number or tendernefs. All this joy terminated happily, fince every one took a part in it. The King and M. the Earl of Arundel, great marefchal of England, and great indeed in all things, took the Queen under their arms, and the Queen her daughter following her, led by Monfieur the Baron of Goring, her chief ufher, with the Princes and Princeffes her children all together, followed by a croud of lords and ladies, afcended into the Queen's chamber, when, after the chief ladies of the court had paid their refpects to her Majefty, one of the moft beautiful circles was formed that I ever beheld.

Certainly I tafted an extreme fatisfaction in feeing fo great a number of foreign ladies thus arranged, but on accofting them, they being dumb as to me, I contemplated them afar off, as ftatues carved by Lifippus, or pictures

Y y y painted

painted by Apelles, to which only speech was wanting to make them pass for miracles; in effect, as nature had taken pleasure to dress their faces with all the charms which can inspire love, their language only reaching my soul through my ears, diverted it from the thoughts of adoring them.

But at length this royal company separated, in breaking this grand circle, where, as in heaven, three beautiful stars of equal brightness shined all together. Their Majesties of Great-Britain, with the Princes and Princesses their children, returned to Whitehall, leaving the Queen in her chamber well satisfied to find herself in so safe and tranquil a port.

The following night was not less beautiful than the day which had preceded it; for the splendor of an infinite number of fireworks, joined to that of as many stars which shone forth at the same time, both the heavens and earth at once seemed equally filled with light; and although one was different from the other, all together had such powerful attractions to make them beloved, that it is credible could the sun have appeared he would not have dared, for fear that his brightness should have been despised. Not to lie, no summer ever exhibited to me a day so beautiful in appearance as that night, which had charms to content all the senses; the eyes lighted with the brightness of fireworks which they themselves had lighted, were gently arrested to their admiration. The ears, attached with like pleasure to the annunciation of the acclamations of joy which all the people had set to songs, to sing them in dancing through the streets, were equally satisfied. The smell had also its pleasures of the cinnamon and rosemary-wood, which were burning in a thousand places; and the taste was gratified by the excellence of all sorts of wine, which the citizens vied with each other in presenting to passengers, in order to drink together to their Majesties healths. All the city appeared at the same time in arms, on fire, and in joy; but these arms, by being agreeable, made only love wounds; the fire burned only insensible bodies, which had been destined to the satisfaction of its avidity, in order to enjoy the sweet light of its flames; and, in fine, this joy not only gave pleasure to the most melancholy, but would have charmed even sorrow herself. Whence she enviously kept herself hid, to avoid the force of these charms.

Truly, if I had not been witness to all these truths, I should have found a difficulty to believe them. Represent to yourself, that all the streets of this great city were so illuminated by an innumerable number of fires which were lighted, and by the same quantity of flambeaux with which they had dressed the balconies and windows, that from afar off to see all this light
collected

collected into one single object, one could not consider it but with great astonishment, so prodigious it appeared by being extraordinary, that if I represent to myself all those flambeaux which at once shone, as well from the top of the palace as in the deepest part of the Thames, I have yet a difficulty to detach my mind from so agreeable a thought; for not to lie, the sea that night appeared so brilliant, that I no longer doubted that the sun set every night in its waves; and at length imagined that a new Phaeton, attempting to conduct the chariot of the moon, had been precipitated from the highest heavens into that element, so luminous was it.——I fear to tire you.

At length this night, or rather this whole day of twenty-four hours, passed away imperceptibly even to the most melancholy, so completely had it filled the mind with pleasure in its course. I can moreover assure you, that a variety of all the different pastimes that can be imagined, having banished sleep from their company, all those who were assembled in a thousand places to celebrate this feat were so enlivened, that they had already forgot the use of rest.

On the morrow M. de Bellieure, ambassador extraordinary from France, came to felicitate the Queen on her happy arrival in London; but during his audience he would never cover himself before her Majesty, although she pressed him to it many times, testifying by that extraordinary respect, that he acquitted himself towards the King his master, in rendering it to the Queen his mother. I can truly say of him, after the public voice, that his name proclaims his merit, since all those who have born it have been raised above the common level to a particular esteem. A race that from age to age serves to decorate the general history, as well as that of France, producing to us nothing less than chancellors, presidents au mortier, and ambassadors. And where any of the same stem have followed the profession of arms, they have caused themselves to be admired by the greatness of their courage, as much as by the force of their understanding.

Monsieur Joachimi, who has been ambassador in ordinary from Messrs. the States of the United Provinces of the Low Countries these twelve or fifteen years, a personage whose probity, joined to his long services, (he having grown old in continual employments of great importance) puts him above the common rank of even persons of his condition; came also an hour after to felicitate her Majesty, on the part of Messrs. the States, on her happy voyage, as having contributed to it by their cares as well as their wishes.

Monsieur

Monſieur Coneo, whoſe merit is ſufficiently known, did not fail, at the ſame time, to come and compliment her Majeſty on her happy arrival, on the part of his Holineſs, which he did with a good grace, and to her Majeſties particular ſatisfaction.

Monſieur Salvieti, reſident of the Grand Duke of Tuſcany in England, acquitted himſelf very worthily in the ſame devoir towards the Queen, on the part of his maſter, and the compliment which he made her, was very agreeable to her Majeſty.

Monſieur Jutiniani, the ambaſſador of the Moſt Serene Republic of Venice, in England, was the laſt in paying his compliments to the Queen, to felicitate her, like the others, on her happy voyage, having arrived ſome days after her in London, which prevented me from inſerting him according to his rank.

Madame, his wife, came alſo to viſit her Majeſty, who received her with all the honours which are due to a perſon of her condition; but I can farther ſay, without flattery, that her virtue, joined to her beauty, merited nothing leſs.

That ſame day the Queen of Great-Britain being come to viſit the Queen her mother, their Majeſties went together, followed by their court, to Somerſet, which is the name of a Houſe that belongs to the Queen of Great-Britain, of which ſhe having given a part to the capuchins, has cauſed a magnificent chapel to be built there, the daily expences of which ſhe defrays out of her privy purſe, or money ſet apart for her private pleaſures, as having none greater than that of exerciſing her piety, as well as all her other virtues.

It was in this beautiful Chapel that their Majeſties heard the *Te Deum Laudamus*, which the excellent muſicians of the Queen of Great-Britain ſung, as a thankſgiving for the happy arrival of the Queen her mother; and after having finiſhed their devotions, walking ſome time in the fine gardens of that royal houſe, they re-aſcended their coaches, and came to St. James's, followed by their whole court, where the Queen of Great-Britain, having taken leave of the Queen her mother, returned home.

The following day the lords of the privy-council came in a body to pay their compliments to the Queen in her chamber, and Monſieur the Earl of Dorſet, great chamberlain to the Queen of Great-Britain, counſellor of ſtate, and of the privy-council, a lord of diſtinction, and of conſideration in all ſorts of qualities, ſpeaking for the whole, ſaid to her :

" That

"That the King her son-in-law, and their Master, having commanded them to come and do their reverences to her Majesty, to offer her their most humble services, this order was very agreeable to them, since in the obeying of it, they had the honour and the satisfaction of acquitting themselves of their duties to the greatest Queen in the world. And that for his particular part, he esteemed himself happy in having been chosen from all the company to address her Majesty, and being enabled, by this opportunity, to assure her he was her most humble and most obedient servant."

The Queen answered:

"That she felt herself much obliged by the honour she received from so illustrious a company, and that she should never forget the testimonies of their good will which they thus rendered her. Thanking him for the trouble he was pleased to take in becoming their speaker, as a matter highly agreeable to her."

At these last words the archbishop of Canterbury, and all the other councellors of state made their reverences to her Majesty, every one according to his rank, which was curious to behold, and worthy of being remarked.

Two days after the Lord-Mayor, dressed in his official robes of crimson velvet, with a gold chain about his neck, accompanied by twenty-four aldermen of London, dressed also in their robes of scarlet lined with martens skin, all well mounted, having their officers carrying the insigns of office before them, came to pay their reverences to her Majesty, and presented her with a large cup of massive gold richly wrought, of an inestimable price. This is a translation of his speech:

Harangue of my Lord-Mayor to the Queen.

"Madam,

"Although we come by the express order of the King your son-in-law and our master, to render this duty to your Majesty, the desires which we have always had so to do, even before your arrival, having forestalled his commands, we shall not have much difficulty to persuade you how agreeable it was to us, since it affords us an opportunity to offer to your Majesty our most humble services in particular, and at the same time on the part of the city, this gold cup. It is true, Madam, that the smallness of these offerings has no proportion to your Majesty's greatness; but when you consider the place you now occupy on earth, that of the greatest

" Queen that ever was, you will not be aftonifhed if this ifland, which
" makes only a fmall part, has nothing in it worthy of being prefented.
" Neverthelefs, the perfection of our zeal, fupplying the defects of our
" power, we hope that this prefent will be agreeable to you, and the more
" fo, as it is accompanied with both our vows and our prayers for the fuc-
" cefs of your defires, and the increafe of your profperity."

The Queen, very fenfible to thefe new teftimonies of good will which my Lord-Mayor had rendered her as well by his words as the prefent, thus anfwered:

" That fhe was forry to be able to repay, with thanks only, the many
" favours fhe had already received, and was ftill receiving by this fine pre-
" fent which the city made her; but that if an occafion fhould offer whereby
" fhe might one day teftify the gratitude fhe felt, fhe would then fhew a
" more worthy acknowledgment, and that in the mean time fhe would dearly
" preferve the remembrance, as well as of the trouble he had taken in par-
" ticular, with all his colleagues."

This action thus terminated with a common fatisfaction both to the Queen and my Lord-Mayor, who retired home well pleafed with the gracious reception with which the Queen had honoured him.

Some days after Monfieur the Vifcount de Fabroni, and Monfieur the Prefident le Coigneux, waiting on the King at Whitehall, they were kindly received by his Majefty, and M. le V. de Fabroni had the honour of conferring with him a whole hour refpecting the Queen's affairs, with which he was well fatisfied, as well as with his perfon, as appeared by the praifes his Majefty beftowed on him both in public and private, as well for his probity as for the extreme zeal which he had for the fervice of the Queen his miftrefs, having been informed many times, and in divers rencontres, of the good and long fervices he had rendered to her Majefty.

They had befides an audience of the Queen of Great-Britain the following day, where they received no lefs honour and fatisfaction than in the firft, as M. le V. de Fabroni had likewife converfed with her Majefty concerning the ftate of the affairs of the Queen her mother. The Queen, her daughter, praifed him highly for his fidelity, and the great fervices he had done her, of which the laft proofs were extremely fenfible to her. M. le P. de Coigneux had alfo all forts of fubject for fatisfaction from that great Princefs, by the efteem which fhe teftified for his merit.

Their

‟ Their Majesties of Great-Britain, in the mean time, visited the Queen from day to day. I say from day to day, for this virtuous Princess visited them in her turn, if not confined to her chamber by indisposition, not being able to take greater pleasure than that of seeing them at all times. I can also besides truly say, that the King and Queen of Great-Britain appeared equally so pleased with the presence of the Queen their mother, that their extreme joy was observable to all who were present.

Nothing was talked of but feasts, balls and plays, to which all the ladies of the Queen and her maids of honour were invited, and they would have added to these rejoicings the diversion of baletz, or musical interludes, if the Queen of Great-Britain had not been pregnant; and besides the sorrowful news of the death of the Duke of Savoy, in putting both courts into mourning, caused a long truce to all sorts of diversions.

During their interval, M. du Peron, bishop of Angoulesme, and great almoner to the Queen of Great-Britain, a prelate whose merit as, famous as his name, makes him peerless among his equals, obtained an audience of their Majesties, followed by all their courts, on Christmas-day, in the chapel of Somerset, where he preached, according to custom, with so much eloquence, that even those that envied him were constrained to become his admirers. For my part I was very well pleased, as being informed by others that he was as eloquent in effects as in words, since he practised all the good he preached.

I shall finish this work at the beginning of this year, asking, as a New-Year's Gift, your approbation of my labours, although I am already recompensed by the glory which remains to me, for having employed my time on so worthy a subject.

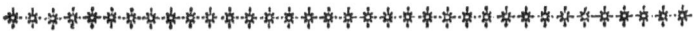

LIFE OF DR. SIMON FORMAN.

DR. SIMON FORMAN was, like the Welch impostor Evans, a pretended astrologer and magician; and to the great impeachment of the sagacity of the age wherein he lived, is said to have levied a comfortable subsistence on the folly and superstition of the public.

The Drawing from which this Plate was engraved, is in the Collection of the Right Honble the Lord Mountstuart, and was communicated by the late ingenious and reverend Mr. Grainger.

The best account of this pretended philosopher is to be found in the Life of Lilly, a fellow-labourer in the vineyard of knavery, and is as follows:

" When my mistress died, she had under her arm-hole a small scarlet bag full of many things, which, one that was there delivered unto me. There was in this bag several sigils, some of Jupiter in Trine, others of the nature of Venus, some of iron, and one of gold, of pure angel-gold, of the bigness of a thirty-three shilling piece of King James's coin. In the circumference on one side was engraven, *Vicit Leo de tribu Judæ Tetragrammaton* +, within the middle there was engraven an holy lamb. In the other circumference there was Amraphel and three +. In the middle, *Sanctus Petrus, Alpha* and *Omega*.

" The occasion of framing this sigil was thus; her former husband travelling into Sussex, happening to lodge in an inn, and to lie in a chamber thereof; wherein, not many months before, a country grazier had lain, and in the night cut his own throat; after this night's lodging he was perpetually, and for many years, followed by a spirit, which vocally and articulately provoked him to cut his throat; he was used frequently to say, ' I defy thee, I defy thee,' and to spit at the spirit; this spirit followed him many years, he not making any body acquainted with it; at last he grew melancholy and discontented, which being carefully observed by his wife, she many times hearing him pronounce, ' I defy thee,' &c. she desired him to acquaint her with the cause of his distemper, which he then did. Away she went to Dr. Simon Forman, who lived then in Lambeth, and acquaints him with it; who having framed this sigil, and hanged it about his neck, he wearing it continually until he died, was never more molested by the spirit: I sold the sigil for thirty-two shillings, but transcribed the words *verbatim* as I have related. Sir, you shall now have a story of this Simon Forman, as his widow, whom I well knew, related it unto me. But before I relate his death, I shall acquaint you something of the man, as I have gathered them from some manuscripts of his own writing.

" He was a chandler's son in the city of Westminster. He travelled into Holland for a month in 1580, purposely to be instructed in astrology, and other more occult sciences; as also in physic, taking his degree of Doctor beyond seas: being sufficiently furnished and instructed with what he desired,

he

he returned into England towards the latter end of the reign of Queen Elizabeth, and flourished until that year of King James, wherein the Countess of Essex, the Earl of Somerset, and Sir Thomas Overbury's matters were questioned. He lived in Lambeth with a very good report of the neighbourhood, especially of the poor, unto whom he was charitable. He was a person that in horary questions (especially thefts) was very judicious and fortunate; so also in sicknesses, which indeed was his master-piece. In resolving questions about marriage he had good success: in other questions very moderate. He was a person of indefatigable pains. I have seen sometimes half one sheet of paper wrote of his judgment upon one question; in writing whereof he used much tautology, as you may see yourself (most excellent Esquire) if you read a great book of Dr. Flood's, which you have, who had all that book from the manuscripts of Forman; for I have seen the same word for word in an English manuscript formerly belonging to Doctor Willoughby of Gloucestershire. Had Forman lived to have methodized his own papers, I doubt not but he would have advanced the Jatro-mathematical part thereof very compleatly; for he was very observant, and kept notes of the success of his judgments, as in many of his figures I have observed. I very well remember to have read in one of his manuscripts, what followeth:

'Being in bed one morning' (says he) 'I was desirous to know whether I should ever be a Lord, Earl or Knight, &c. whereupon I set a figure; and thereupon my judgment:' by which he concluded, that within two years time he should be a Lord or great man: 'But,' says he, 'before the two years were expired, the Doctors put me in Newgate, and nothing came.' Not long after, he was desirous to know the same things concerning his honour or greatship. Another figure was set, and that promised him to be a great Lord within one year. But he sets down, that in that year he had no preferment at all; only 'I became acquainted with a merchant's wife, by whom I got well.' There is another figure concerning one Sir —— Ayre his going into Turkey, whether it would be a good voyage or not: the Doctor repeats all his astrological reasons, and musters them together, and then gave his judgment it would be a fortunate voyage. But under this figure, he concludes, 'this proved not so, for he was taken prisoner by pirates ere he arrived in Turkey, and lost all.' He set several questions to know if he should attain the philosophers stone, and the figures, according to his straining, did seem to signify as much; and then he tuggs upon the aspects and configurations, and elected a fit time to begin his operations; but by and by, in conclusion, he adds, ' so the work went very forward; ' but upon the □ of ☉ the setting-glass broke, and I lost all my pains:' He sets down five or six such judgments, but still complains all came to nothing, upon the malignant aspects of ♄ and ♂. Although some of his astrological judgments did fail, more particularly those concerning himself, he being no way capable of such preferment as he ambitiously desired; yet I shall repeat some other of his judgments, which did not fail, being performed by conference with spirits. My mistress went once unto him, to know when her husband, then in Cumberland, would return, he having promised to be at home near the time of the question; after some consideration, he told her to this effect: ' Margery,' for so her name was, ' thy husband will not be at home these eighteen days; his kindred have vexed him, and he is come away from them in much anger: he is now in Carlisle, and hath but three-pence in his purse.' And when he came home he confessed all to be true, and that upon leaving his kindred he had but three-pence in his purse. I shall relate one story more, and then his death.

One Coleman, clerk to Sir Thomas Beaumont of Leicestershire, having had some liberal favours both from his Lady and her daughters, bragged of it, &c. The Knight brought him into the Star-chamber, had his servant sentenced to be pilloried, whipped, and afterwards, during life, to be imprisoned. The sentence was executed in London, and was to be in Leicestershire: two keepers were to convey Coleman from the Fleet to Leicester. My mistress taking consideration of Coleman, and the miseries he was to suffer, went presently to Forman, acquainted him therewith; who, after consideration, swore Coleman had lain both with mother and daughters; and besides said, that the old Lady being afflicted with fits of the mother, called him into her chamber to hold down the fits with his hands; and that he holding his hands about the breast, she cried, ' Lower, lower,' and put his hands below her belly; and then――He also told my mistress in what posture he lay with the young Ladies, &c. and said, ' they intend in Leicester to ' whip him to death; but I assure thee, Margery, he shall never come ' there; yet they set forward to-morrow,' says he; and so his two keepers did, Coleman's legs being locked with an iron chain under the horse's belly. In this nature they travelled the first and second day; on the third day the two keepers, seeing their prisoner's civility the two preceding days, did not lock his chain under the horse's belly as formerly, but locked it only to one

side.

side. In this posture they rode some miles beyond Northampton, when, on a sudden, one of the keepers had a necessity to untruss, and so the other and Coleman stood still; by and by the other keeper desired Coleman to hold his horse, for he had occasion also: Coleman immediately took one of their swords, and ran through two of the horses, killing them stark dead; gets upon the other, with one of their swords; 'Farewell, gentlemen,' quoth he, 'tell my master I have no mind to be whipped in Leicestershire,' and so went his way. The two keepers in all haste went to a gentleman's house near at hand, complaining of their misfortune, and desired of him to pursue their prisoner, which he with much civility granted; but ere the horses could be got ready, the mistress of the house came down, and enquiring what the matter was, went to the stable, and commanded the horses to be unsaddled, with this sharp speech—'Let the Lady Beaumont and her 'daughters live honestly, none of my horses shall go forth upon this occa- 'sion.'

I could relate many such stories of his performances; as also what he wrote in a book left behind him, viz. ' This I made the devil write with his ' own hand in Lambeth Fields, 1596, in June or July, as I now remem- ' ber.' He professed to his wife there would be much trouble about Carr and the Countess of Essex, who frequently resorted unto him, and from whose company he would sometimes lock himself in his study a whole day. Now we come to his death, which happened as follows: the Sunday night before he died, his wife and he being at supper in their garden-house, she being pleasant, told him, that she had been informed he could resolve, whether man or wife should die first; 'Whether shall I (quoth she) bury you ' or no?' 'Oh Trunco,' for so he called her, ' thou wilt bury me, but ' thou wilt much repent it.' 'Yea, but how long first?' 'I shall die,' said he, ' ere Thursday night.' Monday came, all was well. Tuesday came, he not sick. Wednesday came, and still he was well; with which his impertinent wife did much twit him in the teeth. Thursday came, and dinner was ended, he very well: he went down to the water-side, and took a pair of oars to go to some buildings he was in hand with in Puddle-dock. Being in the middle of the Thames, he presently fell down, only saying, ' An impost, an impost,' and so died. A most sad storm of wind immediately following. He died worth one thousand two hundred pounds, and left only one son called Clement. All his rarities, secret manuscripts, of what quality soever, Dr. Napper of Lindford in Buckinghamshire had, who

had

had been a long time his scholar; and of whom Forman was used to say he would be a dunce: yet, in continuance of time, he proved a singular astrologer and physician. Sir Richard now living, I believe has all those rarities in possession which were Forman's, being kinsman and heir unto Dr. Napper. [His son Thomas Napper, Esq. most generously gave most of these manuscripts to Elias Ashmole, Esq.]

✤✤✤✤✤✤✤✤✤✤✤✤✤✤✤✤✤✤✤✤✤✤✤✤✤✤✤✤✤✤✤✤✤

To the EDITOR of the ANTIQUARIAN REPERTORY.

SIR,

THE story of a Centinel escaping punishment for being found asleep on his post at Windsor Terrace, by a singular proof that he was not relieved at the proper hour, has generally met with credit, and may deserve it. It is not long since a Newspaper mentioned the death of one who said he was the man.

One circumstance of it I think I can correct from my own memory: for the first time I heard it was at Windsor, before St. Paul's had a clock; when the Soldier's plea was said to be that Tom of Westminster struck thirteen instead of twelve, at the time when he ought to have been relieved. This being thought worth enquiring after, proved true, and he was forgiven.

This, and some other particulars it leads me to recollect, you are heartily welcome to, if you think them worth a place in your Repertory.

The Bell, called Tom of Westminster, hung in a strong Clock Tower of stone, over-against the great door of Westminster-hall; and about the beginning of the present Century was granted to St. Paul's, whither it was removed, and stood under a shed in the Church-yard many years before the steeple was cleared of the scaffolding, and fitted for such an ornament.

The Clock had not long been up before the Bell was cracked, and new cast; but with such bad success, that in a few years it was thought necessary to take it down and repeat the experiment.

I myself was at the lowering of it, and lent a hand to the breaking it in pieces; when an inscription on it, copied from the old Bell, engaged the attention

attention of the company; the form of the letters I cannot give, the spelling is, to the best of my memory, as follows:

> Tercius aptavit me Rex, Edwardque vocavit,
> Sancti decore Edwardi figneretur ut hore.

It is to show that the third King gave this Bell, and named it Edward, that the hours of St. Edward might be taken proper notice of.

It was debated whether this King was the third from the Conqueror, but the words did not express this; and as to Edward, the name was plainly given in honour of the Confessor and the devotions paid to him. We could not then settle this matter to our satisfaction, but I think it may be done now.

The Clock Tower was standing till the year 1715; the occasion of its being built, Mr. Maitland's History of London gives as follows:

"A certain poor man, in an action of debt, being fined the sum of thirteen shillings and fourpence, Radulphus Ingham, Chief-Justice of the King's-Bench, commiserating his case, caused the court-roll to be erased, and the fine reduced to six shillings and eightpence, which being soon after discovered, Ingham was amerced in a pecuniary mulct of eight hundred marks, which was employed in erecting the said Bell Tower on the northside of the said inclofure [new Palace-Yard] opposite Westminster-hall Gate; in which Tower was placed a Bell and a Clock, which striking hourly, was to remind the Judges in the Hall of the fate of their brother, in order to prevent all dirty work for the future."

Ingham appears, by Tindal's Additions to Rapin, to have been Chief-Justice in the time of King Henry III. we may therefore suppose the King mentioned on this Bell as donor of it; and then, if any difficulty remains to be cleared up, it is how the Bell should come to be called Tom of Westminster, which was named Edward at its baptism.

I use this word, because among the superstitions of the Church of Rome, one we read of is the ceremony of baptizing of Bells with Godfathers, who make responses for a new one as in baptism of a christian, giving it a name and cloathing it with a new garment, as Christians used to be cloathed, and believing this would make it capable of driving away tempests and devils.

While this opinion kept its ground we may suppose the Bell kept its first name, but that when the Reformation occasioned St. Edward and his hours to be but little regarded, as other Bells of uncommon size were frequently called Tom, as fancied to pronounce that word when stricken; that at Lincoln for example, and that at Oxford, this also followed the fashion, of which, to what I remember of it before it was hung up, I may add another proof, from a Catch made by the late Mr. Eccles, which begins:

> Hark! Harry, 'tis late, 'tis time to be gone,
> For Westminster Tom, by my faith, strikes one.

I cannot tell whether the Monkish verses which have furnished materials for this letter, were remembered at the casting of the present Bell, nor whether you will think it worth while to examine, or to find room for what I now send you; if you do you may possibly hear from me again, for I am one of your well-wishers.

M. Y.

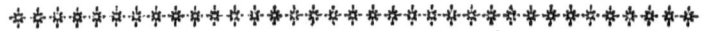

VIEW of OLD LONDON from BLACKHEATH.

THE many picturesque beauties with which Blackheath abounds, will render this Print as respectable an acquisition to the Connoisseur as the Antiquary. The richness of the Fore-ground, the steep ascent of the Hills, which gradually rise above each other, and the view of the River, gives a striking idea of that noble simplicity of nature, which art has in vain attempted to reach. London is seen in the distance, where the eye may distinctly trace St. Paul's, the Tower, Westminster Abbey, and many Parish Churches, forming a most picturesque group of Buildings, and exhibiting to the Spectator the extent and dignity of the old City in its then contracted state, compared with its present splendor.

This Drawing was made by Thomas Wyck, who died Anno 1682. His Works are well known [a], and this View may be numbered among the most capital of his performances. It was communicated by Paul Sandby, Esq. in whose possession it now is.

[a] See Anecdotes of Painting.

THE following curious Inftrument is ftill preferved in the Town Cheft of Wymondham, in the County of Norfolk: It ferves to fhew how low that rapacious Tyrant, Henry the Eighth, would fometimes ftoop to plunder his Subjects. Many fimilar Deeds are extant, and by remaining uncancelled demonftrate that they were never difcharged. Indeed fuch Loans were fo far from being voluntary, that they were frequently extorted by perfonal Threats, and always, like the Free Gifts in France, levied againft the Will of the Contributors or fuppofed Donors.

WE Henry by the Grace of God King of England and of Fraunce Defenfo^r. of the Faith and Lorde of Irelande promyfe by thefe prefents trulye to Contente and Repair to all and Singular fuch Perfounes of thee hundrede of Fourhowe w'in oure Countie of Norff. whofe names be conteyned in a Scedule indented hereunto annexed all and Singular fuch particular fomes of Money as have been by them and every of theym lovingly advaunced unto us by the waye of loone amountynge in the hole to the fome of One hundred threfcor thirteyn pounds Eight fhilling Sterling. In Witnefs whereof to thefe Prefents we Cauled o^r. privey Seale to be fette the Secunde Daye of the Moneth of December the xiiijth Yere of o^r. Reigne

Annexed to s^d Deed }   (Seal Damaged.)

	Fourhowe
Thomas Wodehous Knyght	xlv s.
John Bale	iii li.
James Frofeyke	xlviii s.
Herry Symond	iiij li.
John Kenfey	vj li.
Willm. Weerlyndon	iiij li.
Stephen Burrell	vi li. xiii s. iiij d.
George Brown	xl. s.
Willm Reynold	xlviij. s.
Robert Kenley	iiij li.
John Jufte	xl. s.

Dna

Dna Lovell	xx li.
John Cusshyn	xx li.
Wellm More	x. s.
Roberd Wright	xl. s.
Roberd Cussheyn	xl. s.
Willm Reyner	iiij li.
Nicholas Marche	xl. s.
Roberd Coupper	xliiij.
Edward Down	xl. s.
Stepheyn Petter	iiij li.
Richard Seman	iiij li.
Thomas Canfey	xl. s.
Edward Tilles	xl. s.
Richard Stene	xl. s.
Thomas Fofter	iij li.
John Goche	iij li.
Willm Penyngton Gent	xl. li.
Thomas Cauften	xliiij. s.
John Vyncent	xl. s.
Edward Chamberleyn	ix. li. xs. viij^r.
Edward Kenvett Efquire	xx li.

Sm. tot^l. of this } One Hundred Threfcor thirteyn
Cedule indented } Pounds viij^s

Henry Useal

✧✧✧✧✧✧✧✧✧✧✧✧✧✧✧✧✧✧✧✧✧✧✧✧✧✧✧✧✧✧✧✧✧✧✧

To the EDITOR of the ANTIQUARIAN REPERTORY.

SIR,

THE following Epitaphs I took *verbatim* from the Cover of a Manufcript in the Hand writing of William Roper, Son-in-law to Sir Thomas More, lately in the Poffeffion of Anftis, Garter King at Arms; if it comes within the Plan of your Undertaking, pleafe to infert it, and you'll oblige yours,

T. N.

AN EPITAPH

WRITTEN by Syr Thomas More upon the Death of Henrie Abyngdon, one of the Gentlemen of the Chappel; which Devife he was fayne to put in Meeter, by R... on the Partie that requefted his Travel did not like of verye proper Epitaph ... was firft framed, becaufe it ran not in Rythme, as may appeare at ful in his Latin Epigrammes; whereupon Syr Thomas More fhapt thefe Verfes enfuing, with which the Suppliant was exceedingly fatisfyed, as if he had hit the Nayle on the Head.

Hic jacet Henricus,   Millibus in mille
Semper pietatis amicus: Cantor fuit optimus ille.
Nomen Abingdon erat, Præter et hæc ifta
Si quis fua nomina quærat: Fuit optimus orgaquenifta;
Wellis hic ecclefiâ   Nunc igitur, Chrifte,
Fuerat fuccentor in almâ, Quoniam tibi ferviit ifte,
Regis et in bellâ   Semper in orbe foli
Cantor fuit ipfe capellâ. Da fibi regna poli.

The fame, though not *verbatim* conftrued, yet in effect thus may be tranflated; wherein the learned are not to look for the exact obfervation of quantities of Syllables, which the Authour, in the Latin, did not very precifely keepe.

Heere lyeth old Henry   And fuch a loud Singer
No freend to mifchevus envy, In a thowfand not fuch a ringer;
Surnam'd Abyngdon   And, with a Concordance
To al men moft hartily welcoom A man more fkilful in organce.
Clerck he was in Wellis Now, God, I crave duly
Where tingle a great many belles; Sence this man ferv'd the fo truly,
Alfo in the Chappel   Henry place in kingdoom,
Hee was not counted a mongrel; That is alfo named Abingdon.

✦✦✦✦✦✦✦✦✦✦✦✦✦✦✦✦✦✦✦✦✦✦✦✦✦✦✦✦✦✦✦✦✦

For the ANTIQUARIAN REPERTORY.

AT Langley-Hall, in the parifh of Lanchefter (the antient *Longovicum*) between three and four miles to the north-weft of the city of Durham, is a Mantle-piece of Stone over a large Fire-place, with an infcription thereon in capital letters: the infcription relates to Henry Lord Scrope of Bolton in Yorkfhire, who married Margaret, the daughter of Thomas Lord Dacre of Gillefland in Cumberland. The arms on the fecond quarter are thofe of Tibetot or Tiptoft, an heirefs of which family married an anceftor of the said Henry Lord Scrope, whose coat of arms are engraved with hers, and the same are depicted in the upper windows on the south part of the parish church of Richmond in Yorkshire. The escutcheon by the division on the wife's side, on the right hand looks as if intended for him and his two wives, for he was twice married; but the arms on the side of the wives are so worn away that they are not distinguishable. The uppermost seems as if something like Bars or Barry were in them; Bars were in the arms of Greystock: the other should be Scrope of Upsal, his second wife, whose name was Alice, daughter of Tho. Lord Scrope of Upsal by Margaret his wife, daughter of Tho. Lord Dacres, grandfather of Thomas Lord Dacres above-mentioned.

Henricus Scrope is legible in the second, as Dominus is in the third.

Langley-Hall is now and long has been in ruins: Robert (de Insula) bishop of Durham, by deed granted to William de Insula (or Lisle) free warren in Langley. It afterwards became the estate of the Lord Scroop of Bolton, and then came into the family of Pawlet, by marriage of one of the natural daughters of Emanuel Scrope, earl of Sunderland; and not many years ago was sold by Mr. Pawlet, son of Lord William Pawlet, who was second son of the first duke of Bolton, to Henry Lambton, Esq. of Lambton, late member of parliament for the city of Durham, and is now enjoyed by his brother, Ralph Lambton, Esq. collector of the customs in the port of Sunderland, elder brother of general John Lambton, one of the present representatives in parliament for the city of Durham.

This Drawing was made Anno 1771.

✣✣✣✣✣✣✣✣✣✣✣✣✣✣✣✣✣✣✣✣✣✣✣✣✣✣✣✣✣✣✣✣✣✣✣✣✣

To the EDITOR of the ANTIQUARIAN REPERTORY.

SIR,

THE inclosed Drawing which I send you, is taken from a very curious piece of antiquity in my possession, it is an inlaying or enamelling in Copper. The figure which, I imagine from the Alpha on the right side of his head, and Omega on the left, represents God the Father, is of Brass, as are likewise the outward circles. The other parts are curiously inlayed with enamel of various colours, as red, green, blue, yellow, white, &c. The outside is plain Copper, and by the six holes in the inner circle it appears to have been taken off something, perhaps a Coffin. If it merits a place in your Repertory, it is very much at your service.

I am, Sir, yours, &c.

ANTIQUARIUS.

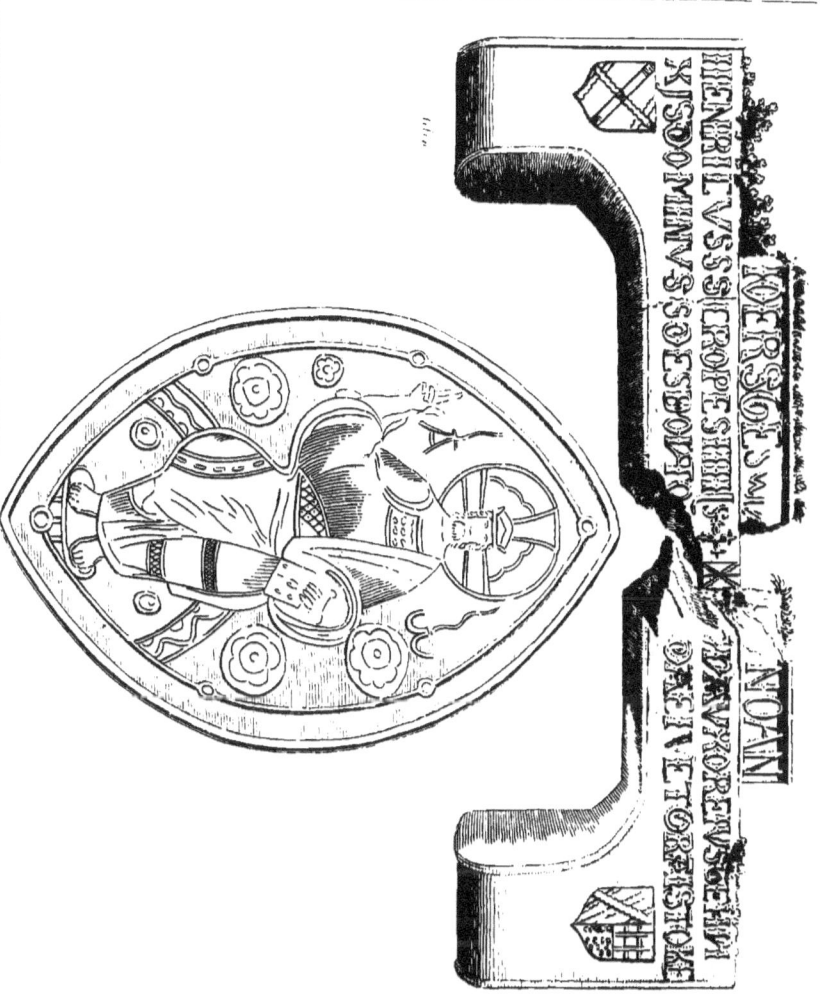

A

AUGUSTINE's St. Canterbury, Great Gate of — 145
Alms-houſe, Rocheſter, Deſcription of 95

B

Banquetting-houſe and Gate at Whitehall, Deſcription and View of 86
Bridge, temporary one, of Black-Friars, Account and View of — 18
Bolton-hall, Deſcription and View of 22
Beef-eaters, the Inſtitution of, and why ſo called — 49
Buſhy Park, old Lodge, Account and View of — ibid.
Bothwell Caſtle, Deſcription and View of — 68
Buck Stone, Gloceſterſhire, Deſcription and View of — 112
Baſingborne, Extract from Churchwardens Books there — 176
Bidding Prayer, Form of before the Reformation — 113
Bath, Roman one, deſcribed 162
Boothole Manor, Extract relating to 215
Bridgenorth Bridge, Deſcription and View of — 217
Bell at St. Paul's, Account ot — 280

C

Capitals, ſome Saxon ones explained 57
Curfew, explained 89
———, Uſe of, and why ſo called ibid.
———, Monſ. Paſquier's Account of 216
Cluer Wall, Seat of C. Windham, Eſq. Deſcription and View of — 109
Combat, Trial by, as in Q. Elizabeth's reign, Account of — 116
Cuntius John, extraordinary Story of 135
Cuſtom, jocular one, at Alnwick in Northumberland — 182
Charter of William I. to City of London — 128
Carfax Conduit, Oxford, Account of 210
Chimney-piece, curious, Account of 217
——— at Langley Hall — 285

D

Dunmow Priory, Ceremony of the Bacon of — 58
———, Oath of — 59
Devil, buying and ſelling of the — 87
Deed of Gift, Form of an old one 118

D

Deed of Henry VIII. at Wymondham, Copy of — 283
Dodſworth, MS of, extract from 173
Druidical Circle near Keſwick Cumberland, Deſcription and View of 240
Dover, Privilege allowed to Felons there, as amended by Henry VII. and VIII. — 175
Deſcription of England and Scotland, by Stephen Perlin — 229

E

Ely Houſe, Account of — 25
Eater, Teeth and Stomach Exploits of a great one — 76
Epitaph on Lady Lavinia Manwood 93
——— abſurd, Collection of — 178
——— in St. Nicholas, Newcaſtleupon-Tyne — 194
——— Latin, on Evan Rice — 214
——— by Sir Thomas More — 285
Edward II. Print of his Cradle 112
——— the Black Prince, Account and Print of — 169
Evans John, the Welch Aſtrologer, Account and Head of — 241
Edmund's Bury, St. Account of a Body found there — 195

F

Form of Surrender of the Monaſtery of St. Francis — 119
Forks, firſt Uſe of — 130
Fiſh, extraordinary, Deſcription of 144
Fordwich, Extract from the Regiſter of 194
Fees appertaining to the Officers of Arms 16
Font, curious, in Orford Chapel, Suffolk, Account and Print of 181
Forman, Dr. Simon, Life of — 275

G

Guildford, divers rude Figures ſcratched on the Caſtle Wall there — 17
Gypſies, Account of People ſo called 53
Ghoſt, extraordinary Relation of one 135
Grave-ſtones, Queries relating to — 156

H

Herald, the Oath of one on Creation 38
——— abridged — 39
——— incorporated by Richard III. 40
Hengiſt, his Maſſacre at Stonehenge 140
Holy Croſs Chapel, Colcheſter, Letter of Indulgence for repairing — 90

Vol. I.

INDEX.

I
Ireland, Etymology of Names of Places in — 40
Jeronimo, Signior, Account of 62—67
Indulgencies, Collection of — 109
Jefferys Judge, Anecdote of — 141
James's Palace, St. Account of, and View of from Village of Charing 197

K
Keswick Waterfall, Description and View of — 97

L
Letters Patent for Incorporation of Heralds and Pourfuivants — 46
Leyr, History of, and Daughters — 157
Letters, numeral, Conjectures concerning — 208
Long Meg and her Daughters, Description and View of — 239
London, Description of the City of, published Anno 1693 — 258
——— Old, View of from Blackheath 283

M
Monument of the Selwyns, Account of 26
——————— of Scarlet, in Peterborough Cathedral — 52
Middleton, Capt. Thomas, some Account of the Valour of — 60
Masques curious, performed before the Earl of Leicester — 101
Mariners Compass, Account of Invention of — 123
MSS in Bodleian Library, Copy of 173
Morpeth Grammar School, Account of 198
Mary de Medicis, Account of her Entry into England — 248

N
Netley Abbey, Hampshire, Description and View of — 244

O
Ordinances used at Tournaments 1 & 29
Offence, Account of three Italian Teachers of — 62

P
Perversion of proper Names — 49
Popish Courant, Relation of — 131
Perhaps and Probably, humble Petition of — 177
Pont y Pridd Bridge in Glamorganshire, Description and View of — 207

Q
Queen's Cross, Northamptonshire, Description and View of — 73

R
Roman Utensils, Description and Print of — 134
——— Bath in Lidney Park, Description and View of — 162

S
Scowls in Lidney Park, Description and View of — 155
Sweating Sickness, Account of 161
Signs, uncommon ones explained 50
Strongbow, Fragment & Monument of 112
Stature extraordinary, Description of two Men of — 120
St. Wenefrede, Life of — 125
Stonehenge, Massacre at — 146

T
Taylor's John (the Water Poet) Voyage to Quinborough in a Paper Boat 68
——— Discovery by Sea from London to Salisbury — 162 & 184
Tintern Abbey, Description & View of 129
Templers, Order for Apprehension of 142
Tutbury, Relation of Ceremonies there 149
Tomb of Earl of Westmorland, Description and Print of — 246

W
Westminster Abbey, Account of 42
Words, not generally understood, Etymology of — 49
William the First, Politic Conquest of 105
Windsor Castle, Description & View of 121
Woodstock Thomas de, Account and Print of — 193
Weston House, Warwickshire, Description and View of — 220

www.ingramcontent.com/pod-product-compliance
Lightning Source LLC
Chambersburg PA
CBHW031901220426
43663CB00006B/723